WESTERN FUTURES:
PERSPECTIVES FROM THE HUMANITIES
AT THE NEW MILLENNIUM

EDITED BY
SUSANNE BENTLEY
BRAD LUCAS
AND STEPHEN TCHUDI

WESTERN FUTURES:
PERSPECTIVES ON THE HUMANITIES
AT THE MILLENNIUM

PUBLISHED BY
THE NEVADA HUMANITIES COMMITTEE
RENO AND LAS VEGAS

A HALCYON IMPRINT

The Nevada Humanities Committee logo is derived from a petroglyph representing a human hand at Rattlesnake Well, Mineral County, Nevada, carved ca. AD 800-1200.

WESTERN FUTURES is published by the Nevada Humanities Committee, 1034 Sierra Street, Reno, Nevada 89503 U.S.A.

ISBN 1-890591-04-1

Cover design concept: Carrie Nelson House

Design and typography: Halcyon Imprints of Nevada

As the ancient bird,
the halcyon,
calmed the waters
in the face of winter gales,
so can the humanities
calm our fears and make safe
our voyage and our young.

The Halcyon series is published annually by the Nevada Humanities Committee through a grant from the National Endowment for the Humanities. *Western Futures* is Volume #22.

Halcyon
Volume #22
WESTERN FUTURES

Editor
Stephen Tchudi

Associate Editors
Susanne Bentley
Brad Lucas

Executive Director
Nevada Humanities Committee
Judith K. Winzeler

CONTENTS

LITERATURE AND LANDSCAPE

TRIANGULATIONS

WESTERN FUTURES

Our Days
in the Olduvai Gorge

BILL COWEE

To stand, to move from the recliner
is to walk through evolution,
bent over like *Australopithecus*,
shuffle all the way back
guided by Mary Leaky to Lucy,
the first jaw,
walking more *Homo Erectus* with each step
until our knuckles clear the floor.
The older we become, the longer
our journey to vertical as the intricate
lattice of vertebrae compresses.
We shrink.
We bend to pick up the newspaper,
realize the distance
to the floor has increased
even though we have grown shorter.
There appears to be an inverse
proportion to this devolution.
So, Lucy, was it difficult to stand
so long ago, to strain upward
against the lock of pelvis and spine?
Even then was there anything worth
seeing on the horizon,
anything of promise
for an aging twenty year old?

Bill Cowee earns his living as an accountant in Mound House, Nevada. He has served as Poetry Editor of Bristlecone, *has been co-director of the Western Mountain Writer's Conference, and is a founding member of the Ash Canyon Poets. Black Rock Press recently published his first book of poetry,* Bones Set Against the Drift.

MILLENNIAL MADNESS

A common theme in American popular culture revolves around a fear of the future and a lament for our losses. We are bombarded with images of our lost connections to one another as caring human beings, our lost connections to a spiritual life, and lost connections to the natural world. Technology, industrialization, and urbanization have cut us off from these sources of renewal, hope, and inspiration. Americans are longing for something, but most of us can't articulate what we long for. We only know the yearning gaps inside us, unfulfilled.

The West has traditionally satisfied this unspoken yearning as a place that can offer a new start, reinvent a life, provide a last hope. The West, with its windy high plateaus, towering forests, snowy mountains, red-rock canyons, and searing deserts may be as much a mythic landscape as it is a reality, a place in the psyche as well as a geographic location, but for Americans, it represents a place where the future can always be better.

As we contemplate our future, we sometimes feel overwhelmed, as though we are standing by some boundless canyon, peeking over the edge with anticipation, delight, and more than a little trepidation. Excitement fills us as we consider the wonders and challenges ahead, but our bodies tense and our stomachs tighten as we feel the uncertainty of our collective prospects. Before us stretch the new millennium, the new West, the new world. We imagine not just one future, but many. This plurality of futures suggests the marvels and hardships humankind will encounter, but more than anything, the myriad possibilities.

This first section of *Western Futures* gives us a look at some of the darker or zanier possibilities. We are not the first people to be concerned about a new millennium. Francis. X. Hartigan's "Millennial Madness" puts current apocalyptic fears about the year 2000 into historical perspective, and tells us "'Millenarianism' suggests belief in a thousand year epoch of history which will end with the destruction of the world." Ken Egan brings this destruction metaphor up-to-date and squarely situates it in the West in "Montana Apocalypse," while Barbara Erickson looks at the lighter side of our fears as she explores why people are drawn to potentially dangerous radon-producing mines in Montana in her article, ". . . And the People Went to the Caves to be Healed."

Cynicism and fear are easy to come by in our troubled society and a world that seems out of control. These essayists remind us that facing our fears is the first step toward overcoming them.

The Last Millennium
Are the Terrors of the Year 1000 True?

FRANCIS X. HARTIGAN

As we enter the third millennium of the Christian era, interest in apocalyptic and millenarian ideas grow in intensity. Religious visionaries and academic historians alike struggle to assess the meaning of the millennial year. Many European historians have long maintained that a great fear, called the "terrors of the year 1000," gripped Europe in 1000, the first millennial year. On the eve of the second millennial year we find apocalyptic fear breaking out in many places including Korea, Japan, and the United States.

In Korea a spiritual leader proclaims the end times are at hand. He coaxes his followers to turn their property over to him and he assembles great riches while his followers await the coming end. The end does not come. He is arrested for fraud. In Japan a terrorist act occurs when sarin gas released into the Tokyo subway killing twelve people, injuring many, and terrorizing millions. The gas attack is allegedly the work of Aum Shinrikyo, a religious movement with followers in Japan and Russia, whose leader proclaimed that the end of the world would occur in 1997, then revised to early September, 1999 ("Fearing"). In the United States an armed confrontation in Waco, Texas between members of the Branch Davidians and federal agents ends in a holocaust. During the confrontation, the group's leader, David Koresh, was writing a commentary on the Book of Revelation which is the main biblical source for Christian millenarianism. Also in the United States a massive bomb at the Federal Building in Oklahoma City kills 167 people. This event and other armed confrontations alerted the American people to the existence of private armies, or militias, some of whom are preparing for Arma-

---

Frank Hartigan is professor of History and Director of the Honors Program at the University of Nevada, Reno.

geddon, the final battle between the forces of good and evil
prophesied in the Book of Revelation, or Apocalype (Rev.
16.16). In March 1997, thirty-nine members of the Heaven's
Gate cult committed suicide to free themselves from their
bodies so that they could be transported by a space ship to
their extraterrestrial "home," according to the statement they
left behind:

> We came from the Level Above Human in distant space
> and we have now exited the bodies that we were wear-
> ing for our earthly task, to return to the world from
> whence we came—task completed. The distant space
> we refer to is what your religious literature would call
> the Kingdom of Heaven or the Kingdom of God. We
> come for the offering of a doorway to the Kingdom of
> God at the end of this civilization, the end of this
> millenium (sic). (qtd. in Gould 52-53n)

What moves people to such drastic behavior? Why do
people kill others or commit suicide over the millennium? All
these groups have in common is the belief that the world will
end soon, on or about the year 2000. This is millenarianism
and it is not new.[1] It is not our purpose to psychoanalyze this
behavior but we note it as a benchmark for considering conditions as Europe approached the year 1000, the first
millennial year. Primary sources are few for this interesting
period yet historians have nevertheless speculated that Europe, especially France, was in the grip of millennial madness. Was it? Was the fear widespread? Historians commonly
refer to this millennial madness as "the terrors of the year
1000." A brief paraphrase of the chapter in a work by historian Emile Gebhardt will illustrate the terrors. Gebhardt
painted a vivid and frightening portrait of Europe on the eve
of the millennium in the eighth chapter of *Au Son des Cloches*.
His chosen venue is Rome: St. Peter's church itself on the
last night of 999. There Romans huddled in prayer begging
God to spare them from the agony to come. Humanity was to
perish in a destruction forecast since David and the Sibyls; it
was the shipwreck of the Church and the funeral of Chris-
tianity. That day a bloody vapor hung about the fabled hills
and towers of the Eternal City. At dusk sad crowds of humble
people abandoned their homes and employment and made

their way to the churches of Rome and the papal palace to await the end.

Gebhardt paints a terrifying picture of the coming end of time. Of course, time did not end, the earth was not destroyed. In fact, Gebhardt made the whole thing up. There is no documentation whatsoever for this event which, had it occurred, must surely have been the most somber New Year's Eve party in history.

"Millenarianism" suggests belief in a thousand year epoch of history which will end with the destruction of the world. The term and idea arise from the Book of Revelation: "And when the thousand years are ended, Satan will be loosed from his prison and will come out to deceive the nations of the earth, . . . to gather them for battle . . . " (Rev. 20.7-10).

In this paper I will explore the year 1000 to see if there existed genuine concern that the end was at hand. In doing so we briefly review the major primary sources and examine the works of major historians to see if the terrors of the year 1000 were widespread and to understand why the issue persisted though many centuries.

The most significant primary source is the eleventh-century Burgundian monk Rodulfus Glaber's, *Historiarum Libri Quinque*, or, if you prefer English, Ralph the Bald's *Five Books of History*. Ralph has the weaknesses of many early medieval writers. He is not well educated, he is poorly informed about the world at large, and he is bit muddled as a thinker and as a writer. In the eighteenth century he was regarded as a barbarian with nothing to offer, but in the nineteenth century he gained status as a source for early French history, and in the twentieth century he is carefully studied as a wonderful window on the Middle Ages who is rich in information about that period. Ralph proclaimed that Europe was in the grip of terror as the millennial year approached and signs and wonders announced the coming disaster. Historians have made much of his proclamation of widespread terror. Yet, although Ralph writes as if 1000 is coming soon, he actually wrote the *Historiarum* about 1040, forty years after the dread event had passed.[2] He was certainly not forecasting the end times, as so many historians have assumed, but, as I have argued elsewhere, he used the millennium as a tool to preach reform in the lives of individual Christians and in the Church

("Rodulfus"). Christians may have been spared the end at 1000 but they still faced final judgement by an angry God.

Another important source is Abbo of Fleury, monk and abbot, reformer and scholar. Unlike Ralph, Abbo is distinguished for his learning and is a harbinger of a new intellectual awakening that reaches full bloom in the twelfth century. This highly credible source says little about the millennium though he lived through the dread year. His sole comment concerning the millennium is to report that in his youth he heard a preacher proclaim that 1000 would bring the coming of the Antichrist and soon thereafter the Last Judgement would follow.[3] Certainly the preacher was a millenarian but he made little impression on Abbo who does not elaborate on this proclamation but passes it on as a mere curiosity. Abbo not only lived at the time of 1000 but he had an important career in the Church as a noted reformer and intellectual, so it is significant that he made no further mention of the millennium.

A third and last primary source requiring our attention is Ademar of Chabannes whose *Chronicle* provides information for the period before and after 1000 (Chavanon). Ademar provides us with a different view of the period than either Ralph or Abbo. Like Abbo, he pays little attention to 1000 and says little that is millenarian. He reveals in his *Chronicle* and in his sermons the existence of considerable religious unrest, especially outbreaks of Manichaeanism. Ademar's report of extensive religious dissent is corroborated by other sources and it attracts considerable scholarly attention at the present time. Richard Landes' recent study of Ademar casts considerable light on the year 1000 and the fact that religious unrest stirred millenarian concerns in some people.[4]

The three principal sources agree on one thing: reform was needed. Ralph sought it in his clumsy, uneducated way by using the prospect of the Last Judgement and "terrors of the year 1000" to scare the populous into reform. Abbo was an active reformer who paid with his life for his commitment; he was murdered by monks who rebelled against his reform efforts. Ademar feared heresy would lead the Christian people astray. All three reflect a grass-roots movement in the Church for reform and as such they are part of a movement begun earlier at the monastery of Cluny in France, at Glastonbury in England, at Gorze in Lorraine, and reaching its culmination later in the eleventh century as it swept upward through the Church hierarchy until the papacy itself underwent reform at the hands of Pope Gregory VII.

It seems reasonable to assume that medieval people about the year 1000 had at least the credulity of people now, on the eve of the year 2000. We can say that perhaps a small minority of people as 1000 approached feared the end of the world just as today a small minority hold similar fears. Neither period had widespread fears. Why, then did historians in the nineteenth century, particularly in France, promulgate a doctrine of widespread terror in Europe as 1000 approached?

The most important historian in answering this question is one of the leading and most influential historians of the century, Jules Michelet. Michelet was widely recognized throughout Europe as a great historian and in France he sat at the top of the pyramid of historians as an educator, archivist, political consultant, and model historical writer. Michelet was a great exponent of the "terrors of the year 1000" and he influenced generations of historians in France and elsewhere.

Michelet gave the terrors prominent place in his monumental and highly influential, *Histoire de France*. Michelet was no Gebhardt; he engaged in no fabrication. He honestly believed that the terrors did occur and that they were extremely important in European history. He read the primary sources we have discussed but he read them through the prism of French nationalism and the political issues that dominated his time. In his role as head of the French National Archives, Michelet buried himself in the sources of French history and became a master of them. He knew the *Histories* of Ralph Glaber very well and used him extensively in the first volume of the *Histoire de France*. He captures the gloom of Ralph's world and uses it to present his case for widespread terror:

> It was the universal belief of the middle age, that the thousandth year from the Nativity would be the end of the world. . . . The idea of the end of the world, sad as that world was, was at once the hope and the terror of the middle age. . . . Christianity had then believed itself intended to do away with sorrow here below; but suffering still went on. Misfortune succeeded misfor-

tune, ruin, ruin. Some other advent was needed; and
men expected it would arrive. (2-132)

The "other advent" that Michelet refers to is the establishment of the nation of France which to Michelet was the true
center of civilization and the hope of the world. Michelet, then,
advocated a secular millennarianism that proffered France
as the answer to human needs. He goes on to say: "The captive expected it [the other advent] in the gloomy dungeon, . . .
The Serf expected it while tracing the furrow, under the
shadow of his lord's hated tower. The monk expected it amidst
the privations of the cloister, ... All longed to be relieved
from their suffering, no matter at what cost!" (133).

Michelet's *Histoire de France* dominated French historical
studies for much of the nineteenth century,[5] so too did his
vivid interpretation of Ralph Glaber's account of millennial
fears. Indeed, Gebhardt's account of Rome on the last day of
999, though fabricated, is based on Michelet's interpretation
of the terrors of the year 1000. Most French historians followed in Michelet's footsteps while a few objected to his belief
in widespread terrors. Thus began the controversy that continues to this day.

Among those who followed Michelet were art historians[6]
who took his structure of the Middle Ages as given and accepted his views of the political and cultural events of the
period: terror spread as the year 1000 approached and a new
order was born after the dread year passed (Batissier 463-
78; Crosnier 18-21). This analysis was ready made for art
historians for two reasons. First, any medieval art historian
knew about the Day of Judgement depicted on innumerable
medieval churches and the fearsome illuminations of the Book
of Revelations, such as the famous Beatus Apocalypse.[7] Secondly, Ralph Glaber reported that after the year 1000 Europe
"took on a white mantel of churches" (98)—a reference to a
building boom that art historians know began in the early
eleventh century. Michelet's interpretation of 1000 made good
sense in light of what art historians already knew.

Michelet's interpretation of 1000 was also influenced by
the political conflicts of his time. He spent much of his life in
conflict with the Catholic Church over the issue of who should
control education in France, the Church or the State. Michelet
was vehement in his opposition to Church control of educa-

tion. Consequently he saw the terrors as an attempt by the Church to manipulate the public into donating property to the Church as the end drew near. Fragmentary evidence exists for this position in some Church documents, though few historians see the evidence as conclusive. The concept of widespread terrors fit Michelet's historical analysis in two convenient ways. First, the terrors marked the "new advent," the emergence of France as Europe's greatest nation, an idea reinforced by the simultaneous founding of France's first great royal dynasty, the Capetians, and the reign of the first French pope, Sylvester II (999-1003). Secondly, arguing that the medieval Church manipulated fears of the end of the world to enrich itself with donated property strengthened Michelet's hand in his opposition to Church influence in nineteenth-century France. Some historians actively opposed Michelet's view that the Church was behind fear of the end of the world.[8] Others attack Michelet's interpretation on the grounds that the evidence does not support it.

Michelet's position on widespread terror held firm until well into the twentieth century. Opposition grew in strength across time and culminated in a direct attack by the noted French medievalist Ferdinand Lot. In an article in *Mercure de France* in 1947 entitled "The Myth of the Terrors of the Year 1000," Lot thoroughly reviewed the primary sources and the secondary literature to conclude that no terrors existed at 1000. Lot accords Michelet the honor of bringing the myth to its full realization and spreading it throughout generations of historians and across the world. Lot concludes that no terror existed but it would be naive, he says, to think that the issue would go away. It has not. He advises his readers that they would do better to concentrate on an apocalypse more meaningful for them: 6 August 1945, the bombing of Hiroshima. Atomic terror is more relevant than any millenarian concerns.

One last work requires our attention: Stephen Jay Gould's *Questioning the Millennium: A Rationalist's Guide to a Precisely Arbitrary Countdown.* Gould, a noted scientist and scientific writer, argues persuasively that there is no basis in mathematics, science, or calendrics for millenarianism; in fact, he finds little basis even in the Bible. His arguments are not new but they are complete. He addresses himself to one area of continuous confusion: actually when was Jesus born and does the BC-AD calendric system accurately record the date of his birth? The BC-AD idea was first annunciated by St. Jerome in the fifth century and calculated by Dionysius Exiguus in the sixth century. Dennis the Short, as Gould prefers to call Dionysius, made two significant errors. First, he miscalculated the birth of Christ by four years, thus Christ was born in 4 BC! Secondly, in setting up the BC-AD system he failed to include a zero year thus reducing the AD system by one year. Accordingly, the year 100 belongs to the first century and the year 2000 belongs to the twentieth century. This error accounts for the fact that the years 1000 and 2000 belong to the previous millennium and the third millennium will not begin until 1 January 2001. Correcting Dennis's two errors leads to the conclusion that the millennial year is 1997, so we are safe, we have made it through! Surprisingly some millenarians have accepted this date, as we have seen in the case of Aum Shinrikyo, including the infamous Archbishop James Ussher, Anglican Primate of Ireland, whose calculations not only gave the precise date for the creation of the world but also its end, 23 October 1997.

In his book Gould smashes the millenarians to pieces. But he does not say that the argument is at an end. No, the argument will go on. Gould recognizes that while many will accept his evidence and proofs some will not. Millenarianists will hold their beliefs regardless of the evidence mustered by scientists, mathematicians, and historians. The most recent prediction for the end of the world known to me as I write this is 5:00 PM, 24 July 1999 ("Fearing"). So it goes with the human race.

We are back to our beginning. Were there millenarian fears at the year 1000? Yes. The primary sources prove it. Were there widespread terrors then? No. The evidence does not support that conclusion. Medieval people seemed to have handled the change of the millennium similarly to people today. A few feared that the end was at hand; most did not. In our time a few can be found in cults and movements such as Aum Shinrikyo and Heaven's Gate; most are not. There is however one great difference between medieval people and ourselves. There is no evidence that medieval people welcomed the new millennium with lavish parties. Around the world party spots are booked to continue the "precisely arbitrary countdown" and to welcome in the new millennium on New Year's Eve 1999 which, of course, is the wrong year.

NOTES

[1]The growing interest in the millennial year has given rise to an organization dedicated to observing the phenomenon. *Millennial Prophecy Report* is published by the Millennium Watch Institute of Philadelphia.

[2]In addition to the year 1000, the year that marked the 1000th since the birth of Christ, Ralph also considered 1033, the 1000th year since the death of Christ, as millennial.

[3]Abbo of Fleury. *Apologeticus*, in *Patrologiae Latina*, 139.

[4]See also Callahan and Frassetto. Bernard McGinn, noted American medievalist, has contributed more than any other American scholar to our understanding of medieval apocalyptic thinking. However, McGinn is not particularly concerned with the year 1000.

[5]See Kippur and Haac.

[6] See Crosnier and Caumont, and also the famous twentieth-century art historian Focillon.

[7]For an engaging discussion of art history and millenarianism in which the Beatus Apocalypse figures prominently see Eco.

[8]See especially the works of Francois Duval.

REFERENCES

Batissier, Louis. *Historie de l'art Monumental. Paris: Furne et Compagnie, 1845.*

Callahan, Daniel. "The Manicheans and the Antichrist in the Writings of Ademar of Chabannes: 'The Terrors of the Year 1000' and the Origins of Popular Heresy in the Medievil West." *Studies in Medieval and Renaissance History* 15 (1995): 163-223.

Chavanon, Jules. *Chronique d'Ademar de Chabannes.* Paris: A. Picard, 1897.

Crosnier, Augustin. *Iconographie Chretienne.* Paris: Derache, 1848.

Eco, Umberto. "Waiting for the Millennium." *FMR America* 1 (1984): 63-92.

"Fearing the End." *The New York Times.* 11 May 1999.

Frassetto, Michael. "Reaction and Reform: Reception of Heresy in Arras and Aquitane in the Early Eleventh Century." *The Catholic Historical Review* 83 (1997): 385-400.

Gebhardt, Emile. *Au Son de Cloches.* 6th ed. Paris: Hachette, 1912.

Glaber, Rodulfi. *Historiarum Libri Quinque.* Ed. John France. New York: Oxford, 1989.

Gould, Stephen Jay. *Questioning the Millennium: A Rationalist's Guide to a Precisely Arbitrary Countdown.* New York: Harmony Books, 1997.

Haac, Oscar A. *Jules Michelet*. Boston: Twayne, 1982.

Hartigan, Francis X. "Michelet and the Year 1000 Controversy." *Proceedings of the Western Society for French History* 20 (1993): 249-55.

———. "Rodulfus Glaber: Apocalyptic Visionary or Reformer?" *Proceedings of the Western Society for French History* 14 (1987): 30-37.

Kippur, Stephen A. Jules Michelet: *A Study of Mind and Sensibility*. Albany: State University of New York Press, 1981.

Landes, Richard Allen. *Relics, Apocalypse, and the Deceits of History: Ademar of Chabannes, 989-1034*. Cambridge: Harvard University Press, 1995.

Lot, Ferdinand. "Le mythe des terreurs de l'an mille." *Mercure de France* 300 (1947): 639-55. Rpt. in *Recueil des travaux historiques de Ferdinand Lot*. Genève: Droz, 1968. 398-414.

Michelet, Jules. *History of France: From the Earliest Period to the Present Time*. Trans. G.H. Smith. New York: D. Appleton, 1845.

Montana Apocalypse
Extremism and Hope in the American West

KEN EGAN, JR.

The foolish In-who-lise and Squaw Kid, instead of keeping their eyes and ears open, kept on dreaming and like all sweet dreams that are too good to be true, theirs had a cruel and rude awakening.
—Andrew Garcia (171)

But I think we're going to have to find new stories to tell ourselves, because the old stories don't have much weight anymore. The old stories keep getting people into trouble around here, in fact; the old stories of going off to wilderness and living in wilderness, in isolation, seeing civilization as corrupt and wilderness as pure, keep getting people killed in Montana.
—Ralph Beer (9-10)

As for my notions of the West, I don't have vast concepts . . . I try to look at what I see as the situation—at how people are doing, at what people are doing—and go from there.
—Ivan Doig ("Interview" 72)

During the spring of 1996, Montana seemed on the verge of apocalypse. On an isolated ranch in north central Montana,

Ken Egan, Jr.'s article in this volume is an excerpt from his book-in-progress, Montana Apocalypse: Dread and Hope in Western Writing. *His first book,* The Riven Home: Narrative Rivalry in the American Renaissance, *appeared in 1997. He teaches western American and American literature at Rocky Mountain College in Billings, Montana.*

self-proclaimed Freemen declared themselves citizens of "Justus Township," an independent, utopian homestead, a purifying defiance of the corrupt national and state governments. Images of Waco circulated in the popular media and in the minds of those living in the society the Freemen had rejected. Fire and destruction seemed imminent, inevitable. Daily reports from "the compound" hinted at weapons stored, violence planned, martyrdom looming. It became a kind of death watch, made all the more absurd by national reporters' attempts to provide "local color" about a region they could neither like nor begin to understand. What made the stand-off even more pregnant with tragedy was the event of exactly one year before, the bombing in Oklahoma City. It was as though some terrible earthquake had sent shockwaves through the western United States, and the after shocks were surging on the high plains.

Montanans could hardly avoid the implications of the bombing in Oklahoma, since that event had brought to the surface an apparently home-grown manifestation of conspiracy theorizing and implied violence: the Militia of Montana. Led by the voluble, strangely personable John Trochmann, the Militia had gained national notoriety on its own terms, even getting a full spread in *The New Yorker*. Preaching the need to return to Constitutional purity and local governance, the Militia promised to lead Americans back to their patriotic roots, complete with local militias that circumvented the corrupt National Guard and the forces of one-world government. Barely concealed behind these patriotic cries in the dark was a politics of hate espousing the necessary segregation of the races. Even more disturbing, the amiable Trochmann hinted at a looming apocalypse, a dire end-time, that would result in the triumph or defeat of the white patriots. His publications (and now Web page) urged acquiring the skills and equipment for surviving a terrible cataclysm, a battle to the end for the soul of the nation, of the world.

As if locals had not suffered enough revelatory shocks, on April 3, 1996, Theodore Kaczynski, every American's vision of the mad man of the mountains, was arrested in Lincoln, a true mountain community that seemed a far remove from either Justus Township or the Militia headquarters in northwestern Montana. The madness had now blanketed the state, completing a puzzle of zaniness, confirming the nation's worst fears about the effects of isolation and exposure to the natural elements in the remote West. It made sense, it seemed, that the Unabomber would emerge from this parodic land of the brave and home of the free. Preaching the need to destroy a decadent, dehumanizing, ecologically destructive technological culture, the Unabomber urged that we assault the monster by any means necessary, including violence. In a discourse ranging from the sublime to the ridiculous, the Unabomber had suggested that only retreat to a Walden-like simplicity could save us from our worst rationalist selves.

Not only had the strangeness covered the state geographically, but it had also demonstrated striking ideological patterns. In all three events, troubled citizens espoused a sense of the end-time approaching, a cataclysm on the horizon. All three agents of virtue demanded the turn from a corrupt, over-regulated, outsized, materialistic national culture toward a localized utopian enclave, a space apart, a community (or cabin) of saints. And all three explicitly or implicitly advocated violence as the necessary means to the end. In fact, since all three voices prophesied apocalypse now, all three urged preparation for a time of tribulation, a time of trial by literal fire, a time of necessary conflict between the light and the dark, the virtuous and the evil, the white and the black. As such, these movements correspond to a pattern of rural radicalism analyzed with skill and bite by Catherine McNicol Stock:

> Far from centers of political and economic power, engaged in the difficult labors of agriculture and extractive industry, increasingly unable to participate in aspects of American culture available to city dwellers, rural Americans have often turned to collective protest to make themselves heard. And because they have also shared a culture of hardship, self-defense, and intolerance, that protest has more often than not manifested itself through acts or threats of violence (7).

It is easy enough to see why such madness had erupted in a seemingly idyllic place at this historical moment. In 1989, the Dakotas, Montana, Wyoming, Idaho, and Washington celebrated the hundredth anniversary of statehood, a jubilee that produced a sobering, even depressing sense of failure. National publications such as *Newsweek* highlighted the isolation, backwardness, and poverty of the high plains: "for the ranchers, farmers, miners and millworkers of this Centennial West, the commemoration is pocked by scarcity and stillborn dreams. The region most emblematic of the nation's grandeur and strength is, today, the region most exploited and ignored" (McCormick and Turque 76). This frenzy of skepticism was fueled in part by the work of Frank and Deborah Popper, urban planners at Rutgers University who advocated returning the Great Plains to a "buffalo commons" in light of the evident failure of settlement in this region.[1] The end of the Cold War perversely fed into a sense of paranoia already inspired by home-grown critiques. Unable to break the psychosis of fear in which we were all immersed for nearly fifty years, many plains residents transferred their distrust of impersonal, oppressive, "evil" empires to the United Nations, the Trilateral Commission, and the federal government itself. The debacle of Ruby Ridge, in this very region, further stoked the fires of fear. Finally, the approach of the millennium itself, replete with a sense of end-time, of passing from one epoch to the next, of entering into some decisive moment of change, added fuel to the fire.[2]

Of course, the world as we know it did not end that spring of 1996. I took a trip to north central and northeastern Montana one year after the spate of madness, curious about scars on the land, a hovering echo of those trying times. The towns and the land were oddly serene. It had been a wet winter, producing excellent winter wheat. Jordan, Circle and other communities made briefly famous had returned to rituals of economic survival in what remains a tough economy for ranchers and farmers. Folks seemed much more interested in discussing crop yields than Freemen. It is tempting, then, to imagine that those bizarre events were aberrant, apart from ourselves. It is tempting to assume that they have nothing to say to us as Westerners, especially those living in the northern-tier states. But that would be a terribly misguided assumption. For all our desire to separate ourselves from the "wackos" of 1996, if we step back to consider the habits of our hearts, the cultural memories we carry, the evidence of landscape and peoples, the Freemen, Militia of Montana, and Unabomber are far from "other." In fact, they are clear if exaggerated images of ourselves, images that we would ignore at our own peril.

Montana can be seen as a microcosm, an exemplar, of the settlement of the West by Euro-American culture. Because of its compressed history, this state provides a case study in the assumptions, methods, and results of that settlement. While it is hardly unique, then, Montana does demonstrate with unusual clarity the strains and consequences of Manifest Destiny. Lewis and Clark journeyed through much of the region on their epoch-making (and now much ballyhooed) trek to the coast. After an era of tentative contact between fur trappers and Native Americans, gold mining became the spur for territorial identity, exploding in 1862 with the finds in south central Montana. At that moment, armed conflict between whites and Indians became inevitable; at that moment, the history of depredation toward native peoples and places accelerated. An interlude of Indian Wars followed, eventually resulting in the creation of seven reservations in what was soon to be the state of Montana. With the apparent removal of natives from the range, and with the mindless slaughter of the buffalo, that range became the available site for the cowboy legend. The era of the open range that lasted so briefly (essentially ten years) would become in many ways the defining story of the high plains, oddly displacing more substantive, more representative stories.

The devastating winter of 1886-87 demonstrated the impracticality of allowing cattle to range over an open terrain without sufficient feed. Ranchers scaled back their dreams of a cattle El Dorado, and settlers increasingly turned toward homesteading and extractive industries such as silver and copper mining. Trails were plowed under and swept away by farmers and massive mining operations. These activities dominated early twentieth-century Montana economics and politics, resulting in sometimes radical labor movements, boom and bust cycles, industry-dominated newspapers, and increasing pressure on the ecology of the place. The Great Depression only exacerbated these trends, though large infusions of federal cash softened the blow to the economy. Post-World War II Montana has resembled much of the West in its increasing internationalization, attention to tourism, interest in education and high-tech industries, and love-hate affair with the federal government.

If nothing else, this Montana chronicle shows the remarkable brevity of that history, a brevity that has profound consequences for our culture. Such a young culture necessarily has fresh memories; it is impossible to repress or evade a past so pressing, so present. This is quite literally true of Montanans living today. I brag that I am a third-generation Montanan, as though such a fact made me indigenous to the place. While that brag separates me from the most recent arrivals, it hardly grants me a title to an aboriginal pride of possession or longevity. But the boast also reminds me that I can trace my roots back to 1913, the year of my grandmother's arrival as a homesteader in the northeastern part of the state. My family has witnessed a majority of the years of this state's existence. That means the history of political strife, economic struggle, and environmental degradation resides in the collective memory of my relatives.

All this suggests that history is alive, is real, is realized in this place, and that the complex, sometimes tragic events live with us. That's why we cannot so simply laugh at the Freemen, the Militia of Montana, and the Unabomber. Our short chronicle tells us that the utopian longing, sense of failure, violence, racism, pride, struggle for control of place, ambiguous relationship with the federal government, and sense of impending doom are very much part of the fabric of our communities. But what, ultimately, is at stake here? What difference does it make that Montanans seem drawn to visions of the apocalypse? Apocalyptic dreaming breeds a desperation and resentment that harms us all. In this sense (as in others), the culture of apocalypse is immature, demanding simplistic answers to complex dilemmas. Perversely, this way of figuring the world feels good, for it allows us obvious answers and thrilling resolutions. The apocalyptic imagination also imposes an abstract schema, a vision of history, upon this particular place. Much as the Puritans transplanted the jeremiad tradition to New England, Montanans have a tendency to imagine this region as the site of battle between good and evil. Rather than ignore or satirize our fringe elements, we should try to make sense of our relationship with them, and then, in a necessary act of survival, propose alternative ways of being in this place. We must, in other words, undertake a dual task of critiquing our own potential madness and embracing an alternative.

To come to terms with both our apocalyptic dread and more hopeful alternative visions, we must honestly confront the ideological legacy of the past century. Interpreting Montana history through the prism of writing about the place, we can see how during the first half century of statehood, Montana nurtured a collection of fantastic dreams that in turn inspired their antithesis, cataclysmic dread. Reading the Montana past through the eyes of traders, cowboys, artists, female settlers, and, especially, American Indians, we see how diverse peoples carried their vivid fantasies of economic, religious, and cultural salvation to these tough places, only to see those visions violently overturned. With astonishing quickness, the hope becomes the dread, the dream the nightmare, the belief the despair. But those same stories often carry the germ of another narrative possibility. Side-by-side with tales of woe move tales of endurance and even recovery, and it is precisely that counter tradition that we must embrace at the turn of the millennium.

Yet we can witness the continuing currency of despair in contemporary Montana culture. With what may seem surprising ease, apocalyptic thinking has transmuted into the stuff of our best literature, dominating the texts of A. B. Guthrie, Jr., D'Arcy McNickle, Richard Hugo, and others. Because of the lingering memory of paradises lost, because of continuing economic struggles and political immaturity, because of Cold War militarism that took up habitation here, Montanans continue to clutch close to their ideological hearts the mantra of end-time. Let me add an important caveat here: by no means do I confuse tragedy with right-wing militancy. Though he often composes in the apocalyptic, despairing mood, Richard Hugo should never be confused with John Trochmann. Quite the opposite. Yet Hugo's engaging poems such as "Degrees of Gray in Philipsburg" and "Montana Ranch Abandoned" demonstrate the regional habit of the heart, the Medusa-like effect of cultural memory on our visions of ourselves.

Fortunately, the alternative tradition of pragmatic thinking and direct action has long served as a counterweight to these more troubling trends. Given the tough weather, geographic isolation, and economic underdevelopment, Montanans have had to find provisional solutions to their immediate difficulties. Visitors to this region often comment on the apparent stoicism, even reticence, of the locals. At first glance the visitor might assume a lack of intelligence, an insular stupidity, if you will. Probe the surface, however, and you often find shrewd, clever, funny, mildly ironic, but rarely cynical folks. By turns stubborn and welcoming, these dwellers on the plains can disarm with their charm and frustrate with their determined convictions. These character traits have evolved as a necessary adaptation to external conditions. I am suggesting that the very events that have encouraged utopian fantasy, racist xenophobia, and violent responses to perceived threats have also nurtured the traits we most admire in citizens of Montana. We discover as much by paying close attention to the writings of many of our significant recent writers, including James Welch, Mary Clearman Blew, William Kittredge, and especially Ivan Doig. Openly espousing the need for "new stories," rejecting the glamorous allure of what Doig has called "Wisterns," peeling back the layers of memory to uncover the unsentimental but nonetheless exemplary conduct of locals, these writers give us a vocabulary for action, a language for choosing to live well rather than mindlessly rebel.

We should attend, then, to writings that dramatize tough, resilient, provisional hope in the region. We can turn away from apocalyptic tragedies toward pragmatic comedies. Though we typically use "comic" to suggest humor or ease, the term has a much more complex meaning. Think here of classic texts such as Shakespeare's *Twelfth Night* and Jane Austen's *Pride and Prejudice*, or more recent narratives such as Willa Cather's *My Antonia* and Toni Morrison's *Song of Solomon*. Comedy tells the story of how an alienated self is reintegrated into society, finding a place, a purpose for being. Such a tale begins in pain, doubt, and confusion, then leads toward salve, hope, and order. If tragedy shows us humanity stripped of dignity and control, comedy reveals a protagonist who grows in stature and knowledge. But that growth is always tempered by a lingering modesty, a perspective on one's limitations, one's follies. An element of the tragic always hovers in the margins of a comic tale. This narrative form thus demonstrates humility and perspective, a knowledge that our solutions are often provisional and incomplete. We seek answers but do not expect their easy arrival. By modifying "comedy" with "pragmatic," I mean to suggest that comic stories in

Montana engage the concrete dilemmas of making a go here, such as struggles over land use, native rights, and economic development.

Consider, for example, Doig's Centennial Trilogy: *Dancing at the Rascal Fair, English Creek,* and *Ride with Me, Mariah Montana* (1984-90). The novelist has granted himself the scope to address Western history from early white settlement to the present day. This intricate family narrative shows the ups and downs for the McCaskill clan, extending from Angus's daring migration from Scotland, to young Jick's tragi-comic take on life at the turn into World War II, to the aging Jick's struggles with his wife's death, his daughter's willfulness, and his ranch's uncertain future. Tragedy does indeed inhabit both the center and margin of this long meditation on the complex fate of being a Montanan. In moments such as Anna Reese's death during an influenza epidemic and Alec McCaskill's meaningless death in the Second World War, the reader is pulled up short, left to wonder about the worth of it all. We also witness settlers almost dying in the attempt to feed starving sheep, ranches failing, homesteaders plowing up valuable rangeland, and an alienating media culture encroaching upon a rural society. Yet at the end, Jick is left standing, firm in his decision to donate his land to the Nature Conservancy. And, in a clever nod toward the well-made novel, Doig has his late-in-life protagonist "move in" with Leona, precisely the cause of family conflict in *English Creek*. The Centennial Trilogy takes us through harrowing passages to arrive at a sustaining possibility: pragmatic hope.

What lessons can we draw from such a set of texts? In contrast to the self-pity of our extremists, we experience endurance, a hanging on, a tough hope. In contrast to immersion in a solipsistic mirror world, we observe a strong sense of the concrete history of this place, including human depredation. In contrast to the violence and melodrama of the male stories, we witness thinking-through, dialogue, and provisional solutions. These alternative stories are not for the faint of heart, but they can sustain us emotionally, spiritually, and politically long after the cataclysmic story has merged into the background noise of late-twentieth-century dread.

A recent controversy in Montana has reminded me of what's at stake in this struggle between extremism and hope for the soul of the West. Lynda Borque Moss, the energetic director of the Western Heritage Center in Billings, proposed American Heritage River designation for the Yellowstone, a precious, meandering, life-giving thread on the high plains. Moss, along with many others living along the river, assumed that this was a win-win situation: local citizens could designate specific sites and projects for funding, and the region would benefit from a federally-funded River Navigator who would help implement the local initiatives. The director went out of her way to emphasize that the Navigator would have no authority to impose or enforce federal regulations in local communities. Yet the result was a firestorm of fear and protest. Of course the idea merited tough discussion, possibly even final rejection. But citizens poured venom upon the idea and its proponent. Why are people in the West so quick to explode into something approaching paranoia? How have we been so hurt, so emotionally maimed, that we resort to shouting matches in lieu of reasoned debate? Can we stop insisting that our way is the only way? Can we figure out a way to "decenter" ourselves, to see from another's perspective, even briefly? I turn back to the books to absorb whatever hope, whatever trust I can. Let's see what we can turn up.

Rick Bass's *The Book of Yaak* (1996) and Spike Van Cleve's *40 Years' Gatherin's* (1977) make an improbable, even wacky pairing. Surely they would have little to say to each other. These two writers seem to inhabit mutually exclusive universes: one is a recent immigrant to the state, while the other is a third-generation Montanan; one seems to represent the political left, the other the right; one inhabits the terrain west of the continental divide, the other the landscape east of the divide. Yet both writers show what a connection to place means for Western citizens: relationship, deep time, community, family, hope. Both writers have a tremendous amount at stake: for Bass, his precious, irreplaceable, irrecoverable Yaak Valley; for Van Cleve, his precious, irreplaceable, irrecoverable "Melville Country." Both men are willing to fight fire with fire to protect something so important, even resorting at times to the name-calling that marred debate on the status of the Yellowstone River. But both are looking for common ground, looking for a way to bridge the divide that separates them from their ideological rivals. Bass, for instance, dwells upon his connection to timbering practices: "I can say that I use wood, and love much about the culture of logging. I love the rip of a saw, the muscularity of it—the smell of wood, the sound and sight of wood. . . . These to me are as much a part of the culture and a part of the wild as the lions and bears and wolves" (27). Or as he puts it with admirable terseness in his "Conclusion": "I believe the simplest and yet most inflammatory belief of all: that we can have wilderness and logging both in the Yaak Valley" (188). You can't accuse Bass of biocentrism. And I suspect Spike would immediately appreciate Bass's desire to live simply and well in his cabin in the Yaak Valley. After all, Van Cleve describes the first three years of his marriage "at the head of the creek" as among the happiest of his life: "We lived well and happy. . . . We just knew we had to be careful of what little we had, so we did fine, because in my book 'poverty' depends an awful lot on a man's state of mind, not just what he's got. . ." (166).

But despite these common grounds, Bass and Van Cleve would disagree fervently on the status of wolves in the region. If Bass describes the wolf as a semi-mystical, potent embodiment of wilderness, Van Cleve sees the animal as a predatory force best eliminated from the range. We're at the heart of the matter here. For all of the intense potential conflicts in this region, none is so public and so polarized as the environmentalist/rancher debate. But I deeply believe that this is a false dichotomy, a false choice. We don't have to allow one or the other perspective to have the final, complete word. What would these two say to each other? We can only guess from their books, but I bet they would begin with good hunting stories, and then share stories about encountering bears in the wild, and then tell about special places in their home terrain, and then (only then) talk about what they're trying to preserve and how they would set about it. They may have to work through language, through what Bass derisively calls "semantics." The word "environmentalist" can instantly send many Westerners into a streak of cussing. But here's a little secret that too few appreciate: many Montanans act on environmentalist principles while barely able to utter the "e" word. And Bass, for all the stereotyping of left-wing agitators, can sink his teeth into the earthiness, the practicality, and the humor of Van Cleve. When all is said and done, these two would share a blood knowledge that could bypass the superficial political divisions.

Of course, there are plenty of forces out there that don't want this kind of healing, this form of rapprochement. It often serves political and economic institutions to keep the pot boiling, the anger raging. If citizens engage in the hand-to-hand ideological combat typified by our most extreme movements in the West, then they likely won't direct their scrutiny toward companies that seek to exploit Montana workers and resources. But there's another force at work here, one deeper and more insidious than overt political and economic interests: the very stories we tell ourselves, the narratives that form our lives. We seem drawn to plots with a classic rising and falling action: begin with conflict, bring that conflict to a climactic resolution, then clean up the loose ends with a satisfying close. More than that, we currently seem to prefer tragic or darkly comic plots, typical of what observers have aptly called a "Gothic America." We are caught, then, in a web of storytelling that drives us apart, or drives us toward open conflict. Our own history and traditions of storytelling reinforce this cultural tendency. No wonder Westerners often incline toward conspiracy theories, the assumption that there's some kind of plot out to get us. It seems an almost inevitable pattern. What I propose here is, by contrast, prosaic, low-key, quiet, undramatic. I'm proposing (along with many more gifted thinkers and writers) that we stop shouting, stop hurting each other, stop falling into the trap posed by apocalyptic tragedy. Wallace Stegner wrote that the West is the native land of hope. We should live up to that charge.

Joseph Kinsey Howard once asserted, "The key to happiness for an individual . . . lies in completeness as a human being, rather than in competence in a particular field; and the happy community is the many-sided, fully functioning community of neighbors to whom democracy is not so much a word as it is an instinct" (qtd. in Roeder 9). We have witnessed manifestations of this possibility in this region recently:

Item: During a conference on A. B. Guthrie, Jr.'s *The Big Sky*, Lee Rostad, a rancher and writer from Martinsdale in central Montana, and Annick Smith, a rancher and writer from Missoula, engage in an intense debate about the relationship between environmental consciousness and ranching. While few issues are resolved, it feels like the beginning of a dialogue that matters, a dialogue that might just lead toward understanding, even community.

Item: A radio program discussing writing by and about Westerners runs for thirteen weeks during the fall of 1997. The program is carried on NPR stations throughout the Northwest. Listeners phone in and converse with writers, scholars, and other callers. The conversations are spirited, heartfelt, and illuminating. Something like community has formed through the airwaves.

Item: During a graduation ceremony at Rocky Mountain College, Janine Pease-Pretty on Top, Crow woman and president of the Little Big Horn Tribal College, delivers a memorable address to graduating seniors, urging them to recognize the natural and the spiritual as central to their lives. She then receives an honorary doctorate. The ceremony concludes to the beat of Crow drummers. It seems fitting.

NOTES

[1]The Poppers have argued that white settlement of the Great Plains has been an ecological and economic disaster. Citing statistics demonstrating the outflow of population from rural areas in this region, they assert that encouraging homesteading on the plains has proven a long-term mistake. They urge returning large portions of the area to a "buffalo commons," a prairie preserve that could both restore environmental integrity and provide a meaningful economic alternative to agriculture. Needless to say, the Poppers' argument has drawn a strong reaction in Montana and elsewhere. For an excellent overview of the buffalo commons concept and its reception in the West, see Anne Matthews, *Where the Buffalo Roam.*

[2]For an informative, edgy account of rural radicalism in our own time, see Joel Dyer, *Harvest of Rage.* Dyer emphasizes rural citizens' despair at losing control of their lives in a time of vertical and horizontal integration of the agricultural market. In "The Current Weirdness in the West," Richard White traces the history of western antipathy to the federal government's involvement in land issues. White notes the irony of this distrust: the federal government has poured more largesse into western states than into any other region. Yet,

"[t]his conservative West . . . sees its genealogy not in the history of federal development in the region but instead in terms of a set of archetypes: the isolated, armed male, the courageous homesteading family, the poor but industrious immigrant. It is no wonder that the regional icon is John Wayne" (9).

REFERENCES

Bass, Rick. *The Book of Yaak.* Boston: Houghton Mifflin, 1996.

Beer, Ralph. "Interview." Morris 2-23.

Doig, Ivan. *Dancing at the Rascal Fair.* New York: Harper and Row, 1987.

———. *English Creek.* New York: Penguin, 1984.

———. "Interview." Morris 66-80.

———. *Ride with Me, Mariah Montana.* New York: Penguin, 1990.

Dyer, Joel. *Harvest of Rage: Why Oklahoma City Is Only the Beginning.* Boulder, CO: Westview, 1997.

Garcia, Andrew. *Tough Trip Through Paradise, 1878-1879.* Ed. Bennett H. Stein. San Francisco: Comstock, 1967.

Matthews, Anne. *Where the Buffalo Roam.* New York: Grove Weidenfeld, 1992.

McCormick, John, and Bill Turque. "America's Outback." *Newsweek* Oct. 9, 1989: 76-80.

Morris, Gregory L., ed. *Talking Up a Storm: Voices of the New West.* Lincoln: U of Nebraska P, 1994.

Roeder, Richard B. "Joseph Kinsey Howard and His Vision of the West." *Montana: The Magazine of Western History* Jan. 1980: 2-11.

Stock, Catherine McNicol. *Rural Radicals: Righteous Rage in the American Grain.* Ithaca: Cornell UP, 1996.

Van Cleve, Spike. *40 Years' Gatherin's.* Kansas City, MO: Lowell, 1977.

White, Richard. "The Current Weirdness in the West." *Western Historical Quarterly* 28.1 (1997): 5-16.

"...And the People Went to the Caves to be Healed."[1]

BARBRA ERICKSON

Tucked away in the Elkhorn Mountains of Montana, about halfway between the cities of Butte and Helena, are six small and obscure mines, doing their best to make a living by attracting visitors. Old mines like these, no longer worked for their ores, are appealing to history buffs, to those interested in mining, and to people who just want to get a feel for a chapter in the American past. But these particular mines have a very different purpose: their owners hope to attract not students of history but people in pain. For a modest fee, these Montana mines offer the opportunity to inhale radon gas as a treatment for various chronic illnesses.

Radon is a colorless, odorless gas that occurs as a radio-active decay product of uranium. Reports that radon is a potential carcinogen have been widely publicized, and in many parts of the country homeowners are actively encouraged to have their homes tested for radon.[2] The people who come to the "Radon Health Mines," as they are called, are aware of the alleged dangers of radon, but they come to the Montana mines regardless, because they believe that the low-dose exposure to radon helps to relieve their arthritis, rheumatism and other painful ailments.

Origin of the Radon Health Mines

The mountainous land along US Interstate Highway 15 is rich in mining history and is the location of many once-thriv-

Barbra Erickson is a doctoral candidate at the University of Nevada, Reno. Her research interests are medical anthropology and the history of medicine. Special thanks are extended to Patricia Lewis for generously providing access to the archival papers of the Free Enterprise Radon Health Mine.

ing and now-abandoned mines and their adjacent towns. Silver, gold, lead, and copper have all played a pivotal role in the settlement of this area, but it was the 1949 discovery of uranium ore at what is now the Free Enterprise Health Mine at Boulder that began the chain of events that would result in today's "radon for health" phenomenon. Wade Lewis (1893-1974), founder of the Free Enterprise Mine, wrote that throughout the 1920s and 1930s a fair amount of prospecting by individual miners was undertaken at the site, during which time small amounts of silver and lead were extracted and sent to local smelters. No exciting finds were made, however, and an eighty-five foot shaft dug sometime around 1939 was simply abandoned.

Even as local gold and silver mining seemed to be dwindling, the use of atomic weaponry in World War II spurred worldwide efforts to locate sources of so-called atomic ores. Lewis, having studied geology and mining engineering at Oregon State College, and having worked as a chemist and assayer for Bay Horse Mines in Oregon, was more than qualified to search for this new atomic "gold," and he hoped to find it in the Elkhorn Mountains. In his book *Arthritis and Radioactivity*, Lewis describes how, in June of 1949, he and his associates Sanford Davis and Edward Miles began a survey of the area with their Geiger counters. They found that the tailings at "the old dump" near the eighty-five foot shaft were radioactive—what would turn out to be the first discovery of commercial uranium ore in Montana (12). Organizing themselves officially as the Elkhorn Mining Company, the three men first leased, then eventually purchased the property, and began to ship ore to Salt Lake City for processing.

Lewis recorded his experience and impressions upon first being lowered down into the old mine shaft on the Free Enterprise claim just days after the uranium was discovered:

> At the time I was lowered into the shaft, it was soon evident that radioactivity was so great at the station 50 feet down that instrument readings were useless. In five minutes the Geiger counter . . . was so saturated with radon gas and its decay elements that the needle exceeded any attempted readings on any scale . . . and on [my] return to the surface [I] found that my clothing was likewise saturated with radon gas. My

hair, hands, every portion of my body and even my
breath were extremely radioactive. Quite evidently I
had breathed a very heavy concentration of radon gas
during the one hour examination . . . [and] my body
and clothing were radioactive for several hours following the shaft trip. (10-11)

In a letter to the Atomic Energy Commission dated July 22,
1949, Lewis reported the geological and chemical findings at
his new uranium mine, also noting,

Last week I was able to get down to the 45 foot level by
rope, monoxide test was negative, but ray count was
high, all my clothing was contaminated and radioactive on return to surface and I am advised . . . not to
spend much time in the shaft without a test of the
gases accumulated there. We are having such a test
made soon.

For two years the Elkhorn Mining Company continued to
ship uranium ore to Salt Lake City, and the concurrent discovery of other properties in the region with similar ores helped
to sustain a boost in the local economy. However, the focus of
this mining boom suddenly changed in 1951. On August 15,
a Los Angeles woman came to visit her husband, a mining
engineer working with Wade Lewis. Wanting to see where her
husband spent his time, she requested to go down into the
mine shaft, and she was lowered to the eighty-five foot level
by steel cable in a narrow mine cage (Lewis 11). The woman
had severe bursitis in her right shoulder and according to
her husband could not even lift a kitchen utensil without
extreme pain. Lewis writes that he "facetiously" suggested to
her, as the cage lowered them down into the mine shaft, that
the radiation there might help her shoulder.

Twenty-four hours later her husband called Lewis to tell
him that his wife was "miraculously" free from pain. The
woman invited a friend of hers in Los Angeles, also suffering
from bursitis, to visit the mine, which she did. Three weeks
later, the second woman was also claiming to be pain-free.
No one knows how the word spread so quickly, but within a
few months a local newspaper reported that "people with arthritis who have heard about this underground 'cure' are

swarming around the Wade Lewis mine" (Hillinger, "Health" 9).

For about six months the Free Enterprise continued to allow people to go down into the mine free of charge, and uranium mining operations continued. But eventually the increasing numbers of visitors became a problem. "We just can't handle this thing . . . " Lewis told a reporter towards the end of 1951. "We would like to help, if this be help, but we aren't set up for it. We can't go into the health business" (Hillinger, "Health" 9). Whatever his initial feelings may have been, by the following February Lewis decided to shut down the uranium mining operation and to re-open as the Free Enterprise Uranium Radon Mine, selling arthritis treatments instead of uranium ore. During the temporary closure, the Elkhorn Mining Company would install an Otis elevator and various improvements to the property that would accomodate arthritic visitors. Almost immediately after this announcement, the Elkhorn Mining Company was deluged with letters requesting appointments for treatment:

March 26-1952

Mr. Wade Lewis
Boulder, MT

Dear Sir

I'm writing to you to see if I could get [an] appointment to visit the mine for a treatment. I've been in terrible pain in my arms and fingers for the last three days that I can't sleep at nite [sic] and trying to work, as I stand and walk for the eight hours I work . . .

* * * * *

Tues. Apr. 1 [1952]

Dear Mr. Lewis.

Mrs. B. called me yesterday and said to get in touch with you about taking Mr. C. into the mine. His back is like a board and pains a lot and now his elbows are getting stiff. He also has that mean palsy caused from hardened arteries and I have a strong feeling that if the arthritis can be helped so can those arteries which are filled with calcium. He is able to get around, and we have a friend who would go with him, for he also is hobbling around with arthritis.

I know you aren't open to visitors now, but we would like to go in as soon as possible when you are ready. What a miraculous thing you have unearthed and it must give you great satisfaction to be able to help such terrible suffering . . .

* * * * *

June 14th [1952]

Dear Sir,

We've been informed your mine will be open to patients this coming week so I'm very interested as I'm only 36 and getting so badly crippled with arthritis . . .

* * * * *

June 26, 1952

Gentlemen:

Please send us information on what is offered arthritis sufferers at the FreeEnterprise Uranium Mine . . . My husband is able to walk short distances with the assistance of a crutch, cane and attendant but cannot sit in or get up from an ordinary height chair or bed . . . . He has been disabled by arthritis . . . for over three years and having tried almost everything offered in the line of drugs as a possible cure without relief is very anxious to see if going into a uranium mine might give him the relief from pain he has been seeking . . . .[3]

* * * * *

On June 23, 1952, the Free Enterprise Uranium Radon Mine officially opened for treatments. At first visitors were charged a fee of $100 for four visits, but by the end of the month the management reduced the price to $10 per visit. In any case, the uranium mining business had unexpectedly turned "golden" in a way no one could have anticipated. Almost immediately other old mines in the area began to claim curative powers, some getting their names in local newspapers even before the Free Enterprise grand opening. The Herzer Mine, the Comstock Mine, the Sunset, the Merry Widow Mine (also called the Basin Arthritis Mine), the Radon Tunnel, Silver Shields Uranium Mine, the Sunshine Mine, the Alhambra Mine, Uranium Mountain Mine, and the Moonlight Mine had all had write-ups in the *Boulder Monitor* by the end of 1951, complete with photographs of eager customers and testimonials of their successful "cures." According to *True Magazine* (1954), in their first two years of operation the mines as a whole were visited by more than 100,000 people seeking treatment, and of these more than 60,000 left their names and addresses, apparently willing to be contacted about their experiences (Bailey 31).[4]

The Nature of the Treatment

The brochures published by the mines today claim, as did Wade Lewis in his 1955 book *Arthritis and Radioactivity*, that low dose exposure to radon gas "stimulates the glandular system, causing your glands to produce more hormones and stimulate other glands to greater activity" (Lone Tree Mine brochure). In 1949 the discovery of the synthetic corticosteroids ACTH and cortisone promised relief for people suffering from inflammatory diseases such as arthritis. Although arthritis responded favorably to increased amounts of corticosteroids, the synthetic steroids unfortunately caused numerous side effects. With the inhalation of radon gas in small regular doses, the radon mines claimed, "the body uses its own steroids" having been stimulated by the radiation to produce them, and health is improved (Merry Widow Mine brochure). The "proper amounts of visits . . . allows Mother Nature to cleanse the body of certain waste materials (i.e., dead tissue cells, decayed food materials, and acids) which hamper the proper function of the endocrine glands, especially the pituitary, parathyroid, and adrenal glands" (High Ore Health Mine brochure). The radon gas in the tunnels "works to break down impurities in the body so that they might be picked up by the blood for elimination from the body. Radon leaves the body naturally within 3-4 hours after each visit" (Earth Angel Health Mine brochure).

The six mines note in their literature that the premises have been inspected by Montana regulatory agencies; that their water has been pronounced pure for drinking purposes; and that neither pregnant women nor children under the age of eighteen should visit the mines without the express prescription and advice of a licensed Montana physician. The optimum treatment program consists of thirty-two one hour visits, taking two to three visits per day, for a total of about three hours exposure per day. Between visits, it is recommended that the client come out into the fresh air, let the radon dissipate from his or her lungs, drink plenty of water, and rest a great deal. This alternation of treatment and rest has been found, according to the mine owners, to be the most beneficial in terms of symptom relief. The Department of Health and Environmental Sciences of the State of Montana does not actively regulate these mines; however, a representative visits randomly to measure the levels of radon within each mine, and makes recommendations about the number of hours to which a client should be maximally exposed. At the time of my first visit, the summer of 1997, the last testing had been done in 1991, with results as shown (table, previous page). As of 1994 the National Research Council, working on behalf of the

Radon Mine Concentrations[5]	
(picoCuries/liter)[6]	
Mine	*Radon Concentration*
Free Enterprise	491 to 890
Merry Widow	1297
Earth Angel	491 to 844
High Ore	233 to 234
Sunshine	176.6 to 202.2
Lone Tree	1000

Environmental Protection Agency, had not determined precisely what dose of radon, if any, could be considered safe (3).

Mining for Health in the 1990s

Today there are currently six radon mines in operation in the Elkhorn Mountains. The numbers of visitors coming to find arthritis relief can no longer be described as they once were in the *Los Angeles Times* : "Ailing Thousands Flock to Mines Seeking Cure (1972)," but enough people still come to keep the mines competing for the business. Four of these mines are near Basin, a tiny hamlet along I-15 that was once a booming gold mining town before the turn of the century. The Free Enterprise and the Lone Tree Mine are just outside of Boulder, six miles north of Basin.

Boulder is a small town of about 1800 people at the intersection of I-15 and Highway 69, and as the Jefferson County Seat it boasts an historic courthouse, the county fairgrounds, and a post office, along with a bowling alley, several small bars and eateries, and surprisingly, an espresso stand. Three aging motels still cater to the business brought by the mines, but although every summer perhaps five hundred out-of-towners arrive in Boulder alone to sit in the radon mines, it doesn't seem to be enough economic incentive to spur renovation or expansion. Neither has the mine business persuaded anyone to invest in building new restaurants; mine visitors enjoy the quaintness of Boulder and Basin for a time, but after a week or so of small town café food, most people end up driving the thirty-odd miles to Butte or Helena for a meal.

All six of the mines are located within a few miles of each other, so that once arrived, mine visitors can freely make the rounds and decide which of the mines they prefer. All of the mines enjoy a similar scenic grandeur. The highway that links the mines runs alongside the Boulder River through a narrow canyon of grassy hillsides covered thickly with conifers. Just as the highway reaches Boulder, the canyon opens up into a wider valley, with tree-covered hills surrounding wide stretches of sagebrush, wildflowers, woodlands, and cattle-grazing pastures. Yet each of the mines, although close geographically, has its own distinctive characteristics. Radon health treatments are a competitive business, and through the years the mine owners have tried to capitalize on the unique qualities of their mines. As a result, each mine has a particular "personality" and tends to attract a loyal following of visitors who prefer one mine over the others. The location, the scenery, the amenities, and the inside of the mines themselves all contribute to the uniqueness of each mine location.

Visiting the Elkhorns in 1997 and 1998 I had the opportunity to try out five of the mines and to talk to many of the people as they took their treatments. There are several major differences between the mines which can be noted immediately. The Free Enterprise, the original "radon health mine," is the only one which is actually located underground. The radon tunnel where people take their treatments is eighty-five feet down, and must be reached by an elevator. The other mines consist of horizontal tunnels that one simply walks into. One of them, the Lone Tree, was never actually a working mine; its tunnel was dug specifically for radon mine visitors. Another major difference between the mines is that some of them are "dry," while others are "wet." The wet mines have either a stream which flows through them, or water which seeps from the rocks and collects in a pool somewhere along the tunnel's length.

The Free Enterprise, with its underground tunnel, is attractive to people who feel that having to go underground somehow makes the radon therapy seem more "real" and more "effective." Other people don't like the idea of going underground at all, and are somewhat fearful of the eight-story elevator shaft. For those who don't care to go underground, the Free Enterprise also has an upstairs "radon room" which is sealed off by double doors from the reception area. Fresh air mixed with radon-laced air is pumped into the "radon room" from the mine tunnel below, and wall monitors show the radon level to be just as high as that in the tunnel. However, several people told me that they didn't care for this room; it seemed too much like their own living rooms at home, and "didn't feel like it was healing" because it didn't look like a mine. The other mines, like the Merry Widow, are walk-in mines with horizontal tunnels: the preferred choice for those who can't take the closed off "trapped underground" feeling of the Free Enterprise. But the walk-in mines have their drawbacks for some people too. Fred, an Idaho podiatrist, doesn't like any of the walk-in mines; he says they "just feel like a hole in the mountain."

People also have preferences about the presence or absence of water in the mine tunnels. The air temperature in
these tunnels is consistantly about 50 to 60° F., and for some
visitors the presence of water added to the chilly temperature
makes it too uncomfortable. Others enjoy the presence of
water, saying they like the echoing sounds of dripping and
trickling in the tunnels. The Merry Widow Mine actually capi-
talizes on its water in a number of ways. The Merry Widow
has set up some of its seating so that the client faces the wall
of the cave, where a flowing stream runs along a bedrock
channel. Buckets and hoses are attached at intervals, so that
clients can soak their feet, hands, knees or elbows in the 40°
F. water. At one point in the tunnel an alcove holds a stone
"bathtub," allowing total body immersion for people who think
that soaking in the radon water will speed the healing process. Like the other mines, the Merry Widow also encourages
its clients to drink "plenty" of the radon-saturated water, saying that it helps to "flush out" the impurities that will be collecting as the radon gas helps to "break them down." Both
the Free Enterprise and the Merry Widow sell water contain-
ers for fifty cents per gallon.

I spent most of my time at the Free Enterprise, which
seemed appropriate due to its status as the original radon
health mine. A sign in downtown Boulder directs the would-
be visitor to turn onto a sidestreet, which quickly becomes
gravel. The road passes under the Interstate, which has so
little traffic on it that it seems like a deserted bridge, and
winds uphill for two miles past sagebrush and the occasional
cow. The Free Enterprise building sits on the top of a small
hill, surrounded by a parking lot and a row of RV hookups.
There is a fine view of Boulder from here, and the RV camp-
ers park their vehicles right at the edge of the hill where they
can overlook the valley. Part of the attraction of the place is
the quietness, as well as the sage- and evergreen-scented
breeze that always seems to be blowing. A person can imagine feeling healed here.

Inside is a pleasant room with three small tables and various chairs. Large windows all around let in plenty of light
along with the panoramic view. To the rear of the building is
the "radon room," for people who dislike the underground
tunnel, as well as for arthritic dogs and cats. Coffee is available in the reception area, and clients can either sit there

between treatments, or go out to their motor homes. A shelf is piled with blankets which clients can borrow to ward off the chilly air down in the tunnel. When it's time to go down, the clients crowd into the elevator, which is painted a rather startling pink. The ride is slow and quiet, although there is an intercom left on all the time in case of problems.

Once down at the bottom of the shaft, the tunnel opens off to either side. The walls of the tunnel are the native rock, with huge wooden support beams spaced throughout the length of it. The tunnel is approximately one hundred yards long all together, and along the walls are old bus benches and padded seats of assorted shapes and colors. Card tables and chairs are placed at each end in widened-out areas. It feels cool, but not uncomfortable, and the air smells fresh. The tunnel is well-lit, and people read, play cards, chat, or doze in their chairs all along the length of the corridors.

On every wooden beam dozens of names and dates are inscribed, some with cryptic messages about their healing experiences, and hundreds of business cards have been tacked or stapled onto the wood. Names and dates are also carved into or written on the stone walls. One of the plastic chairs has printed on it in marker pen, "Roy's healing chair." There are places where annual visitors have written each successive year, for example "Ray and Linda: 1987, 1988, 1989, 1990, 1991" and so on. The people are eager to tell me about their illnesses and about their healing successes. They tell me that in July and August (it is now June) the place will "really get packed" and that usually someone has a guitar, and they sing and laugh. Certain "regulars" come at the same time every summer and plan on seeing friends made at the mines from year to year. Several people tell me that in July "busloads of Amish people" arrive from Pennsylvania and Ohio.

The Free Enterprise works hard to be friendly and personal, but at the same time the owners have made every effort to manage it professionally. It has been in the Lewis family continually since 1949, and was recently purchased by Patricia, the granddaughter of Wade Lewis. She and her husband make their living from the business, and they have tried to make it profitable even as they make improvements in the place. They charge more than any of the other mines but keep their share of loyal customers because of the amenities, the professionalism, and the sense of confidence and competence exuded at the Free Enterprise.

Patricia has set up a Web page, and regularly communicates with researchers in the United States who believe there may be a scientific basis for low-dose radiation therapy.[7] She is also in contact with several "Radon Spas" in Austria and Germany, where radon tunnels are used in conjunction with mineral baths, all of which is covered by health insurance.[8]

After the Free Enterprise, the Merry Widow Mine is probably the most popular, and it certainly is the most well-known radon mine in Basin. Unlike the sagebrush and sweeping vistas of Boulder Valley, Basin Gulch is green and lush, and it attracts visitors who prefer the shady trees and stream surrounding the mine here. Campsites, RV hookups, and cabins are available here, and visitors can simply walk up a short slope to the mine entrance, which leads directly into the side of the mountain. Like the other mines, the Merry Widow has numerous testimonials written, drawn, carved, and tacked onto the walls.

Another variation on the theme is found at the Sunshine Health Mine, also near Basin. This mine is reached by taking a gravel road about a mile into the hills to a tiny valley surrounded by grassy pine-covered hills. The owners here compete for the radon business by giving their place a resort-like atmosphere. An artificial pond is stocked with rainbow trout, for anyone who wants to fish. Flowers are planted along the road, and the cheery, well-maintained yellow-and-white office building sits right next to the mine entrance, which is also landscaped with flowers and shrubs. The office has a laundromat, a gift shop and a hot tub. The Sunshine rents cabins, mobile homes, and duplexes for a very reasonable price, which includes full furnishings, kitchen and appliances, and a TV/VCR, and the office even rents videos. The distinctive stamp of the owners is visible inside the mine tunnel as well. The Sunshine is a wet mine, and the water collects in a small grotto which the owner has decorated with hanging pots filled with plastic flowers. The furniture inside this mine is nicer than that of any of the other mines, and visitors seem to have a wonderful time playing cribbage and board games in the well-lighted rooms.

Mining for Hope

A survey of the mine visitors quickly reveals a locus of specific illnesses and complaints common to the group. By far the most common of these diseases is arthritis, but some other typical complaints named include lupus, rheumatism, multiple sclerosis, emphysema, allergies and psoriasis. Mine visitors in the 1990s are more sophisticated and knowledgable about health care than many were in the 1950s, but the hope of pain relief remains fundamentally the same. Most visitors today have seen their physicians, and many have seen specialists as well; yet there is often little that can be done for their chronic conditions with the exception of taking pain medication and curtailing activities. Many of the mine visitors hope the radon treatment will help them cut down on their medications, and as for the danger of radon, most simply dismiss it. As several people said to me, "wouldn't you try anything to get rid of this pain?"

As most of the people will tell you, it seems almost irrelevant whether or not the radon is actually helping their arthritis; the point is that they *feel* better, and however this happens it is alright by them. A Minnesota woman told me, "If it's the placebo effect that's making my pain and stiffness go away, then fine! Being here at the mine is still what's making it happen!" Another thing that keeps people coming to the radon mines is that the vast majority of them are older folks, post-retirement. They are willing to play the odds that by the time any harmful effects of radon struck them they would be long gone anyway.

In any case, Montana is a beautiful place to take a vacation. One couple, visiting the Free Enterprise for their thirteenth year, said that their first visit was the "best vacation we ever had!" Sitting down in the mine they met other couples with whom they have formed lasting friendships, and they often arrange to go to Boulder at the same time of year so that they can visit with each other. The fresh air, the companionship and the peace and quiet of these Elkhorn Moun-

Following pages: Poems and testimonials by visitors to the mines. Photographs of the region by the author. Text continues, page 49.

Main Street, Boulder, Montana

Grocery shopping in Boulder

*Sign along the interstate
near Basin, Montana*

*Entrance to the Earth Angel
Mine*

*Grafitti at the Free
Enterprise mine*

tain communities may be part of the therapy. And in addition, the radon mines have not only given hope and relief to those in pain, but have inspired lasting friendships, fervent testimonials, artwork, and poetry.

Go to the Elkhorn Mines

The Elkhorn Mine country is the place to be,
If you have arthritis as you and me,
Then go to the Elkhorn Mine.

If it's in your arms and you can't hug your money,
I tell you now, that's not funny,
Then go to the Elkhorn Mine.

If it's in your feet and you can't look neat,
And always have to sit right on your seat,
Then go to the Elkhorn Mine.

If it's in your knees and it hurts to sneeze
Then get out in the nice fresh breeze,
And go to the Elkhorn Mine.

If it's in your hands, more than you can stand,
Get in your car and cross the land,
And go to the Elkhorn Mine.

If it's in your toes or maybe your nose,
As that's the way arthritis goes,
Then go to the Elkhorn Mine.

If it's in your fingers and you can't knit,
That's when you feel like having a fit,
Then go to the Elkhorn Mine.

If it's in your back and when you go to fix a snack,
You feel like you've been hit on a railroad track,
Then go to the Elkhorn Mine.

Now the last place to have it may be in your head,
But if it is though it never was said,
Then go to the Elkhorn Mine.

Now I had it in my hand,
So I jumped the bus and crossed the land,

Notes and business cards in the radon tunnel of the Free Enterprise mine

Waiting room, Free Enterprise

Main building, Free Enterprise

July 1967

Bless this tunnel
 O'Lord we pray,
Make it safe by night
 or day.
Bless all who in
 its tunnels walk
Bless the radon
 God's gift to man
We thank you,
 Dear God
For men like Mr. Lewis
Who shares with *all*
 people.
May the Good Lord
Bless us all
 we pray.

-Mr. & Mrs. Klier,
and Mrs. Strackbein

A Trip to the Doctor

I thought I'd see my doctor
    I wasn't feeling right.
My aches and pains annoyed me
    and I couldn't sleep at night.
The doctor could find no real disorder,
    he wouldn't let it rest.
He said with all my Medicare and Blue Cross,
    I ought to have more tests.
So to the hospital he sent me
    (I didn't feel that bad!)
But he told them to check me—
    for everything that could be had.
So they flouroscoped and stethoscoped,
    and my aging frame displayed.
Lying naked on an ice-cold table,
    while my gizzard was x-rayed.
Then they checked me for worms and parasites,
    for fungus and for crud.
And pierced me with long needles,
    to get samples of my blood.
Then doctors came and checked me over,
    they probed and pushed and poked around.
Then to make sure I was living,
    they had me wired for sound.
And when the tests were all concluded,
    what they found would fill a page.
What I've got will someday kill me,
    For my ailment is: OLD AGE.

-Birdie Coombs, Age 99

Buckets for soaking hands and elbows at the Merry Widow Mine

Painting made in the radon tunnel by a visitor

Way across Minnesota to Montana so great,
To Boulder and wasn't too late,
So now I am better and feel real fine,
Just because I went to the Elkhorn Mine.

-Reath Vincent (no date)

Mining the Future

Patricia Lewis and the other mine owners believe that their radon helps people, and they hope that eventually their finances will allow them to build the sort of restaurants and hotels that tourists of the 1990s expect. The Elkhorns are between Yellowstone and Glacier National Parks, and with the right sort of publicity the mine owners envision Boulder and Basin as a convenient and beautiful stopping place for vacationers. Alternatively, Pat dreams of a Boulder Health Resort, similar to the resort at Bad Gastein, Austria, where people could have radon treatments, massage, mineral baths, and the rest of it.

This is probably not an impossible dream. According to recent studies, the United States seems to be undergoing a surge of renewed interest in so-called "alternative" medical treatments, and these tend to be used most frequently for chronic illnesses such as backache and arthritis (Eisenberg 1998). People have come to expect fast and continuing relief or cures from modern medicine, and when this fails, anything that sounds promising is likely to be tried, especially if testimonies to the remedy's effectiveness are popularized (Kronenfeld and Wasner 1120). Arthritis is particularly prone to the use of alternative remedies or folk remedies, and as long as the pain and symptoms seem to be relieved, the scientific explanation of how and why it works is typically only of secondary concern (1120). It could be that the growing tendency for Americans to use "alternatives," coupled with the frequent use of "alternative" remedies for arthritis, will work in favor of the radon mines. Visitors to the radon mines say they want to "get off the medicine cycle" because the prescription drugs they have been taking cause them problems. They would not generally describe themselves as being "against" the conventional medical system in any way; they simply want relief, and are "willing to try anything." From the perspective of the visitors, trying radon therapy for arthritis seems quite rational. The question for the mine owners now is whether the radon mines will have enough "pull" to attract the numbers of people they need to sustain themselves economically. The European mines have managed to market themselves as resort destinations, successfully enough to draw in thousands of visitors annually; but for the present the six mines of the Elkhorns remain obscure, known for the most part only by word of mouth from people who have found relief from their pain.

The success of European radon mines notwithstanding, the future of "Radon Health Mines" in Montana will depend on the conclusions of medical science in the United States. Although the EPA has taken the position that radon at any dose is dangerous, there is a growing body of research that seems to contradict this.[9] The Boulder and Basin mines will have to keep informed of the status of this research, and they will have to decide whether or not they want to act on it. In order to make Boulder and Basin a true tourist destination, the mine owners will have to commit themselves fully to the financial investment such an effort would entail. They will also need to decide if they want to wait for mainstream medical approval of radon therapy, or if they want to concentrate on appealing to proponents of alternative medicine. Until then, the mine owners can only hope that people in pain will continue to make their journey, encouraged by the positive experiences of previous visitors.

Mining has been the source of prosperity in this area of Montana for more than a century. First with gold and silver, then with uranium, and now with radon, these mines have provided a living to local residents. But mining the future must be focused on bringing people into the area. Instead of shipping ore out, these modern day mines are trying to sell an intangible product: the hope of health. The owners will have to decide if they truly believe in their product, or if they will let the "radon for health" phenomenon go the way of the gold, silver, and uranium ores that are no longer mined.

NOTES

[1] Newspaper clipping from a scrapbook kept by Wade Lewis, dated Saturday, May 16, 1953. The name of the newspaper was not included in the clipping.

[2] See, for example, the EPA Radon and Radionuclide Emission

Standards Hearing Before the Procurement and Military Nuclear Systems Subcommittee, October 6, 1983, first session of the Ninety-eighth Congress (and other similar Congressional hearings devoted to the health effects of ionizing radiation exposure and indoor radon gas). Also see Hendee (1995), Cross (1995), Thomas and Goldsmith (1995) for examples of the public perception of health risks from environmental radiation exposure.

[3]Letters courtesy of Pat Lewis, granddaughter of Wade Lewis and the current owner of the Free Enterprise Radon Health Mine in Boulder, Montana. Although most of the letters were destroyed, an estimated 3000 still remain in her possession.

[4]It is impossible to say how many people actually came to the mines in these first few years. Looking through the local newspapers in 1952-1954 shows just how keen the competition was for the arthritis business. In January 1953, for example, the *Boulder Monitor* reported that 45,000 visitors had used the Merry Widow Mine since it opened for business the previous June, but whether this figure is exagerrated or not is unknown.

[5]Source: State of Montana, Department of Health and Environmental Sciences, September 6, 1991.

[6]A picoCurie is the equivalent of one part per trillion per liter of air (Walchuk 2).

[7] See for example, Jim Muckerheide, 1995a and 1995b; and T.D. Luckey 1994 and 1996.

[8]See, for example, A. Falkenbach and N. Wolter 1997; O. Henn 1956; "Development," *British Journal of Rheumatology* 1997.

[9]See note 7.

REFERENCES

Bailey, Seth Tom. "True Reports on the Underground Cure for Arthritis." *True Magazine* Dec. 1955:16-20+.

Cross, Frederic T. "Evidence of Cancer Risk from Experimental Animal Radon Studies." Young and Yalow 79-88.

"Development of Rheumatoid Arthritis During a Radon Thermal Cure Treatment." Abstract #259. *British Journal of Rheumatology.* XIVth Annual General Meeting (April 1997). Bad Gastein, Austria, 1997.

Earth Angel Health Mine Brochure, 1996.

Eisenberg, David M. "Trends in Alternative Medicine Use in the United States, 1990-1997. Results of a National Follow-up Survey." *JAMA* 280 (1988): 1569-75.

EPA Radon and Radionuclide Emission Standards. Hearing Before the Procurement and Military Nuclear Systems Subcommittee First Session of the Ninety-eighth Congress. (6 Oct. 1983).

Falkenbach, A. and N. Wolter. "Radonthermalstollen-Kur zur Behandlung des Morbus Bechterew." *Research in Complemen-*

tary Medicine (1997): 277-83.

Hendee, William R. "Public Perception of Radiation Risks." Young and Yalow 13-22.

Henn, O. "Combined Treatment by Radium Emanation and Hyperthermy (Subterranean Tunnel Treatment) of Bad Gastein (Bockstein)." *American Medical Association Journal* 161 (1956): 917.

High Ore Health Mine Brochure, 1996.

Hillinger, Charles. "Health Mines: Infirm Seek Magical Cure." *Los Angeles Times* (January 26, 1972): 9.

————. "Ailing Thousands Flock to Mines Seeking Cure." *Los Angeles Times* (January 26, 1972):12.

Kronenfeld, Jennie, and Cody Wasner. "The Use of Unorthodox Therapies and Marginal Practitioners." *Social Sciences and Medicine* 16 (1982): 1119-25.

Lewis, Wade V. Letter to the Atomic Energy Commission 22 July 1949. Free Enterprise Radon Health Mine Papers. Boulder, MT. 1955.

————. *Arthritis and Radioactivity.* Rev. ed. Seattle: Peanut Butter Publishing, 1994.

Lone Tree Health Mine Brochure, 1996.

Luckey, T.D. "A Rosetta Stone for Ionizing Radiation." *Radiation Protection Management* 11 (1994): 73-79.

————. "The Evidence for Radiation Hormesis." *21st Century Science & Technology* 9 (1996): 12-20.

Merry Widow Health Mine Brochure, 1996.

Muckerheide, Jim, ed. Extended abstracts of papers presented at the 1995 Winter Meeting of the American Nuclear Society. *Transactions of the American Nuclear Society* 73 (1995).

———— "The Health Effects of Low Level Radiation: Science, Data and Corrective Action." *Nuclear News* 38 (1995): 26-30.

National Research Council, Committee on Health Risks of Exposure to Radon (BEIR VI). *Health Effects of Exposure to Radon: Time for Reassessment?* Washington, DC: National Academy Press, 1994.

Thomas, Terry L., and Robert Goldsmith. "Department of Energy Radiation Health Studies: Past, Present, and Future." Young and Yalow 41-50.

Walchuk, Mary. "Everybody into the Pool! Determining Residential Radon/Lung Cancer Risk." *The Health Physics Society's Newsletter* 23 (1995): 1+.

Young, Jack P., and Rosalyn S. Yarow, ed. *Radiation and Public Perception: Benefits and Risks.* Advances in Chemistry Series 243. Washington, DC: American Chemical Society, 1995.

RHETORIC AND CHANGE

Life in the West demands more than attitude and endurance—
it requires a clear sense of place and a renewed vigilance for
increasing waves of change. With the urge to preserve frontier traditions and sustain regional character, Westerners confront powerful forces, out of necessity, in our deliberations
about changing communities, attitudes, and ways of living.
Of these forces, the contested terrain of scientific inquiry is,
at times, no less threatening or complex than the impending
demands of military and industrial institutions, but these
arenas of conflict determine the shape of the future. More
importantly, we look to possibilities of mediation and consensus among the various factions that would lay claim to
what each considers rightfully its sense of "how things should
be done" in the West.

We begin this section by following discussions with the
stark presence of nuclear power, which is too often surrounded
by avoidance and misunderstanding. Sue Roff takes us
through the data and dangers surrounding the mining, processing, and disposal of uranium, otherwise known as
"yellowcake" (a term that rhetorically diverts our thinking from
sickness and waste to innocuous pastry). Providing balance
for the knowledge of nuclear dangers and scientific warn-
ings, Susanne Bentley's "Scientific Writing as Persuasion"
narrates the tale of one researcher and his efforts to raise
local awareness of issues surrounding the longevity of Lake
Tahoe. Taken together, these discussions sketch a spectrum
of possibilities for science, progress, and community—and
the potential for their mutual reinforcement and coexistence.

With Keith Sargent's "Growth and Consequences," we
read a primer of sorts for non-economists: a concise and co-
gent survey of the issues involved with continued development and urban expansion in the West. Sargent suggests that

uncontrolled growth is not an inevitability; and although a clearer understanding of growth dynamics is a good start, it will take citizen action, interest groups, and voter turnout to shape the development of the places we call home. Ultimately, the future of the West depends on the active participation of Westerners, and as Daryl Wennemann suggests in "The Future of Work and the Worker," even the idea of community in our current "post-capitalist" society cannot be taken for granted. Traditional notions of community are readily challenged and often under siege, and shaping the way we think of ourselves and our communities may be one the greatest challenges we face. However Westerners envision work and play in the years to come, the question of community may be the force that guides our journey together.

Let Them Eat Yellowcake

SUE RABBITT ROFF

Uranium—yellowcake—is abundant in the earth's crust, forty times more abundant than silver. But it is also highly toxic. The mining of uranium poisons the miners and the communities exposed to leachings from the tailings. Used indiscriminately as radium in medicines or in luminous paint in the 1920s and 1930s, it resulted in bone cancers and leukemia. As a component of nuclear weapons it pollutes the immediate environment as well as resulting in fallout during tests. Used for non-military energy purposes in power plants around the world for forty years, it now constitutes a major radioactive waste disposal problem.

The cycle of uranium mining, detonation and disposal tends to involve the same communities—whether they are the Aboriginal Australians who live alongside the mines and the Maralinga and Emu Field test sites; the Navajo, Lakota, and Hopi of the Four Corners (Arizona, New Mexico, Colorado and Utah) downwind of the Nevada Test Site; the Inuit, Ojibway Nation and Dene Indians of Canada caught between the US's Alaska test site and the old Soviet sites at Novaya Zemlya and Semipalantinsk or the Tibetans who are forced to mine uranium for the Chinese. India, Bolivia, Brazil and Peru also mine uranium and have areas of high background radiation from their uranium deposits. Several African countries produce

Sue Roff is a social scientist who teaches in the Centre for Medical Education of Dundee University Medical School in Scotland. She is particularly interested in the interface between quantitative and qualitative data, especially in the area of the health hazards of nuclear weapons. Her books include Overreaching in Paradise: United States Policy in Palau since 1945 *(Juneau: Denali, 1990) and* Hotspots: the Legacy of Hiroshima and Nagasaki *(London: Cassell, 1995).*

uranium for France's weapons and power plants. Namibia's uranium was appropriated by South Africa. The former Czechoslovakia and East Germany supplied uranium to the Soviet regime.

The same communities are exposed to the hazards of mining the ore, the fallout from its detonation in weapons tests, and now are expected to provide disposal sites for the partially depleted residue of an element that has a half life of thousands of years. Many Marshall Islanders are willing to accept radioactive waste from the nuclear powers—forty years after they suffered extensive exposures to radioactive fallout from the US nuclear tests.

Uranium occurs as an oxide, as pitchblende, or as an oxide combined with vanadium and potassium, known as carnotite. The ore contains 5-50% silica and uranium mining often also therefore entails a risk of silicosis. The crude ore is often crushed at the mine and turned into a uranate, known as yellowcake, which is packed into drums and transported to the users. The primary consumers are the nuclear energy and weapons industries, but yellowcake is also used in ceramics manufacture and in the chemical industry. The chief danger is from the dust inhaled by workers at all stages of the extraction and production processes. But the tailings can also poison local communities and enter the water systems of large regions. Flora and fauna are equally at risk of long term contamination.

When Australia was embarking on major uranium mining in the 1970s, Charles Kerr warned that

All parts of the mine and mill complex are potential sources of uranium exposure from uranium and its decay products. Uranium miners are exposed to external radiation from the rock surface and, most importantly, to inhalation of radon gas. Radon is produced by the radioactive decay of radium: its most important isotope is radon 222 which decays with a half-life of 3.8 days to a series of short-lived alpha-emitting decay products (radon daughters). Radon and its particulate decay products, if inhaled, are a potent source of lung cancer. [1] ("Uranium" 583)

Professor Kerr pointed out that the problem didn't stop there:

> The residue remaining after the production of yellowcake is the finely ground material known as tailings. This contains all the radioactive decay products of uranium which were responsible for most of the radioactivity in the original ore. Milling results in the creation of huge piles of tailings. One decay product, thorium 230, has a half-life of about 76000 years and decays into radium 226, radon 222 and radon decay products. Significant concentrations of radiation are emitted for over 100,000 years. (583)

Fiona Martin and colleagues from the Cytogenetics Laboratory at the British Nuclear Fuels Sellafield installation comment that

> [t]he processing and enrichment of uranium to produce fuel for nuclear reactors encompasses a variety of chemical processes and results in a range of potential types of chemical and radiological exposure. . . . The metabolism of uranium has been extensively reviewed. Long term retention is primarily in the bone, but after administration, high concentrations of uranium first occur in the kidneys. This is particularly true for soluble uranium, which is easily absorbed into the blood. Work with laboratory animals has shown that fatal doses to the kidney are much lower than those expected to produce radiation effects in bone, and therefore the toxicological hazard to the kidneys is considered the limiting factor when setting dose limits for chronic exposure. Effects of radiation may become significant for inhaled uranium particularly if the material is insoluble and is retained in the lungs. (98-102)

Regan and Morgan note that uranium usually constitutes only 0.5% of the ore from which it is derived but can be found at higher grades. Uranium 238 decays to radium 226 which in turn decays to radon 222 which is a gas and emits alpha radiation as do three of its daughters, polonium 218, 214 and 240: "These substances diffuse from the rock into the mine air, where they become attached to particles of dust or moisture on which they may be inhaled into the lungs" (185-204). The alpha particles have a range in tissue just sufficient for them to damage the nuclei of the basal cells of the bronchial epithelium by ionisation and it is assumed that this damage may later lead to malignant change.

Harting and Hesse observed a marked increase in the frequency of lung cancer among miners in Bohemia more than a century ago. Vich and Pacina have reported on the incidence of lung carcinoma in uranium miners in Czechoslovakia in the late 1970s.[2] Tomasek and colleagues studied 4320 uranium miners in West Bohemia who started work at the mines during 1948 to 1959 and worked there for at least four years. They followed this group until the end of 1990. The workers had high radon exposures as well as high arsenic levels in two of the mines, and exposure to dust. Their chances of dying of lung cancer increased fivefold in relation to the rest of the community.

The connection between uranium mining and smoking as causes of lung cancer was explored extensively in a study of American miners between 1950 and 1967 (Lundin et al.). The miners experienced a six-fold increase of mortality from lung cancer against the expected rate and the likelihood of dying from this disease was clearly related to the calculated cumulative exposure to radiation expressed in working level months. In the early 1970s other researchers (Archer et al.)[3] found that cigarette smoking among uranium miners increased their likelihood of death from lung cancer. A similar study of workers at the Radium Hill mine in South Australia between 1952 to 1987 also found an elevated level of lung cancer among those most heavily exposed to radon (Woodward et al.)[4].

In 1985 Gregg S. Wilkinson of the Epidemiology Group at the Los Alamos National Laboratory studied mortality from gastric cancer in those New Mexico counties which have commercially significant deposits of uranium. Seven of the thirty two counties displayed stomach cancer rates through the 1970s for white males above the 90th percentile when compared to US rates and female rates in all of these counties also exceeded the 90th percentile (307-12). Five of the nine counties revealed significantly elevated mortality rates among white males, and six for white females. According to Wilkinson,

"These findings demonstrate that all counties in New Mexico with commercially significant uranium deposits, or uranium mining and milling operations, are also characterised by high mortality rates for gastric cancer" (312). Since the findings were similar for both males and females, the cause was less likely to be employment in the uranium operations alone than environmental pollution arising from them. He notes that use of adobe bricks is a common building practice throughout New Mexico, and housing constructed on soil containing high levels of uranium and thorium may result in the inhabitants being exposed to high levels of radon and radon daughters "depending on the type of housing and associated air exchange rates" (312). The exposure may come from the food chain from animals grazing on such soil. The tailings have been shown to have high levels of trace elements such as arsenic, cadmium, selenium, molybdenum and lead as well as compounds such as cyanide. Most of these are known to be carcinogenic or otherwise highly toxic. Other researchers detected raised levels of 226Ra and 210Po in the liver and kidney tissues of cattle from the Ambrosia Lake region of New Mexico, which has been the site of extensive uranium mining for thirty years and contains several underground mines, a processing mill and two large tailings piles (Lapham et al.). Concentrations of 226Ra were found in vegetation around tailings in Wyoming (Ibrahim and Whicker, "Plant/Soil"). Another study found much greater uptake of 230Th than previously reported in such vegetation (Ibrahim and Whicker, "Comparative")[5].

Other researchers found evidence of renal toxicity or kidney malfunction among 39 men who worked in the yellowcake drying and packaging operations at a Colorado uranium mill as compared to 36 local cement plant workers (Thun et al.). They concluded that "The data presented suggest reduced renal proximal tubular reabsorbtion of amino acids and of low molecular weight proteins, consistent with uranium nephrotoxicity" (90).

Dupree and her colleagues studied 995 white males who had worked for more than a month in uranium processing jobs at the Linde Air Products Company in upstate New York between 1943 and 1949[6]. This workforce was unusual in that it was no healthier than the general white male population of the surrounding area, whereas a workforce usually exhibits the "healthy worker effect." This means that workers as a group are less likely to be ill with cardiovascular and other circulatory diseases and most other conditions than the general population of their gender, which includes those too ill to work as well as healthy men. But these men were working in the plant during the war years, after the military services had selected the healthiest men, and had a lung cancer rate of 100—parity with the other men in the community, as were their incidence rates for cirrhosis of the liver. But even so their laryngeal cancer death rate was more than four times that expected (SMR 447). And the number of men at the factory who had died of pneumonia was more than double (SMR 217) that of the other men in the community (100-07).

The same held true of a study of men who worked at the Eldorado Resources Limited Beaverlodge uranium mine in Saskatchewan between 1948 and 1980 who also failed to demonstrate a healthy worker effect. These men experienced high rates of mortality throughout their age groups from lung cancer due to exposure to radon decay products and industrial accidents, according to a study by Howe et al("Components").[7]

Studies of the human metabolism of uranium and its products have resulted in better understanding and monitoring of depositions through inhalation into the lungs (Barber and Forrest). Many uranium mines also use urine bioassay techniques to check the exposures of their workers (Reif).

But the communities in the vicinity of uranium mines are also exposed to environmental hazards from the leachings of the tailings of the separation process. James Garrett, a Lakota Indian and Director for Environmental Affairs of the Cheyenne River Reservation, told the World Uranium Hearing in Salzburg in 1992 that

> In the 1970s, during the so-called energy crisis when gasoline and petroleum were supposedly scarce, gigantic multinational corporations came into the southern Black Hills and started drilling holes wherever they felt like it; deep into the ground—they were looking for uranium, and . . . because it was too expensive to properly cap off those holes—the uranium that they found mixed in with underground water aquifers and travelled underneath the ground to the wells that are

drilled on the Pine Ridge Reservation—a distance of about 50 miles.

In 1979 one of the Indian nurses working at the Pine Ridge hospital noticed a dramatic increase in spontaneous abortions and birth defects. Mr Garrett said,

> You know, the nuclear fuel cycle, in our country at least, begins and ends on Indian homelands. They come and they dig it up. They contaminate the whole countryside with their dust that blows around and that gets into our aquifers. They take it away and do whatever they want with it. They tell all the people of Europe, it's a good clean industry. But I'm here to tell you that now they're knocking on our door because they can't find any place to store the damned stuff for eternity. They come to our homeland and they want to lease some land for 10,000 years!

Lorraine Rekmans, an Ojibway Indian journalist, has reported higher levels of ovarian and uterine cancers, coronary heart diseases and chronic obstructive lung disease in the communities around the Elliot Lake uranium mines in Ontario, Canada, once considered the uranium capital of the world. George Blondin, Elder of the Dene Nation in the Northwest Territories of Canada, told the Salzburg meeting that

> [a]round 1950, there was a boom in Canada and in the United States for uranium. Everybody started looking for uranium, and they found all kinds of uranium in Canada including United States. Not long after that there was another mine discovered not very far from Great Bear Lake towards Yellowknife, and that mine was about 80 miles from the biggest community of Indian people. There was about 1,500 people living in that community, and the river flows right by that community. And that mine, it exists around 15 years. It's the same thing, they dump their dump right in there, a small piece of lake, maybe two or three miles round. So the people there, after investigating what's going on around that lake, it was . . . the trees wouldn't grow any more, they all dried up, and the birds—and

there was no birds coming there. And it was a good hunting ground, but resource people tried to explain to the people that it was quite safe to go there, but a lot of other people, they scared the Indians off that area, so they didn't go to that area until today, they didn't go to that area anymore because of—you could see the evidence that the uranium-ore waste, what it does; the trees are dead, the birds don't go there anymore, there is no more beaver, there is no more muskrat, that we can't go there anymore. So, this is the kind of experience that the Indian people have in uranium mining. And it scares people, it still scares them today. . . . the Elders, they are complaining, in one life span they recognise there's something wrong with the earth. No ducks coming round, no much fish, fish are not very healthy, caribou is not very healthy, moose is not very healthy, and people tell us we have acid rain in the country, and it scares people.

Clulow and colleagues found Radium 226 in the inactive uranium tailings at Elliot Lake, Ontario which other researchers also found in the flora and fauna[8]. As early as 1981, Moore and Sutherland found clear correlations between proximity to the mine tailings and increased levels of heavy metals and radionuclides despite the chemical bonding with the sediment of the Great Bear Lake.

A study of Navajo birth outcomes in the Shiprock uranium mining area of New Mexico from 1964 to 1981 found evidence of greater risk for mothers living nearest to the tailings of the mine—even greater than that of the men who worked in the mines. Gamma radiation data for residential sections of the mining area taken in 1988 and 1989 showed exposures of 1.7-5.2m Sv y-1 in contrast with standards for public exposure of 0.25m SV y-1. This was near homes built of radioactive dump rock (Shilds et al.).

Mays et al. reported a study of two boys who had played on uranium tailings, one of whom was diagnosed with leukemia at the age of fifteen although they reserved judgement as to whether this was induced by the radium 226 in the mill waste.

The United States stopped producing highly enriched uranium for weapons in 1964 and plutonium production ended in 1990. Nevertheless there are still an estimated 248 metric tons of weapons grade plutonium and 2,285 metric tons of highly enriched uranium on the planet —nearly half of it produced by the United States (McGirk 11). That does not include the 122 metric tons of reactor-grade civilian plutonium recovered from spent or irradiated nuclear fuel and another 532 metric tons of reactor grade plutonium in civilian spent nuclear fuel. The amount of plutonium on the planet grows by more than sixty tons a year. There is increasing fear that reactor-grade plutonium can be used in weapons, of at least the same yield as those used on Hiroshima and Nagasaki.

Nine US nuclear weapons manufacturing plants have qualified for the Environmental Protection Agency's "Superfund" National Priorities List of the worst contaminated sites in the country. Decontaminating the ground water or aquifers of sites such as Hanford in Washington State may be beyond the technology presently available, spreading as they do over more than 150 square miles. There is also more than 100 million gallons of radioactive waste stored around the United States, much of it at Hanford.

The potential for catastrophe can be seen from the similar situation at the Soviet plutonium manufacturing plant, Mayak Production Association in the southern Urals about 2000 miles southeast of Moscow. The city of Chelyabinsk is now regarded as the most contaminated region in the world, since some 76 million cubic metres of nuclear waste water, laced with strontium 89 and strontium 90 as well as caesium 139, were dumped in the river system from 1949 to 1967. People living in villages along the Techa and Iset rivers were exposed to radiation from their garden water, their drainage systems, and their drinking water. International studies have been undertaken since 1994 to assess the health consequences. Elaine Gallin of the US Department of Energy says, "The point is to have a much more accurate estimate of the risk for workers in the nuclear industry, in clean ups and near waste sites" (qtd. in Cornwell 21). One study has already found that of 1479 workers exposed to plutonium, 105 had died of lung cancer, twice the expected rate.

At the end of 1980 the US Uranium Registry tissue program was established to enable researchers to compare the presence and distribution of uranium *in vivo* with results of analysis of tissue obtained at autopsy. Individuals who had worked at uranium fuel fabrication plants were contacted and asked to sign 5 year autopsy agreements:

> While this agreement provides permission for an autopsy, experience has shown that a standard autopsy permit may be required at the time of death to satisfy hospital authorities and local legal requirements. For this reason, it is imperative that the next of kin be aware of the program and be agreeable to the volunteer's participation in the Registry tissue program. The next of kin receives a $500 stipend when the autopsy is completed, as a gesture of appreciation for the registrant's willingness to participate in the program and to allow tissue to be taken for analysis, and for co-operation in keeping the USUR informed of the participant's place of residence. (Moore and Breitenstein 373-76)

Tissue from the skeleton, lungs, tracheobronchial lymph nodes and kidney are frozen and sent to Richland, WA for radiochemical analysis. The first 17 individuals worked with uranium in various forms at the AEC, ERDA and DOE Fernald Ohio plant as well as Hanford.

In a Utah study, lungs of seven uranium miners were studied for their uranium and thorium content:

> The lung tissues were transferred to 4-1 beakers and heated on a hot plate at a low temperature to remove formalin. 232U and 229 Th tracers were added and sufficient nitric acid was added to immerse the tissues which were then heated strongly to remove most of the organics. Finally, 100 ml concentrated sulfuric acid was added and heated strongly with occasional additions of nitric acid and H2O2, to remove traces of organics. Most of the sulfuric acid was removed by evaporation and the residue was dissolved in 1:1 HNO3 by heating. The solution was centrifuged and the clear solution was transferred to another beaker leaving some insoluble material in the centrifuge tube. This insoluble material, mostly silica, was then dissolved in a mixture of HF and HNO3 in a Teflon beaker. The HF was then removed by heating slowly and the resi-

due dissolved in HNO3 was then transferred to the bulk of the solution. Ten mg of iron carrier were added and uranium and thorium were coprecipitated with iron hydroxide by adding ammonium hydroxide.

Eventually the precipitate was dried and electrodeposited on to platinum discs for measurements with alpha spectrometers. It was found that the concentration of 230Th were about 30 times higher than those found in non-miners dying at comparable ages from the same region (Wrenn et al. 385-89).

At the same time researchers at the Argonne National Laboratory were finding that uranium was being retained much longer in the chests of exposed workers than predicted by the International Commission on Radiological Protection (ICRP). This suggested that "in epidemiologic studies of early uranium workers, late effects on lymphatic tissues should be examined in addition to lung and bone cancer" (Keane and Polednak 391-402).

Studies of pulmonary retention of plutonium and americium oxides in a worker who had been accidentally exposed to inhalation of these substances led researchers at the UK Atomic Energy Research Establishment to conclude, "It would appear that, both for inhaled 238PuO2 and 241 AmO2, predictions based on the ICRP's clearance model can grossly underestimate the long-term irradiation of systemic sites." An Austrian researcher commented that "Lung cancer is commonly regarded as the most important somatic effect due to inhalation of alpha-emitting nuclides. Candidates for cancer induction are cells receiving radiation energy which is sufficient to induce malignant transformation, but insufficient to kill or sterilize the cell." (Hoffman 419-29)

His research indicated that

For higher doses, i.e. many multiple hits, the specific energy distribution for the hot spot is centered at higher specific energies than for a uniform distribution. Also a smaller percentage of cells is hit in a defined tissue volume. This means that a smaller number of cells receives higher radiation doses. Both facts lead to a decreased number of non-lethally damaged cells in the hot spot case. Since the cells in the vicinity of the particulate will receive more frequently lethal doses, the distribution of the non-lethally damaged cells will become more porous. At high doses a hot spot will be, therefore, less effective in radiation carcinogenesis than uniform source. (419-21)

In other words, low dose long term exposure might be more carcinogenic than high dose short exposures.

In October 1995 President Clinton's Advisory Committee on Human Radiation Experiments reported a series of experiments in which non-consenting patients had been injected with uranium and other radioactive substances as part of a programme of research authorised by the Atomic Energy Commission (792). Similar experiments were reported in the UK. The Committee found that at least several hundred uranium miners died of lung cancer and surviving miners remain at elevated risk because of their exposure to radon well in excess of levels known to be hazardous when they were the subject of government study as they mined uranium for use in weapons manufacture. They recommended lowering the criteria for compensation for lung cancer for uranium miners, urging that

[t]he grave injustice that the government did to the uranium miners, by failing to take action to control the hazard and by failing to warn the miners of the hazard, should not be compounded by unreasonable barriers to receiving the compensation the miners deserve for the wrongs and harms inflicted upon them as they served their country. (815)

President Clinton subsequently announced a multi-million dollar compensation programme for US uranium miners. The Radiation Exposure Compensation Act of 1999 seeks to raise the level of compensation to $200,000 and expedite claims. The United Mine Workers of America is particularly concerned to press for fair access to compensation and to improve safety condtions for those still working with uranium.

Far from disappearing, the market for uranium has proliferated since the collapse of the Soviet Union. All grades of uranium from reprocessed to weapons grade are now reported to be available for sale in Kabul and Peshawar and other places bordering the former Soviet Union. Iran, Iraq, North Korea, Libya and Pakistan are reported to be the most active customers (McGirk 11). As always, the buyer needs to beware, since one military expert trying to monitor the trade was reported as saying that much of the material "could be just radioactive waste scooped off the rubbish heap of some Russian hospital" (11). New uranium mines are being developed in the Ukraine, Russia, Kazakhstan, Uzbekistan, Mongolia, India and Australia as well as Malawi and Brazil.

In Australia, not only has a new mine been developed with a World Heritage-listed national park of great significance to the Aboriginal people, but activists report that Environmental Impact Statements are required to meet lower standards than previously.

NOTES

[1] See also Kerr ("Hazards") and Cawte. A novel about uranium mining in Australia is B. Wongar's *Gabo Djara* (London: Macmillan, 1987).
[2] See also Pirchan and Sikl; Suda et al. [in Czech]; and Vich and Kubat [in Czech].
[3] See also Hornung and Meinhardt; Kohler; Roscoe et al.; Loomis et al.; Tirmarche et al.; and Thomas et al.
[4] See also Petterson and Koperski; Leach et al.; Wise; and Strong and Levins.
[5] See also Ibrahim and Whicker, "Ground Distribution"; Mason et al.; works by Snelling; Shearer and Sill; and Ruttenber et al.
[6] See also Cookfair; Hickey, Crawford-Brown, and Tankersley; Matanoski et al.; Polednak and Frome; Rowland et al.; Waxweiler et al.; Whittemore and McMillan; Waggoner et al.; Lundin et al.; Halpern and Whittemore; and Bertell.
[7] See also Howe, et al., "Lung Cancer"; Macdiamird et al.; Brandon et al.; Saccomano et al.; and Tawn and Binks.
[8] See also Waite et al.; Murray et al.; Wren et al.; and Cloutier et al

WORKS CITED

Archer, V. E., et al. "Uranium Mining and Cigarette Smoking Effects on Man." *Journal of Occupational Medicine* 15 (1973): 204.

Barber, Jerry M., and Robert D. Forrest. "A Study of Uranium Lung Clearance at a Uranium Processing Plant." *Health Physics* 68 (1995): 661-69.

Bertell, R. "Estimates of Uranium and Nuclear Radiation Casualties Attributable to Activities Since 1945." *Medicine and War* 4 (1988): 26-27.

Brandon, W. F., et al. "Chromose Aberrations in Uranium Miners Occupationally Exposed to 222 Radon." *Radiation Research* 52 (1972): 204-15.

Cawte, Alice. Atomic Australia: 1944-1990. Independent Committee of Inquiry into the Nuclear Weapons and Other Consequences of Australian Uranium Mining. Sydney: Total Environment Centre, 1984.

Cloutier, N. R., et al. "Transfer Coefficient of 226Ra from Vegation to Meadow Voles, Microtus pennsylvanicus, on U Mill Tailings." *Health Physics* 50.6 (1986): 775-80.

Clulow, F. V., et al. "Uptake of 226Ra by Established Vegetation and Black Cutworm Larvae, Agrotis ipsilon (class Insecta: order Lepidoptera), on Uranium Mill Tailings at Elliott Lake, Canada." *Health Physics* 55.1 (1988): 31-35.

Cookfair, D. L. "Lung Cancer Among Workers at a Uranium Processing Plant." *Health Physics Society, Epidemiology Applied to Health Physics: Proceedings of the Sixteenth Midyear Topical Symposium, Albuquerque, NM, January 10-14, 1983.* US Department of Energy Report CONF-830101. Springfield, VA: National Technical Information Service, 1984. 398-406.

Cornwell, Tim. "Low Seepage System." *The Times Higher Education Supplement* 1 Mar. 1996: 21.

Dupree, Elizabeth A., et al. "Mortality Among Workers at a Uranium Processing Facility, the Linde Air Products Company Ceramics Plant, 1943-1949." *Scandinavian Journal of Work and Environmental Health* 13 (1987): 100-07.

Garrett, James. *Poison Fire, Sacred Earth.* Salzburg: The World Uranium Hearing, 1992.

Halpern, J., and A. S. Whittemore. "Methods for Analyzing Occupational Cohort Data with Application to Lung Cancer in US Uranium Miners." *Journal of Chronic Diseases* 40 [Supplement 2] (1987): 79S-88S.

Harting, F. H., and W. Hesse. "Der Lungenkrebs, die Bergrankheit in der Schneeburger Gruben." *Vischr. Gericti. Med.* (1879): 31.

Hickey, J. L., S.D. Crawford-Brown, and W. G. Tankersley. Occupational Exposures of Workers to Chemicals and Radiation During Uranium Processing at the Linde Ceramics Plant, 1943-1949. ORAU Technical Report no. 243. Oak Ridge, TN: Oak Ridge Associated Universities, 1985.

Hofman, W. "Microdosimetry of Plutonium in Lungs." *Health Physics* [Supplement 1] (1983): 419-29.

Hornung, R., and T. Meinhardt. "Quantitative Risk Assessment of Lung Cancer in US Uranium Miners." *Health Physics* 52 (1987): 417-30.

Howe, Geoffrey R., A. M. Chiarelli, J. P. Lindsay. "Components and Modifiers of the Healthy Worker Effect: Evidence from Three Occupational Cohorts and Implications for Industrial Compensation." *American Journal of Epidemiology* 128.6 (1988): 1364-75.

Howe, Geoffrey R., R. C. Nair, H. B. Newcombe, A. B. Miller, and J. D. Abbatt. "Lung Cancer Mortality in Relation to Radon Daughter Exposure in a Cohort of Workers at the Eldorado Beaverlodge Uranium Mine." *Journal of the National Cancer Institute* 77 (1986): 357-62.

Ibrahim, S. A., and F. W. Whicker. "Comparative Uptake of U and Th by Native Plants at a U Production Site." *Health Physics* 54.4 (1988): 413-19.

———. "Ground Distribution Patterns of Selected Radioactive, Chemical, and Physical Contaminants from Dispersion of Uranium Mill Tailings." *Health Physics* 58.3 (1990): 321-28.

———. "Plant/Soil Concentration Ration of 226Ra for Contrasting Sites Around an Active Uranium Mine-Mill." *Health Physics* 55.6 (1988): 903-10.

Keane, A. T., and A. P. Polednak. "Retention of Uranium in the Chest: Implications of Findings In Vivo and Post-mortem." *Health Physics* 44 [Supplement 1] (1983): 391-402.

Kerr, Charles. "Hazards to the Health of Uranium Workers and the Regional Population." *Social and Environmental Choice: The Impact of Uranium Mining in the Northern Territory.* Ed. Stuart Harris. Australian National University, 1980.

———. "Uranium: Health Risks from a Nuclear Power Industry." *The Medical Journal of Australia.* 29 Oct. 1977: 583-86.

Kohler, D. "Lung Injury Caused by the Inhalation of Radioactive Substances." *Praxis und Klinik des Pneumologie* 42 [Supplement 1] (1988): 263-64.

Lapham, S. C. "Health Implications of Radionuclide Levels in Cattle Raised Near Uranium Mining Facilities in Ambrosia Lake, New Mexico." *Health Physics* 56.3 (1989): 327-40.

Leach, V. A., et al. "A Study of Radiation Parameters in an Open-Pit Mine." *Health Physics* 43.3 (1982): 363-75.

Loomis, D. P., et al. "Micronuclei in Epithelia Cells from Sputum of Uranium Miners." *Scandinavian Journal of Work and Environmental Health* 16.5 (1990): 355-62.

Lundin, F. E., E.M. Smith, V .E. Archer, and D. A. Holaday. "Mortality of Miners in Relation to Radiation Exposure, Hard Rock Mining and Cigarette Smoking—1950 through September 1967." *Health Physics* 16 (1969): 571-78.

Lundin, F. E., et al. "An Exposure-Time Response Model for Lung Cancer Mortality in Uranium Miners: Effects of Radiation Exposure, Age and Cigarette Smoking." *Energy and Health.* Ed. N. E. Breslow and A. S. Whittemore. Philadelphia: SIAM,

1979.

Macdiamird, W. D., et al. "Chromosomal Changes Produced by Irradiation in Uranium Miners." *Mammalian Chromosome Newsletter* 9 (1968): 36.

Martin, Fiona, et al. "A Cytogenetic Study of Men Occupationally Exposed to Uranium." *British Journal of Industrial Medicine* 48 (1991): 98-102.

Mason, T. J., et al. "Uranium Mill Tailings and Cancer Mortality in Colorado." *Journal of the National Cancer Institute* 49.3 (1972): 661-64.

Matanoski, G. M., et al. "Cancer Risks in Radiologists and Radiation Workers." *Radiation Carcinogenesis: Epidemiology and Biological Significance*. New York: Raven Press, 1984. 83-96.

Mays, C. W., et al. "Radium 226 Dose to a Boy from Playing on Mill Tailings." *Health Physics* 61.2 (1991): 203-07.

McGirk, Tim. "Iranians 'buying ex-Soviet uranium.'" *The Independent* 28 Mar. 1996: 11.

Moore, J. W., and D. J. Sutherland. "Distribution of Heavy Metals and Radionuclides in Sediments, Water, and Fish in an Area of Great Bear Lake Contaminated with Mine Wastes." *Archives of Environmental Contamination and Toxicology* 10.3 (1981): 329-38.

Moore, R. H., and B. D. Breitenstein, Jr. "The US Uranium Tissue Program." *Health Physics* 44 [Supplement 1] (1983): 373-76.

Murray, M. L., et al. "Estimation of Long-Term Risk from Canadian Uranium Mill Tailing." *Risk Analysis* 7.3 (1987): 287-98.

Newton, D., et al. "Differential Clearance of Plutonium and Americium Oxides from the Human Lung." *Health Physics* 44 [Supplement 1] (1983): 431-39.

Petterson, H. B., and J. Koperski. "Investigation of Aerial Dispersion of Radioactive Dust from an Open-Pit Uranium Mine by Passive Vinyl Collectors." *Health Physics* 60.5 (1991): 681-90.

Pirchan, A., and H. Sikl. "Cancer of the Lung in the Miners of Joachimsthal." *American Journal of Cancer* 16 (1932): 681.

Polednak, A. P., and E. L. Frome. "Mortality Among Men Employed Between 1943 and 1947 at a Uranium Processing Plant." *Journal of Occupational Medicine* 23 (1981): 169-78.

Regan, R.B., and W. K. C. Morgan. "Respiratory Cancers in Mining." *Occupational Medicine: State of the Art Reviews* 8.1 (1993): 185-204.

Reif, R. H. "Uranium in Vitro Bioassay Action Level Used to Screen Workers for Chronic Inhalation Intakes of Uranium Mill Tailings." *Health Physics* 63.4 (1992): 398-401.

Roscoe, R., et al. "Lung Cancer Mortality Among Nonsmoking Uranium Miners Exposed to Radon Daughters." *Journal of the American Medical Association* 252 (1989): 629-33.

Rowland, R. E., et al. "Dose-Response Relationships for Female Radium Dial Workers." *Health Physics* 44 [Supplement 1] (1983): 15-31.

Ruttenber, A. J. "The Assessment of Human Exposure to Radionuclides from a Uranium Mill Tailings Release and Mine Dewatering Effluent." *Health Physics* 47.1 (1984): 21-35.

Saccomano, G., et al. "Chromosome Aberrations as a Biological Dose-Response Indicator of Radiation Exposure in Uranium Miners." *Radiation Research* 76 (1978): 159-71.

Shearer, S. D. Jr., and C. W. Sill. "Evaluation of Atmospheric Radon in the Vicinity of Uranium Mill Tailings." *Health Physics* 17.1 (1969): 77-88.

Shilds, L. M., et al. "Navajo Birth Outcomes in the Shiprock Uranium Mining Area." *Health Physics* 63.5 (1992): 542-51.

Snelling, R. N. "Environmental Survey of Uranium Mill Tailings Pile, Mexican Hat, Utah." *Radiological Health Data Reports* 12.1 (1971): 17-28.

———. "Environmental Survey of Uranium Mill Tailings Pile, Monument Valley, Arizona." *Radiological Health Data Reports* 11.10 (1970): 511-17.

———. *Radiological Health Data Reports* 10.11 (1969): 475-87.

Strong, K. P., and D. M. Levins. "Effect of Moisture Content on Radon Elimination from Uranium Ore and Tailing." *Health Physics* 42.1 (1982): 27-32.

Suda, J., et al. "Clinical Pattern and Treatment Results in Professional Bronchogenic Carcinoma Due to Radioactive Radiation." *Studia Pneumologica et Phtiseologia Czechoslovaka* 32 (1972): 259.

Tawn, E. J., and K. A. Binks. "A Cytogenetic Study of Radiation Workers: The Influence of Dose Accumulation Patterns and Smoking." *Radiation Protection Dosimetry* 28 (1989): 173-80.

Thomas, D., et al. "Temporal Factors Modifying the Radon-Smoking Interaction." *Health Physics* 66.3 (1994): 257-62.

Thun, Michael J., et al. "Renal Toxicity in Uranium Mill Workers." *Scandinavian Journal of Work and Environmental Health* 11 (1985): 83-90.

Tirmarche, M., et al. "Epidemiological Study of French Uranium Miners." *Cancer Detection and Prevention* 16.3 (1992): 169-72.

United States. Presidential Advisory Committee on Human Radiation. Final Report. Washington: GPO, 1995.

Vich, Z., and M. Kubat. "Lung Cancer Caused by Radioactive Substances." *Radioaktivita a Zivotne Prostredie* 5 (1982): 290.

Vich, Z., and V. Pacina. "Lung Carcinoma in Uranium Miners, Czechoslovakia, 1976-1980." *Neoplasma* 34.2 (1987): 211-15.

Waggoner, J. K., et al. "Radiation as the Cause of Lung Cancer Among

Uranium Miners." *New England Journal of Medicine* 273 (1965): 181-88.

Waite, D. T., et al. "The Effect of Uranium Mine Tailings on Radionuclide Concentrations in Langley Bay, Saskatchewan, Canada." *Archives of Environmental Contamination and Toxicology* 17.3 (1988): 373-80.

Waxweiler, R. J., et al. "Mortality Patterns Among a Retrospective Cohort of Uranium Mill Workers." *Health Physics Society, Epidemiology Applied to Health Physics: Proceedings of the Sixteenth Midyear Topical Symposium, Albuquerque, NM, January 10-14, 1983.* US Department of Energy Report CONF-830101. Springfield, VA: National Technical Information Service, 1984. 428-35.

Whittemore, A. S., and A. McMillan. "Lung Cancer Mortality Among US Uranium Miners." *Journal of the National Cancer Institute* 71 (1983): 489-99.

Wilkinson, Gregg S. "Gastric Cancer in New Mexico Counties with Significant Deposits of Uranium." *Archives of Environmental Health* 40.6 (1985): 307-12.

Wise, K. N. "Dose Conversion Factors for Radon Daughters in Underground and Open-Cut Mine Atmospheres." *Health Physics* 43.1 (1982): 53-64.

Woodward, A., et al. "Radon Daughter Exposures at the Radium Hill Uranium Mine and Lung Cancer Rates Among Former Workers, 1952-87." *Cancer Causes Control* 2.4 (1991): 213-20.

Wren, C. D., et al. "Ra226 Concentration in Otter, Lutra Candensis, Trapped Near Uranium Tailings at Eliott Creek, Ontario." *Bulletin of Environmental Contamination and Toxicology* 38.2 (1987): 209-12.

Wrenn, M. E., et al. "Uranium and Thorium Isotopes and Their State of Equilibria in Lungs from Uranium Miners." *Health Physics* 44 [Supplement 1] (1983): 385-89.

Scientific Writing as Persuasion
Rhetoric and Rethinking the Environment at Lake Tahoe

SUSANNE BENTLEY

The place where I live, Lake Tahoe, is renowned for its surreally crystalline blue waters. To hike on the conifer-lined high trails that rim the lake, viewing it from above, gives a wondrous perspective of the lake's vastness. And its breathtaking blue. However many shades of blue exist in the spectrum visible to human eyes must be found somewhere in the water at Lake Tahoe. From Rubicon Point, where it's possible to take in the entire body of water from an east-west view, the twenty-two mile length of the lake spreads out in a panorama from left to right, and Lake Tahoe resembles an immense, inland ocean. An air of mystery always swirls around me when I come here. I stand two hundred feet above the white-capped surface on one of the black, windswept cliffs shooting like ramparts up from the water. Here, no beach gives way to a gradual, soothing drop. Instead, the lake bottom falls away deliberately. Only a little distance from shore, the water is twelve hundred feet deep and the luxuriant blue of a priceless sapphire.

Samuel Clemens, who would later become known to readers as Mark Twain, observed the spectacular beauty and remarkable clarity of the world's tenth-deepest lake when he visited in the early 1860's, calling it the "fairest sight the whole Earth affords" (134).

When Clemens came West for the Comstock Lode silver boom, he visited Lake Tahoe in 1861. In *Roughing It*, he would later chronicle how clear the water here was before European settlement. After he and a friend silently drifted over the surface in a small boat, faces to the water, he recalls,

---

Susanne Bentley works for the Tahoe Regional Planning Agency and writes about environmental issues at Lake Tahoe and the West.

> So singularly clear was the water, that where it was
> only twenty or thirty feet deep the bottom was so per-
> fectly distinct that the boat seemed floating in the air!
> Yes, where it was even eighty feet deep. Every little
> pebble was distinct, every speckled trout, every hand's
> breadth of sand. (138)

Sometimes, Clemens would swerve the boat suddenly to avoid
granite boulders "as large as a village church" only to float
over them and realize that the danger that appeared to be
coming straight out of the water at them was actually "twenty
or thirty feet below the surface" (138).

Clemens' account is significant because he came here
before Lake Tahoe was settled. His description is haunting:
"Down through the transparency of these great depths, the
water was not merely transparent, but dazzlingly, brilliantly
so" (138).

At the time Samuel Clemens was waxing rhapsodically
about Tahoe's pristine beauty, lumbermen were cutting ten
thousand board feet of timber a day on the lake's east shore
to send over the mountain to Virginia City to shore up the
hundreds of miles of mines, fuel steam pumps and build a
new city (Strong 27-29).

During the Comstock's twenty-year heyday, entire
mountainsides in the Lake Tahoe basin were clear cut to provide for the insatiable hunger for timber. Lake Tahoe environmental historian Douglas H. Strong says that "lumber (including sawed mine timbers) valued at more than $80 million
came from the forests of the Tahoe and Truckee basins" during those peak years (30). With the surrounding hillsides de-
nuded, spring runoff from the deep Sierra snowpack brought
heavy loads of sediments and nutrients into the lake to start
the first cycle of environmental degradation.

After the veins of silver and gold diminished, Tahoe went
back to a period of near quiet, with the forests growing back
and relatively little human disturbance—a period University
of California, Davis, limnologist Charles Goldman describes
as "Lake Tahoe's 'Golden Age' during the period of 1920-1950;
a time of outstanding water quality" (*Conflict* 1).

The golden age didn't last long, however. Post-World-War-
II prosperity, the proximity of three of the country's largest
cities, and the advent of casino gambling brought hordes of

people and extensive development. This started a new cycle of watershed disturbance with building construction, road cuts, ski resort and golf course development, destruction of essential wetlands, and near-extinction of some native plants. But while the lake was able to recover on its own from the deforestation of the Comstock era, this new cycle of environmental destruction is more far reaching.

Goldman calls Lake Tahoe a microcosm for the environmental problems of the twentieth century, and this is due, in part, to its unusual geology ("Microcosm" 93). Lake Tahoe is essentially a basin, and its large volume of 156 cubic kilometers and relatively limited watershed contribute to its historic clarity. The lake is twenty-two miles long and twelve miles wide with a surface elevation of 6,223 feet. Lake Tahoe sits in a three-hundred-fifteen square mile depression surrounded by mountains, and the lake comprises approximately forty percent of the basin.

Alterations to the watershed and airshed in the surrounding environment, whether human-caused or natural, are eventually manifested in the water quality of the lake. The lake also has a retention rate of at least six hundred years, meaning that once pollution enters the lake, it is essentially there to stay. By studying the Lake Tahoe environment, scientists have a compressed view of how human actions affect other environments. Goldman says:

> Reviewing the various problems while maintaining a focus on the lake itself may provide useful guidance in other similar situations, both foreign and domestic, where planners, in the face of increasing population pressures, hope to maintain environmental quality during the inevitable urbanization of areas adjacent to sensitive freshwater or marine ecosystems. ("Microcosm" 93)

Lake Tahoe is a classically Western nitrogen-limited lake and "ultra-oligotrophic," meaning it is naturally poor in nutrients but rich in oxygen. Nutrients in the form of eroded soils, which produce phosphorus, and from air pollution, which produces nitrogen oxides, continue to pour into the lake despite more than eighty-million dollars that have been spent in public erosion-control projects. "If current levels of pollution continue," Goldman says, "the lake will lose its famous clarity in about thirty years" (*Conflict* 1).

In this article, I will look at two of Goldman's early journal articles on Lake Tahoe and attempt to see how his writing and public discourse have forged the contemporary debate over the environmental future of the lake. Goldman has achieved national and international prominence, and I am curious to see how he used language to go beyond the recording of scientific data to shape readers' ways of thinking and to contribute to our understanding of environmental ethics.

The Social Context of the Articles

To fully appreciate the validity of the texts, it's important to not regard them only as isolated pieces of writing; it is also essential to explore the social situations in which the texts occur.

Twenty-five years ago, Lake Tahoe was centered in the midst of a battle as its sleepy, summer-cabin neighborhoods were transformed seemingly overnight. Development and real estate interests controlled local governments, and no regional planning agency with enforcement capabilities existed. Casinos expanded, and at the southern end of the lake the biggest casino yet, the Park Tahoe, which would later become Caesars Tahoe, prepared to open in Nevada. New residents poured into the basin to fill service-industry jobs, while houses, apartments, roads, gas stations, banks, motels, restaurants and stores became a fungus-like urban blight on the pristine mountain landscape (Strong 52-55).

Marketers promoted Lake Tahoe as "America's All-Year Playground," but the accompanying development seemed to be destroying the very source of income and inspiration. Erosion-prone hillsides were cut away for roads and housing developments, while meadows, which formerly filtered out sediments from runoff before it reached the lake, became enclaves of waterfront homes and boutiques. Smog choked the air during the summer, and the lake's environmental quality experienced a steep decline, losing over a foot of clarity a year.

The El Dorado County Planning Commission's 1959 master plan for the southern end of the lake envisioned a population of two hundred thousand people by 1984 (Strong 52), and many community leaders were calling for a freeway system to encircle the lake with motels, shopping malls and houses blanketing the mountainsides (119-23). The California Department of Transportation planned to build a bridge across Emerald Bay, the spectacular glacier-carved cove of turquoise-colored water that is one of the most photographed sites in the country (Strong 68-70). Residents and visitors engaged in blistering debates over these issues in newspapers, public meetings, post offices and grocery stores.

Environmental advocates, though, were often seen by mainstream Tahoe society as the enemy, with groups like The League to Save Lake Tahoe filing several lawsuits to stop any further alterations to the environment. Property rights advocates and developers also sued the US Forest Service and the Tahoe Regional Planning Agency, or TRPA, which had been created by Congress as a bi-state agency to regulate further development in the basin, on the grounds that the TRPA's regional plan was unconstitutional and the agencies took property without compensation when they prevented landowners from developing certain environmentally sensitive parcels in the 1980s (148-57). One lawsuit made it to the US Supreme Court twice, but the high court refused to hear the case, and fourteen years after it was first filed, the case, which has more than four-hundred plaintiffs, is still unresolved. With so much fighting going on among the various special interests, and the area of concern encompassing two states, five counties, various small communities and two municipalities, agreement on what was best for Lake Tahoe's environmental future was at an impasse.

The Significance of the Research

In 1959, with a grant from the National Science Foundation, Goldman began conducting research by rowing a thirteen-foot wooden boat around the shoreline areas and out to the depths of the lake. He took water samples, observed algae growth on rocks and repeated a practice that a previous researcher, John LeConte, recorded in the *Overland Monthly* in 1883: lowering a white disc down to see how far it was visible (seephoto, p. 89). LeConte actually used a white dinner plate, and he recorded that he could see to a depth of well over 100 feet (Goldman, "Fragile" 10).

Because of Goldman's long-term, continuous monitoring, he was able to build a base of data that undeniably showed the decline of the water's clarity in relation to the growth of urbanization in the surrounding watershed. When he began conducting his research at Lake Tahoe, he was a professor of zoology and the Director of the Institute of Ecology at the University of California, Davis, and one of the few scientists in the country studying watershed management of inland waters.

A grant from the National Science Foundation funded his earliest research, and he founded the Tahoe Research Group (TRG) through the UC Davis College of Agricultural and Environmental Sciences Department. TRG conducts pioneering research on the physics, chemistry, and biology of lake Tahoe and the surrounding watershed, and this research "laid the scientific groundwork necessary to protect water quality from further degradation" (*Conflict* 6).

After studying Lake Tahoe for nearly four decades, Goldman and his team of researchers know that human development is the cause of nutrients flooding into the lake from soil erosion and runoff. These nutrients, including nitrogen, phosphorus and iron, feed the microscopic plant life that explodes into algae blooms that cloud the lake and occur throughout the shorelines and shallow areas of the lake as far out as five miles from the shore.

Mats of Algae Piled Up Along the Shore

At the time Goldman started rowing his boat out into the lake to record algae growth, developers were making plans to cover the hills and mountainsides surrounding the lake with homes, apartments, condos, shopping centers, hotels, freeways, and ski resorts. One Sacramento developer, A.E. Wilson, who developed the Tahoe Paradise and Meyers areas at the South Shore, produced a promotional film in 1959 that followed a family on their vacation to Lake Tahoe as they decide to purchase one of his newly built vacation homes in a project proclaimed as "a fabulous monument to recreation and good living." As the camera pans the modern home and the happy family, the narrator says, "Four years ago there was practically nothing here. But now, our street is in, our home is built—changes; progress all around."

This was the era of boosterism and expansion. Visitors loved the fast action available twenty-four hours a day at the rapidly extending casino strips at the south and north shores of the lake. Lake Tahoe held the promise of economic riches, not only at the casinos, but also to those savvy enough to get in on the ground floor of development. Plans for major housing developments were in the works for Incline Village at the North Shore, and the South Shore's Tahoe Keys, which would be built on a crucial wetland that filtered out sediments from the Upper Truckee River before they reached the lake (Strong 52-55). Heavenly Valley Ski Resort was growing, and Squaw Valley was preparing to host the 1960 Winter Olympic Games (123-26). The viewpoint of regarding nature as a resource to be exploited was in full force, and no one wanted to hear any troublesome rumblings from an esoteric university professor.

As the 1959 promotional film closes, its message perfectly reflects the mood of the times. The family journeys back home over the mountain after a rejuvenating stay in their new Lake Tahoe home, and dad tells us, "Bobby learned how to ski last winter, and for the first time I went deer hunting and shot my first buck. No," he laughs, "I'm not that good—just plain lucky. There was plenty of game around Tahoe Paradise.

"Across the street over there," he points, "they're building an ultra-modern motel. And they're working on our own private lake—right here—about 40 acres of it. There's just one word for it: fantastic. But then, that's the way they do things up here."

A few years later, Goldman published "The Bad News From Lake Tahoe" in the *Journal of California Tomorrow*, published by a non-profit organization dedicated to environmental education. Goldman's opening photograph shows a hand scraping algae off a sifting screen with the caption:

> Nine years ago, when I began studying Lake Tahoe, the rocks along the shore showed only a slight growth of attached algae. Last spring, one could collect handsful almost anywhere in the shallows, and waves piled up mats of the detached material along the shore.

While the boosters called for more growth and expanded development, Goldman was discovering ominous signs that urbanization was ruining the lake's environment, and he made those findings known through his public discourse.

From Nature as Object to Nature as Spirit

When people think of writing by scientists, we usually don't think so much of the writing style as the information presented. Scientific language is, as Charles Bazerman says, popularly thought to be "a transparent transmitter of natural facts" (14). But, he points out, the way science is presented through the writer's rhetorical choices "[shapes] the kind of thing we consider contributions to knowledge" (15).

Rhetorical theory has built on Aristotle's definition of rhetoric as "the faculty of observing in any given case the available means of persuasion" (153) to evolve into a tool to explore our discourse about social and ethical issues. The rhetorical occasion includes a speaker or writer (the rhetor), an audience to which the message is directed, and a purpose for the message. In order to be effective, the rhetor must consider what might motivate the audience, and classical rhetoric centers on three forms of persuasive appeal: the appeal to reason (*logos*), the appeal to the rhetor's authority and credibility (*ethos*), and the appeal to emotion (*pathos*). Rhetoric gives us a way to create meaning from what goes on around us. Rhetoric encompasses more than the elements of persuasion in text or speech, however; it is everything around us that has the underlying goal of influencing and is essentially "the human effort to induce cooperation through the use of symbols" (Brock et al. 14). With this background in mind, I am interested in seeing how science writing goes beyond the purely objective and how this rhetorical triangle of *logos, ethos,* and *pathos* can provide a framework for looking at these articles.

Environmental rhetoric scholars M. Jimmie Killingsworth and Jacqueline S. Palmer have observed a "continuum of perspectives on nature . . . whose poles designate three human attitudes toward the natural world" that I find helpful in considering the rhetoric of environmental discourse (11). On one side is the view of "Nature as Object," which would include traditional or mainstream science and government; in the middle is "Nature as Resource," which includes business and industry; on the other end is "Nature as Spirit," which includes the poetic discourse we use to articulate our response to the beauty and emotional power of nature (11-13). This continuum gives us a format for thinking about the "motives" and "scene"—to borrow Kenneth Burke's terms (992)—from which texts arise, as well as possible audiences for the texts.

It is likely most people could situate themselves along all three places on the continuum at various times, but an essential philosophy that drives our beliefs and actions stems from one area. For example, scientists view nature as object in order to conduct research and quantitative analysis. The view of nature as resource propels economic forces as divergent as mining, tourism and agriculture, and all of us are consumers of nature and rely on its abundance for survival. The third view, "nature as spirit," considers nature as an integrated entity, of which humans are only one part. Ethical action goes beyond the ethics of human relationships and encompasses all creatures and natural landscapes. From the "Nature as Spirit" perspective, indiscriminate violations of nature are violations of ethics, and rhetoric provides a tool to initiate discourse and perhaps move others from their place on the continuum toward this view of ethical action.

Killingsworth and Palmer show the necessity for scientists to consider the importance of rhetoric if they are to affect beneficial changes in our attitudes about the environment: "technological and bureaucratic solutions to environmental problems will be ineffective—or impossible—unless accompanied or proceeded by free and broad access to special knowledges and relevant information as well as by deep psychological and social adjustments" (2). We can think of this point of view as eco-humanism or social ecology, which would fall into the "Nature as Spirit" end of the continuum, while traditional science lies at the other end, with "Nature as Object" (11). What, then, is the place of ethics in scientific writing? If ethics is the relationship of one person to another or to a community, and environmental scientists are observing and reporting data back to the community about the natural world that supports the community, do scientists have a responsibility to bring in their personal beliefs when those beliefs can affect the future of habitats, including those of the human species?

My study is informed by Aristotle's idea that the goal of rhetoric is "not simply to succeed in persuading, but rather to discover the means of coming as near such success as circumstances of each particular case allow" (153). Rhetoric in science writing moves the written work from the objective, scientific "fact" to the ethical "possibility."

In "The Land Ethic," from *A Sand County Almanac*, naturalist and forester Aldo Leopold initiates a new ethic in humans' relationship "to land and to the animals and plants which grow upon it." In contemporary American culture, we still think of the land as "property" we use for economic gain, a concept that gives us "privileges but not obligations." This has been the traditional philosophy taken by those who seek to exploit the landscape for economic gain. For Leopold, though, a new ethics is within our reach, one that will extend the Golden Rule from the individual and society to the natural world (238-39).

Most scientific writing considers reality as something to be described objectively. Data is gained through observation and meticulously recorded, with emphasis on conciseness and academic thoroughness and concern only with the facts. The "[p]rinciple aim is to refer to a world rather than construct a world" (Killingsworth 104). In the writing I will examine here, Goldman builds on a scientific objective style and grounds his claims in solid research and his experience as a scientist, but he extends his thinking through biocentric ethics and rhetorical appeals to move readers to accept, or at least consider, new ways of thinking. He moves beyond the scientific fact and posits an openness to ethical possibilities.

How One Scientist's Rhetoric
Brought About an Environmental Awakening

These two early articles arose during a tumultuous time in the history of Lake Tahoe's environment at the height of a development frenzy. When Goldman published "The Bad News From Lake Tahoe" in the *Journal of California Tomorrow* in 1967, treated sewage was sprayed on the surrounding hillsides, where it subsequently flowed into the lake with the spring runoff, while at the same time, the construction boom was creating significant land disturbance. These factors contributed to overloading the lake with nutrients, which feed algae that cause the lake to cloud and loose clarity. The major premise of his article was to raise public awareness about the harm these human disturbances were causing the environment.

"Danger Signs for Tahoe's Future," co-written with University of California, Davis, physicist Thomas A. Cahill, was also published in the *Journal of California* Tomorrow eight years later and is based on cumulative "qualitative measurements of the lake's water [that] have shown a disturbing trend of increasing fertility" (1). This article also discusses recent research into a new threat: air pollution.

By carefully looking at how the language and text accomplish the work of persuasion and what is imbedded in the language, I hope to make discoveries about the ways these texts contributed to raising the public's consciousness about environmental problems at Lake Tahoe, and consequently, how this writing contributed to creating the collaborative effort to protect and restore the environment that now exists in the Tahoe Basin. This collaboration and the resulting open discourse among people with diverse viewpoints, which Goldman's public rhetoric helped to shape, can serve as an example for other communities experiencing conflicts over environmental issues.

In each article, Goldman creates what Kenneth Burke has termed "identification" between the lake and humans by showing us that we are not separate from our environment. Goldman explains complex scientific research by breaking it down into manageable parts, such as giving readers images with which to identify, analogies related in a narrative style, or easily visualized comparisons between Lake Tahoe and other lakes that were once like Tahoe but are now polluted with "pea-soup-colored masses of blue-green algae" ("Bad News" 1). Goldman uses visual rhetoric, as well, to build identification, such as photos showing entire hillsides that were cut away for development and their subsequent erosion, massive sediment plumes pouring directly into the lake, or Goldman pulling nets full of algae from a dock in a lakeside marina. Readers are able to identify with these representations of a ravaged environment because often they, too, have had similar such experiences. Vague problems of worldwide pollution seem overwhelming, complex, and beyond our reach, but through identification, Goldman has presented graspable parts of a complex whole with which readers can build per-

sonal involvement. Identification gives us a way to link ourselves with larger issues.

Identification and what Burke calls "consubstantiability"
or a shared substance between an individual and some other
person or property, does not replace persuasion, but rather it
enhances it. Identity also coexists with, and arises from, division, and this division creates the need for rhetoric. Burke
says Aristotle's *Rhetoric*: "deals with the possibilities of classification in its partisan aspects; it considers the ways in which
individuals are at odds with one another, or become identi-
fied with groups more or less at odds with one another" (1020).

Rhetoric is the means by which these opposing groups
create a dialectic exchange of views with the goal of moving
beyond this partisanship. According to Burke, "Identification
is affirmed with earnestness precisely because there is division. Identification is compensatory to division. If men were
not apart from one another, there would be no need for the
rhetorician to proclaim their unity" (1020).

To read Samuel Clemens' account of the clarity of Lake
Tahoe one hundred years before, and then to read Goldman's
articles, one might conclude that Goldman was observing an
altogether different lake:

> Lake Tahoe is being polluted. To deny this fact is com-
> parable to saying that a man receiving a daily dose of
> arsenic in his breakfast coffee is not being slowly poi-
> soned. If the poisoning continues, the steady accu-
> mulation in the man's system will eventually kill him.
> If the pollution of Lake Tahoe is not stopped now, the
> pollutants will continue to accumulate in the lake, and
> in time, the lake will turn from clear blue to turbid
> green. ("Bad News" 1)

Thus begins the 1967 article, "The Bad News From Lake
Tahoe." Goldman then invites the reader into the discussion
with a question: "Why, then, do some insist that Lake Tahoe
is not being polluted?" (1).

Goldman builds his argument by comparing Lake Tahoe
to Clear Lake, another California lake that receives an overabundance of nutrients from its surrounding watershed that
"have cluttered its once transparent waters with pea-soup-
colored masses of blue-green algae," a situation he believes

precipitates the fate of Lake Tahoe. Goldman juxtaposes the "transparent waters" of Lake Tahoe with some unappealing sounding organic matter. To his claim that Lake Tahoe is being polluted, he refutes opponents by showing that they are "applying irrelevant standards" to constrict the definition of pollution: "To apply narrow, conventional standards of water quality to a lake valued above all for the clarity it is beginning to lose is unrealistic" (1).

He explains *eutrophication*, the process by which lakes become more fertile, in accessible terms, and tells us "man's current technological practices are accelerating it fantastically. Lake Erie, for example, has eutrophicated to near ruin in a single generation" (1). The choice of the word "fantastically" invites the reader in to make a judgment. Does that word mean that the ways we pollute lakes are outlandish or too crazy to be believed?

Then there are the images of destruction and utter waste conjured up by "ruin." And further appealing to the reader's sensibilities, Goldman doesn't say "in twenty-five years," but rather "in a single generation," which makes his time frame not only tangible, but also haunting. This single phrase connects the destruction images to the human species. He furthers this generational connection toward the end of his article when he says, "The pollution of today is already a sad legacy for many generations to come" (4).

Goldman's article presents his viewpoint clearly. He says at this point, "Man's potential for destroying the great natural beauty of Tahoe must be recognized and controlled. Every disturbance of the watershed has its influence on the lake" (4). He then brings in another human-consumption-of-food metaphor as he relates another narrative to explain a concept:

> We think of the primeval lake as existing on a balanced nutrient budget, like a lean man on a balanced diet. If his diet becomes too rich, he will put on weight. The lake's youthful vigor, by this analogy, is being sapped by the tons of nutrients trucked daily into the watershed, to end up in the myriad garbage dumps, septic tanks, and sewage-disposal systems in the basin. (2)

Goldman then shows how the lake, like the lean, healthy man, will "fatten" and grow unhealthy from the overabundance of nutrients "available because of man's occupation of the watershed." Here, he has clearly brought an objective appeal to logic together with the rhetorical appeal to *pathos* to reach readers on a more personal level.

Throughout the article, he continues to build on his scientific research to inform readers about the harm urbanization—with its accompanying road building, construction, erosion, and inadequate sewage-treatment systems—causes the lake. In one section, he says, "To understand how precarious is Lake Tahoe's future as a remarkable aquatic resource, one must look beneath Lake Tahoe's blue surface to the myriad of aquatic organism whose life and death will greatly affect the lake's future" (3).

Again, Goldman explains the cycles of aquatic life in accessible terms and shows how the nutrient overload is altering the food web and killing plants and animals. Up until this section, which appears in the last one-third of the article, Goldman has been using the impersonal, third-person voice, but here he brings in the first person, inviting his reader to see what he sees first hand.

"I have recently begun to examine the depths of Lake Tahoe with underwater television and sonic probing of the bottom," he says, and he goes on to discuss how coring samples are being taken to record the changes in the rates of sedimentation that have already occurred. "This record of the lake's past history can tell us a great deal about the future" (3). Here, the "us" seems to include not only the scientific community, but the larger community of the public concerned about Lake Tahoe.

After bringing the reader into the article, Goldman calls for "decisive action" and the creation of a "regional administrative agency which has the power and uses it to establish and enforce strong controls on sewage and solid waste disposal and on the appalling erosion of the watershed." He closes with the thought that, without actions to halt the pollution, "the clear blue waters of the lake will soon be only a matter of historical interest in California and Nevada—and the rest of the world" (4).

The reader then sees a six-page series of photos showing the various polluting activities Goldman discusses in his article. There is a runoff canal collecting "waste-laden street drainage" that pours directly into the lake, frozen sewage effluent that was sprayed across a landscape to create a "spectacular winter sewage icicle display," other sewage spray operations, aerial views of subdivisions that clearly show their impact on erosion and runoff into the lake, road cuts and subsequent mudslides, a garbage dump "from which runoff waters carry debris and plant nutrients in solution," and probably the most telling: a two-page spread of ski resorts at Incline Village at the North shore and Heavenly Valley at the South shore taken after the spring thaw (4-9). The photos show entire mountainsides washed away and collapsed due to the disturbance of native vegetation. The landscapes resemble those devastated by massive earthquakes. These photos tie Goldman's appeals to *logos* and *pathos* together. The evidence backing up his verbal argument is there in black and white, and the ravaged landscape appeals to our emotions, for are we not accustomed to regarding nature and mountain landscapes as a source of beauty?

The author has also very subtly built on the appeal to *ethos*. The section of the journal in which the article appears is titled *A Scientist Reports*, which establishes a framework of authority for the article and its author. We know from the biographical information presented on page one that the author is "professor of Zoology and Director of the Institute of Ecology at the University of California, Davis" and "his research speciality is the study of inland waters." The biographical statement also tells us Goldman was at the time of publication "president of the American Society of Limnology and Oceanography" (1). This serves to establish his credibility, and phrases such as "Nine years ago when I began studying Lake Tahoe" and "I have recently begun to examine the depths of Lake Tahoe with underwater television and sonic probing of the bottom," (3) enhance this credibility further. Goldman lets readers know there is an "I" behind the research, and this "I" has a good deal of experience. Also, "underwater television and sonic probing" devices were only available to serious, well-funded researchers in the early 1960s, and although

Following pages, Lake Tahoe and Dr. Goldman. Text continues, p. 90.

Above and right: Lake Tahoe, seen here from the south-west shore, holds enough water to cover the state of California to a depth of fourteen inches. Known for its exceptionally clear, blue water, the third deepest lake in North America is losing its clarity due to human-caused environmental disturbances. Photos by the author.

Below and left: Dr. Charles Goldman at work. When he first began taking measurements in 1968, the visibility into Lake Tahoe was more than one hundred feet. The average measurement for 1998 was only sixty-six feet. Photos: Tahoe Research Group

this likely was not the author's intention, including this phrase helped build his credibility as an authority with readers.

A Worsening Situation After "The Bad News"

"Danger Signs for Tahoe's Future" was published in the *Journal of California Tomorrow* eight years later, after some of the changes Goldman had been calling for, such as the establishment of a regional planning agency and the exportation of sewage out of the basin, had been enacted. This was, however, part of the most contentious period in Lake Tahoe's history. The Tahoe Regional Planning Agency, or TRPA, created by an act of Congress in late 1969, was controlled by local representatives who placed economic interests ahead of environmental interests. Environmental historian Douglas H. Strong called its initial planning and regulatory efforts

> largely ineffective. In fact, the TRPA plan was vitiated before its approval. The Governing Body approved so many new developments during the period of preparation of the plan—reportedly 95 percent of the projects brought before it—that rapid growth was assured for years to come. (153-56)

Calling on local officials to do the painful work of denying further development was like asking the fox to guard the hen house. On the California side of the basin, local governments were largely controlled by construction interests and tourism-dependent business—in Nevada, by casino interests. Local governments, with six of the ten seats on the TRPA's governing board, essentially controlled the agency. One *Los Angeles Times* editorial said the TRPA was incapable of planning anything except "gambling casinos and shopping centers," while the *San Francisco Chronicle* described the agency as an "impotent pygmy" (qtd. in Strong 175).

Between June 1973 and July 1974, the TRPA approved a major expansion of Harvey's Resort Casino and the construction of three major casino-hotels at Stateline. The Park Cattle Company Hotel would be a fourteen-story, 446-room complex, which all California members of the governing board opposed, but under the TRPA's dual majority rule, only a majority vote from each state could block construction. The other two new casinos would be built three-quarters of a mile from Stateline, creating a new gambling hub. The 960-room Hotel Oliver and 560-room Tahoe Palace would consume 80,000 square feet of space for the buildings and include parking for 3,400 vehicles. Just three local Nevada members voted for approval, while the other seven members voted against it, but due to a clause in the bi-state compact that called for a dual majority rule vote from both states, the new casino-hotels gained automatic approval (Strong 163-65).

If all four of the approved casino-hotels were constructed, said a TRPA staff report, more than eight thousand new housing units would be needed for at least 24,000 new residents, and ten additional traffic lanes would need to be added on the California side of the state line. Led by the League to Save Lake Tahoe, a series of lawsuits and subsequent appeals to block construction followed (Strong 166).

In spite of the legal battles, the south shore would soon see the construction of more shopping centers and subdivisions, as well as casino expansion. In 1972, Bill Harrah turned his casino/showroom into a major casino with an eighteen-floor hotel (Strong 162).

Goldman and Cahill open "Danger Signs For Lake Tahoe" with an ecocentric, or nature-centered, appeal: "The clear, blue waters and fresh alpine air at Lake Tahoe have helped to make it one of the world's most beautiful places," but they then move down the continuum to nature as resource, pointing out how "[d]evelopment within the basin, stimulated by an expanding population and exploitation of Tahoe's highly valued resources, threatens to transform the lake basin into the very kind of environment from which many seek to escape" (1).

This article was written after the Tahoe Research Group at the University of California, Davis, had been established, and the authors refer to the university and the research connected with it. Because of the time elapsed between this and the earlier article, and because of the establishment of the Tahoe Research Group, this article relates more scientific data than "The Bad News From Lake Tahoe," and it sets forth a stronger appeal to *ethos*.

In the rhetorical tradition, *ethos* is the character of the communicator and its power of persuasion or "the shared concerns of speaker and audience" (Bizzell and Herzberg 29).

Aristotle says that *ethos* may actually be the "controlling factor in persuasion" (133), and the rhetorical power of these articles comes from the establishment of a constructed persona, or voice, that arises from the *ethos* to represent the author.

Wayne Booth expounds on the notion of persona as a created "second self" that authors construct to communicate meaning (71). Booth is referring here to the rhetoric of fiction, but his concepts are equally applicable to non-fiction writing. I contend that skilled science writers construct a persona to reflect or create an impression as a means to influence audience perception, or, as author H. Lewis Ulman says, "persona refers to a rhetorical construct that focuses an audience's 'perceptions of a source of communication' and establishes general expectations of the 'value and importance' of an author's message" (50). Skilled writers use these strategies, according to Roger D. Cherry, to "enable them to portray themselves in written text [in] a way that contributes to the optimum effectiveness of a given text" (269). Thus, the creation of ethos and persona in these texts can be a strategic rhetorical device if executed with care.

The *ethos* of this piece arises from the objective scientific voice. Goldman has at this point been conducting his research for sixteen years, and the data he has to draw on are well grounded. This article shows contour maps of the lake and the results of synoptic studies to measure the fertility of water masses conducted over a four-year period.

Because so much research had now been conducted at the time of this article's publication, Goldman could also draw on data collected showing the magnitude of air pollution in a study conducted by the California Air Resources Board. As in the earlier article, Goldman brings in photographic evidence to back up his arguments. This time, we see thick algae growth clouding the water, as well as heavy air pollution clouding the atmosphere. The opening photo shows a panoramic view of the lake, but the opposite shoreline is barely visible. The caption reads: "Dramatic views of mountains across the blue waters, long associated with Lake Tahoe, are now often obscured by atmospheric haze extending outward from the shore" (2). Another photo shows the Stateline casino corridor packed with cars and reads: "Increasing motor-vehicle traffic, concentrated along the shores of the lake, is contributing substantially to the decline of air quality. A 1973 study of air pollution at Tahoe compared Stateline, Nevada, to downtown Los Angeles at the peak of its smog season" (6). These photos, along with their captions, further the appeal expounded in the text based on scientific research and also appeal to our emotions. The photos shake our idea of pristine nature and show us the real effects of our human presence on this landscape.

In the text, Goldman refers to his research supported by the national Science Foundation's RANN program (Research Applied to National Needs) as it relates to measuring changes occurring in Lake Tahoe's air and water quality. Tables and graphs illustrate data that show areas of greatest water pollution and a breakdown of pollutants in the air. His remarks reflect a position that this scientific research is irrefutable, saying, "The decline in Tahoe's air and water quality is no longer a matter of conjecture. Scientists have now documented the deterioration and are making the information available to the public" (6). In the same passage, he also addresses the controversy surrounding the adoption of a new land ethic:

> The evidence is presented in the midst of a continuing controversy over land development at Tahoe. Environmentalists, developers and politicians alike are engaged in often heated exchanges concerning the merits of conservation versus development in the basin, with viewpoints ranging from advocacy of unlimited economic growth to the complete halting of development. (6)

Here, he acknowledges the varying perspectives across the continuum, and he ends the article with a reflection on the role of science in this debate, saying, "It is not the scientist's wish to intensify polarization of opinion; his role is solely to record environmental changes as they occur in the basin and to make the findings public" (6).

In both articles, Goldman establishes a subtle identification between the reader and the lake as a place of "solace and refuge from the turmoil of city living" ("Danger" 1). While he uses the impersonal voice of the scientist reporting in the third person in each, i.e., "it is hoped that" "the decline in air quality at Tahoe is causing concern," ("Danger" 1, 8) and, referring to damage from grazing, "This can be documented by shifts in vegetation patterns and by the appearance of barren ground where the cattle and sheep congregate" (2), the writing in the earlier piece, "The Bad News From Lake Tahoe," establishes more of a rapport between the reader and the author.

The bulk of "The Bad News From Lake Tahoe" is written in the third person, but Goldman occasionally uses the first person "I" and "we." In this article, he takes only five paragraphs to break out of the impersonal third person and say, of the threat of domestic pollution, "To understand this threat, we need to look at the gradual thickening of the mats of attached algae and bacteria on the boulders in the shallows." This "we" brings the reader into the scientist's realm to see the "clear and undeniable biological testimony that the lake is being polluted" ("Bad News" 1). He ends this piece by bringing the reader back in with the notion of identification: "Until that time [when a regional administrative agency with enforcement powers is created], we can look forward to acceleration of the pollution" ("Bad News" 4).

In the 1975 article, "Danger Signs For Tahoe's Future," Goldman and his co-author, Thomas A. Cahill, stay with the impersonal third person scientific reporting, but there are phrases that establish an identification between the reader and the subject matter, such as, "The clear, blue waters and fresh alpine air at Lake Tahoe have helped to make it one of the world's most beautiful places. For generations, its scenic beauty has offered solace and refuge from the turmoil of city living" (1), and "A large part of Tahoe's appeal is the scent of pine and the fresh mountain air one associates with the high Sierra. Nowadays, this fragrance and purity are often replaced by dust and fumes from automobile and truck traffic" (4). This article also contains graphs and tables that illustrate pollution levels in the water and pollutants in the air that provide evidence for the authors' argument that "Further deterioration in air and water quality at Tahoe can be expected if unrestricted development and population growth are allowed in the basin" (6).

With the publication of over four hundred peer-reviewed journal articles and scientific papers, Goldman has a myriad of articles that reflect the traditional impersonal voice of scientific writing. I chose these two articles because they were written more for the lay person and made scientific writing accessible, and because of the time and social context in which they occurred. Using the public discourse of community meetings, letters to the editor and lawsuits over land use as a barometer, I would say that when each of these articles was published, many people aligned themselves with the "nature as object" or "nature as resource" perspective. It is possible that, not only because of Goldman's scientific research, but also his ability to convey his findings in a rhetorical discourse that built identification with his audience, more people are now moving toward the land ethic end of the continuum in the communities around Lake Tahoe.

Toward a Discourse That Applies the Objective to Build Interest in the Subjective

Goldman builds on a scientific objective style and grounds his claims in solid research and his experience as a scientist, but he extends his thinking through biocentric ethics and rhetorical appeals to move readers to accept, or at least consider, a new way of thinking and adopting a new perspective on the continuum.

He has embraced the objectivity of science, but the appeal that lies at the heart of these articles considers action as social responsibility. Through his writing, Goldman has always advocated the absolute need for solid scientific research to ground social and economic decisions about the environment. "Political decisions in planning at a place like Tahoe need a scientific basis," he says ("Danger" 6).

In the years that have ensued since the publication of "The Bad News From Lake Tahoe" several things have changed. Sewage disposal, which prompted the article, has improved, and sewage is now pumped out of the basin. A number of state regulatory agencies from California and Nevada have been established, including the federal Tahoe Regional Planning Agency, which Dr. Goldman called for in his early articles. The University of California, Davis, and the University of Nevada, Reno, conduct regular and ongoing research, and they participate with agencies and other groups to implement policy solidly founded in scientific research. Goldman's pioneering research has also contributed to understanding the processes of ecosystems and how impacts from urbanization stress the environmental health of lakes, and this research has assisted in formulating watershed management plans throughout the West and in Siberia.

What may be the most visible indicator that someone is listening occurred in the summer of 1997 when a series of workshops on water quality issues, forest ecosystem restoration, recreation, tourism, and transportation in the Lake Tahoe basin culminated with President Clinton's Lake Tahoe Presidential Forum. Dr. Goldman delivered the keynote address at the opening workshop, and Lake Tahoe's environmental problems received national attention, a commitment from the federal government for better efforts to solve the problems, and an infusion of federal money.

Lake Tahoe is far from saved, though. The lake continues to lose over one foot of clarity each year, and Goldman predicts the lake will go from deep blue to turbid green in the next thirty years if current levels of pollution continue (*Conflict* 6). He contends:

> With a continuation of the rate of decline in clarity that has been actually measured since 1968, we can predict from existing data that by the end of the next 30 or so years Lake Tahoe will have lost one-half of its extraordinary transparency. In total the lake will have lost 62 feet or 19 meters of transparency since 1968. ("Opening Address" 1-6)

Goldman's research, though, has played a major role in turning the political debate over the fate of Lake Tahoe around from a highly combative atmosphere to one of collaboration. These days, former enemies sit together at the table to work toward a common goal: the protection of the Lake Tahoe basin environment. Professor Goldman's research and writing has had a major influence on expanding the public's knowledge and perceptions and was instrumental in initiating this complete turn around.

Rochelle Nason, executive director of the League to Save Lake Tahoe said, "When people with different interests sit down together to try to find common ground, the first thing they need to agree about are the basic facts of the matter. For many years, business and development representatives denied that human activity was having an impact on Lake

Tahoe." Nason said Goldman's scientific research provided the common ground needed to move forward. "Dr. Goldman's research eventually convinced everyone that the lake is in serious trouble," she said. "Only when his work led to agreement on the problem could we finally start working to find a solution" (interview)

There are those who value wilderness for its own sake, those who look for the monetary value in the resources nature can provide, those who seek to preserve the bio-diversity of nature and keep the environment in tact as a legacy for future generations, those who value nature for the income it can produce through tourism, and those who believe regulations to protect the environment will impede economic growth. People interested in Lake Tahoe's future represent a range of these perspectives, but Goldman's research and the writing he published about that research helped to bring these myriad viewpoints together. "The reason we have a partnership now with all the players from the public and private sectors is because of Dr. Goldman's research," said Jim Baetge, executive director of the Tahoe Regional Planning Agency. "When people ask, 'How can you justify spending over $900 million in the next ten years on environmental protection projects at Lake Tahoe,' we can answer 'Because we are comfortable with the research'" (interview)

Lake Tahoe is a place where civilization and wilderness collide. We can extrapolate from the struggles to deal with humans' impact on the land here to the global struggles of preserving disappearing habitats, reducing water and air pollution, and solving the problems of overpopulation. What happens at Lake Tahoe can provide lessons for other communities in sensitive environments.

When Interior Secretary Bruce Babbitt came to Lake Tahoe for the 1997 Presidential Forum on the environment, he said that the environmental issues encountered at Lake Tahoe

> reverberate throughout the American West. The issues we confront here came to Tahoe first. . . . By looking at Lake Tahoe, communities can learn, first, what not to do to cause harm, and second, how to build consensus to deal with environmental degradation.

Referring to the collaborative efforts of Tahoe's governmental agencies, environmental advocates, business leaders, and private citizens to solve the pending environmental catastrophe, Babbitt said, "What you have done in this basin as neighbors is way ahead of any other process anywhere in the country. The rest of the world is watching" (public address).

In a speech delivered during his visit to Lake Tahoe, President Bill Clinton also commented on how the efforts among diverse factions working to preserve the basin's environment can be a model for other communities:

> Your cooperation to protect Lake Tahoe is, frankly . . . an outstanding model for the work we have to do to protect all kinds of national treasures and deal with all kinds of environmental challenges in the new century . . . [O]ne of the reasons that I wanted to come here was . . . to show the nation that there is a place where environmentalists and business people and ordinary citizens, where Republicans and Democrats, where tribal leaders and governmental people, where everybody is working together in common cause recognizing that there cannot be an artificial dividing line between preserving our natural heritage and growing our economy.

Goldman's forty years of research and public rhetoric had a tremendous effect on bringing about this consensus. He closes "Danger Signs for Tahoe's Future" with a reflection on the role his research plays in the political debate, saying, "By providing planning agencies with this information, particularly information applicable to the long-range effects of alternative development plans for the basin, it is hoped that guidelines for wise land-use policies will be adopted" (6). And here, he brings in the entire range of perspectives on the continuum:

> No one can deny the esthetic values—or, indeed, the health and economic values—of clean air and sparkling clear waters at Lake Tahoe. Through sound and strictly enforced management practices, these essential features of Tahoe's unique beauty can be preserved for this and future generations. (6)

Professor Goldman's research at Lake Tahoe has provided indisputable proof of the connection between land development and the degradation of the environment. He has published four books and over four hundred scientific articles, and he has produced four documentary films that have worldwide distribution. In 1990 he was a member of a UNESCO team to qualify Lake Baikal as an International Heritage Lake and Senior Scientist for the National Geographic Baikal project (Tahoe Research Group).

In late 1998, he was presented with what may be the most prestigious recognition yet: the Albert Einstein World Award of Science, which included a diploma, a commemorative medal, a check for $10,000. An international jury of the Interdisciplinary Committee of the World Cultural Council, consisting of eminent scientists including twenty-five Nobel Prize winners, selected Goldman. The Albert Einstein award was created to recognize those members of the scientific community whose scientific and technological accomplishments have progressed science and benefited humanity.

Goldman has bridged the esoteric language of writing about scientific research and, through rhetoric, presented his analysis and expert knowledge to the public in accessible terms using narrative and analogy in order to forge an opening of dialogue, focus attention away from conflict over what courses of action to take to a move toward collaboration, and set in motion unprecedented ways to re-think the Lake Tahoe environment. This is one example a rhetoric of the twenty-first century: a rhetoric that provides ways to develop within communities a new communication in which the lay person is informed in areas that were previously reserved for the scientists and bureaucrats, and political power is not concentrated solely in the hands of those who have access to complex scientific data and can interpret it. By making his work approachable to the lay person, Goldman empowered individuals to participate in the discourse that sets public policy.

From the beginning, Goldman took the stance that something must be done to stop the urbanization and the increasing pollution of Lake Tahoe. He built on the traditional scientific method of observation, analysis, and classification and in turn used his objective research to lead a pro-active stance for altering the course of environmental destruction at Lake Tahoe.

With the perils facing the environment in the West now and in the future, we can no longer think about the landscape as a separate "thing" placed here as a backdrop for our pleasure. Humans are connected to the environment, and the language of scientific research helps give us a common ground for our discourses. The words we use to talk about the environment hold power: the power to keep us in old, destructive ways of thinking, the power to change our way of looking at the environment and our place in it, and the power to affect the environment we leave as a legacy to our children.

REFERENCES

Aristotle. *Rhetoric*, Book I. Trans. W. Rhys Roberts. New York: Modern Library, 1954. Rpt Bizzell and Herzberg 151-60.

Babbit, Bruce. Public address. Lake Tahoe Presidential Forum Forest Ecosystem Restoration Workshop, 30 June 1997. Hyatt Hotel, Incline Village, Nevada.

Baetge, Jim. Telephone interview. 5 April1999.

Bazerman, Charles. *Shaping Written Knowledge: The Genre and Activity of the Experimental Article in Science.* Madison: U of Wisconsin P, 1988.

Bizzell, Patricia and Bruce Herzberg eds. *The Rhetorical Tradition: Readings From Classical Times to the Present.* Boston: Bedford Books, 1990.

Booth, Wayne C. *The Rhetoric of Fiction.* 2nd ed. Chicago: U of Chicago P, 1981.

Brock, Bernard L., Robert L. Scott, and James W. Chesebro, eds. *Methods of Rhetorical Criticism: A Twentieth Century Perspective.* 3rd ed. Detroit: Wayne State UP, 1989.

Cherry, Roger D. "Ethos Versus Persona: Self-Representation in Written Discourse." *Written Communication* 5.3 (1988): 251-77.

Clinton, Bill. Public address. "Opening Remarks by the President and Vice President," Lake Tahoe Presidential Forum. Hyatt Hotel, Incline Village, NV. 26 July 1997.

Goldman, Charles R. "The Bad News From Lake Tahoe." *Journal of California Tomorrow* Winter 1967-68.

———. "The Fragile Ecosystem of Lake Tahoe." *Environment* 31.7 (1989): 6-31.

———."Lake Tahoe: A Microcosm for the Study of the Impact of Urbanization of Fragile Ecosystems." *The Ecological City.* R.H. Platt et al., eds. Amherst: U of Massachusetts P, 1994. 93-105.

————. "Opening Address of the Lake Tahoe Presidential Forum Water Quality Workshop." Tallac Historic Site, So. Lake Tahoe, CA. 18 June 1997.

Goldman, Charles R., and Thomas Cahill. "Danger Signs for Tahoe's Future." *Journal of California Tomorrow* Spring, 1975.

Goldman, Charles R. and John E. Reuter. *Lake Tahoe Moving Beyond the Conflict: Past, Current and Future Scientific Contributions by the Tahoe Research Group.* Davis: University of California, Davis Center for Environmental Research, 1997.

Killingsworth, M. Jimmie, and Jacqueline S. Palmer. *Ecospeak: Rhetoric and Environmental Politics in America.* Carbondale: Southern Illinois UP, 1992.

Leopold, Aldo. *A Sand County Almanac and Sketches Here and There.* 1949. New York: Oxford UP, 1979.

Nason, Rochelle. Interview. 3 May 1999.

Strong, Douglas H. Tahoe: *An Environmental History.* Lincoln: U of Nebraska P, 1984.

Tahoe Research Group. "Founding Members—Charles R. Goldman." (Dec. 15, 1998). Apr. 9, 1999 <http://trg.ucdavis.edu/clients/trg/who/default.html>.

Tahoe Research Group. "Charles Goldman Receives Prestigious Einstein Award." (Sept. 1998). 9 Apr. 1999. <http://www.development.ucdavis.edu/tahoe/trg_update_sept_98>.

Twain, Mark. *Roughing It.* New York: New American Library, 1962.

Ulman, H. Lewis. "Thinking Like a Mountain." *Green Culture: Environmental Rhetoric in Contemporary America.* Ed. Carl G. Herndl and Stuart C. Brown. Madison: U of Wisconsin P, 1996.

Wilson, A. E. Promotional film for Lake Tahoe land development project. 1959.

Growth and Consequences
The Future of the West

KEITH SARGENT

The future of the West can be summarized in one word: "growth." For the past five years, the West has experienced the fastest growth of any region in the US and this is expected to continue, according to the US Bureau of the Census. Currently the West has eight of the top ten fastest growing states and seven of the top ten fastest growing cities (see Table 1). Furthermore, during the next quarter of a century, seven Western states are projected to be among the top 10 fastest growing areas. But what will this growth bring and at what cost?

There are a variety of reasons why people in the past have moved to the West. In the first half of the 20th century, logging and mining were the major growth industries attracting new residents. In the 1930s legalized casino gambling in Nevada contributed to growth as did an increase in farming made possible by irrigation. The building of Hoover Dam, to control the Colorado River and provide electricity to the growing Western cities, attracted even more residents to the region. Likewise, the development of atomic weapons in Washington brought an influx of new residents as did the testing of those weapons at the Nevada Test Site. Some of those who moved to the desert regions were simply trying to escape allergy problems.

Keith Sargent grew up in Las Vegas and is now an economist in the Economy and Environment Division at the EPA in Washington, DC. He welcomes your comments and questions and can be reached at (202) 260-2231 or by E-mail at sargent.keith@epa.gov. The views expressed in this paper do not necessarily reflect the official position of the US Environmental Protection Agency.

Ranking	Fastest growing states (1995-2000)	Fastest growing metropolitan areas (1900-1997)	
		Region	Percent
1	Nevada	Las Vegas, Nevada	48
2	Arizona	Larado, TX	38
3	Idaho	McAllen, TX	33
4	Utah	Boise City, ID	30
5	Colorado	Naples, FL	29
6	New Mexico	Phoenix, AZ	27
7	Georgia	Fayetteville, AR	27
8	North Carolina	Austin, TX	25
9	Oregon	Wilmington, NC	25
10	Wyoming	Provo, UT	24

Source: US Bureau of Census

Table 1: Fastest Growing States and Metropolitan Areas

But new residents have caused the loss of the amenities that originally attracted them to the West. Many of the mining towns became ghost towns when the ore disappeared, and the over-harvesting of the timber caused a steady decline of jobs in the Western logging industry. Irrigation from water supplied by the aquifers and rivers allowed the new residents to recreate the lush lawns and gardens found in the East, along with golf courses and backyard pools in a desert landscape that averaged only 4 inches of rain a year, thereby leading to water scarcity and land subsidence. Many brought Eastern vegetation to the West, filling the air of Arizona and Nevada with the pollen that caused severe allergic reactions among many of the residents. The open spaces became built up, causing crowding and traffic congestion on what had once been the lone prairies.

But even with these losses, the growth of the West has, and will, continue. In fact, the West is still exceptional in regards to population and growth rates. Currently, the 100 largest US cities have a median growth rate of 2.3%, a median population of 323,000, and a median density of 3,331 people per square mile ("Cities"). Six of the ten biggest cities are in the West, with four of these six showing growth rates above the median (Houston, San Diego, Phoenix, Dallas, and San Antonio).

Advantages and Disadvantages of Growth

While the future trends in Western growth are easy to predict, the consequences of this growth are not. Some consequences are obvious, such as increases in water use, electric power, roads, and pollution. The need for more public services (such as public education, and police and fire protection) and infrastructure (roads, water, power, and sewer lines) will also increase. It is also likely that the population density of cities will increase, resulting in more stress being put on the existing services and infrastructure. But other consequences, such as urban sprawl, higher taxes, and increasing crime (which are already occurring) do not necessarily have to continue if appropriate measures are taken.

However, in addition to the negative elements, growth may also bring positive changes to a city. For example, growing populations may bring increases in tax revenue, lower the per capita costs of providing public services, allow a greater variety of restaurants, and may give rise to more shopping malls, art galleries, theaters, and orchestras. In addition, more public services that depend on economies of scale can be provided, such as increased bus services, larger hospitals, and bigger airports.

Optimal Growth

The relevant question thus becomes, "Do the positive benefits of growth outweigh its costs?" If that question is answered in the affirmative, then the next question to examine is whether the net benefits of growth are being maximized. In other words, "Is the optimal amount of growth taking place?" To answer these questions, a little economic theory is needed.

Suppose that the cost of moving (e.g. hiring a moving company) is a *private cost* paid for by the new resident. However, the new resident also imposes additional costs (called *external costs*) on the new city, such as increased road congestion and more air pollution, since these costs are not paid for by the new resident, he or she ignores them. Therefore, the total *social costs* (the sum of the private costs plus the external costs) of moving will be greater than the private costs.

When families decide to move to a new city, they compare only the private costs of the move to the benefits they expect to obtain. If the expected benefits exceed the costs, then they move. However, since the rational individual compares only private costs to private benefits, and ignores the external costs, this results in more people behaving rationally, social welfare is not maximized.

More importantly, growth and urban sprawl is encouraged by federal, state, and local subsidies that lower the cost to new residents even further. New public services and infrastructure needed in the growing suburbs are subsidized by existing city residents through existing taxes. Federal tax policy encourages the purchase of homes and lowers the cost of mortgage payments, while zoning laws and favorable tax treatment for commercial developers encourage strip malls in the suburbs.

This economic model assumes only the existence of external costs, but external benefits also exist. So an additional question arises: "Are the additional social costs imposed by a new resident greater than the additional social benefits the new resident adds to the city?" Or to put the question more precisely, "Does growth pay for itself?"

Does Growth Pay?

Asking whether growth pays for itself is another way of asking whether the net social cost of a new resident is positive or negative. One way to answer this question is to examine whether city and local government revenues rise faster than the growth rate and the increase in public service expenditures. If these revenues rise faster, then growth pays for itself in economic terms. Unfortunately, many things that people value have no price, such as good health, clean air, a short commute to work, or a quiet park. Since more pollution, noise, and traffic congestion occur with growth, the external costs that growth imposes on residents are not included in the cost of public expenditures. Therefore, even if revenues rise faster than growth and expenditures, the non-monetary costs of growth may not be covered.

However, developers claim that growth is the solution, not the problem. C. Doug Johnson of Abat-Johnson Enterprise Inc., a Southern Nevada general contracting firm, stated: "People don't understand that growth is bringing necessary services to the community" (Caruso). Since the necessary services for a new community are such things as water, electricity, new roads, and new schools (which are difficult to pack into a moving van), transporting them presents a bit of a problem, and it would be interesting to hear how Mr. Johnson does his packing.

Naturally, Mr. Johnson does not mean to be taken literally. Growth brings an *increase in demand* for services and, over time, an *increase in the supply* of services will result. However, as anyone who has taken an introductory economics class (and not slept through it) can tell you, an increase in demand that is not offset by an *equal* increase in supply will cause a rise in the price of the good. Thus, the delay in the needed growth of community services for the new residents will cause the price of services to rise for existing residents. The question that needs to be examined is therefore, "Will the cost of services rise as a result of growth?"

Fortunately actual studies of the impact of growth on services have been done. A 1991 study by the firm of Arthur Anderson, "The Fiscal Impact of Population Growth in Nevada" found that growth did not pay and that expenditures rose faster than revenue, resulting in a need for increasing taxes (according to the Nevada Taxpayers Association). However, the Nevada Taxpayer Association pointed out that the higher expenditures resulted from (1) increases in the Consumer Price Index (CPI), (2) policy decisions to expand government programs and services, and (3) cost shifting made necessary by additional state and federal government regulations. The Association concluded that although Nevada's revenue increased faster than the CPI and Nevada's growth rate combined, the local governments' expenditures were increasing faster than the increase in revenue. In other words, growth can pay for itself, if expenditures don't increase faster than the per capita growth rate.

Helen Ladd, examining 248 large US counties or county-equivalents in 1993, found a more complicated relationship between population growth, taxation, and per capita expenditure. She found that both high *and* low (or negative) growth rates caused increases in expenditures and the tax burden. Furthermore, she concluded that slowdowns in the rate of population loss or slow increases in population tended to reduce the total tax burden relative to income.

While Ladd's study cannot distinguish between spending and the quality of service provided, nor explain how population growth affects the type of spending, it is helpful in explaining general trends, and she suggests that "in rapidly growing areas, development does not pay its way" because population growth results in an increase in per capita spending, and average and per capita tax rates increase in rapidly growing areas ("Effects" 216). Furthermore, in another study done in 1994, she found that in fast growing areas (i.e. above 7%) current residents may experience declines in services *and* a rise in the local tax burden.

Reasons for Western Growth

Since it appears rapid population growth, as now seen in many Western states, usually does not pay its way, how can a more optimal growth rate be achieved? To understand the best ways to manage growth, it would be useful to know the reasons behind the growth. According to the US Census Bureau, the main reason for Western population growth is due to migration. So why do people move from the East to the West?

Movement to the *suburbs* is motivated by the quality of the schools, personal safety, and lower taxes (21st Century Commission), but Yu Hsing found that *interstate* migration was influenced by changing tax burdens, employment growth, the level of income, heating degree days, violent crime, and metropolitan area populations.

However, a look at the data shows no obvious reasons for the attraction of the West. *The World Almanac* gives the median size of US cities (but not the larger metropolitan regions) as 323,000 with 14 Western cities ranking above the median and 12 below it. The population density of 12 Western cities is above the median density of 3,331 per square miles and 14 are below it, while the median unemployment rate is 5.3% (surprisingly it ranges from a high of 13.1% in Stockton, California to a low of 3.1% in Huntington Beach, California). Here the West has 12 cities with higher levels of unemployment and 14 below. What then explains the startling difference in the cities' growth rates? 23 Western cities have growth rates higher than the US median of 2.3 percent, with only three below it, all in California (Los Angeles, San Francisco, and Oakland).

A current reason suggested for Western population growth is the growth of new jobs and the low unemployment rates, but this is difficult to prove. Using recent data from the 100 largest US cities, the relationship between a city's growth rate, total population, population density, state and local tax rates, and the unemployment rate can be examined using a simple linear regression (Table 2).

The regression results show that the population of the city has no significant influence on the growth rate, but surprisingly, population density does have a strong and significant negative effect. Also surprising is the fact that neither the tax rate nor the unemployment rate has a significant effect. Dr. Harvey Molotch of the University of California, Santa Barbara, also found that there was no statistical correlation between the growth rate and unemployment rate. One often hears that lower tax rates in the West are one of the reasons people move, but this is also not borne out in the regression and even a simple look at Table 3 gives no evidence for this belief, since only six of the 11 Western states have tax rates below the national median.

The relationship between tax levels and migration between cities and states has generated a great deal of economic theory. In 1956 Charles Tiebout developed a model that explained

Variable	Coefficient	Std.. Error
Intercept	11.79	4.70**
Population	0.10	0.07
Density	-0.66	0.20*
Unemployment	-.10	0.24
State/Local Tax	-.051	0.42
Adjusted R^2	0.18	—
* and ** indicate significance at the 10% and 1% confidence levels respectively.		

Table 2: Determinants of the Growth Rates of the 100 largest cities.

how all communities would have the level of taxes and services desired by their residents; otherwise they would move to another community that better reflected their interests. However, there are several critical assumptions: (1) a system of fiscal federalism exists where the tax rates and expenditures are set by local governments; (2) people are free to move; (3) the costs of moving are relatively small; and (4) there are a sufficient number of alternative communities offering different levels of taxation and services. Since his landmark study, several studies have been conducted, giving some limited support to the Tiebout hypothesis.

Do we find, then, that the growth of the West is compatible with the Tiebout hypothesis? It is difficult to draw firm conclusions because of the wide variety of tax structures in different states and cities (Federation of Tax Administrators). There are a wide variety of combinations of corporate taxes, income taxes, property taxes, and use taxes, all with different brackets and exemptions. The Tax Foundation has at-

State	State/ local taxes as % of income	50 state ranking	State/ local & federal taxes as % of income	50 state ranking
UT	12.7	7	36.1	11
NM	12.4	8	35.1	20
CA	12.0	10	35.8	14
WA	11.8	14	36.4	8
ID	11.7	15	35.0	24
NV	11.3	26	36.2	10
OR	11.3	27	34.8	30
AZ	11.0	31	34.9	28
CO	10.8	35	34.9	26
MT	10.7	38	33.5	40
TX	10.5	43	34.2	34
50 state average	11.5		35.5	
			Source: Tax Foundation	

Table 3: State Taxation Rates

tempted to analyze the overall average tax burden for residents based on the average person (See table 3).

It is also hard to draw strong conclusions from the regression since many important variables may have been left out, such as the corporate tax rate. However, Michael Nelson reviewed how state and local taxes affected the location decisions of firms and did his own econometric study, and concluded that existing studies on the relationship between the two factors are "sparse and often contradictory," but his findings "suggest relative changes in state and local taxes on products and labor are of more significance as a location determinant than relative changes in the state corporate income tax" (13-30).

Consequences of City Growth

The primary growth of the West is occurring in cities. In one important aspect, cities share with factories increasing returns to scale, up to a point. If there are increasing returns to scale for city services, then as the population grows, average costs (i.e. the tax burden) should decrease, assuming the same level and quality of service is provided.

Ladd's studies suggest that there is an optimal growth rate, but is there an optimal city size that would result in the lowest possible cost for a given level of service? Although the variations in city size are enormous, "larger cities consistently have higher per capita taxes" according to Eben Fodor. Thus, it appears that many factors besides taxation rates and levels of service determine the size of a city. Otherwise, we would be able to develop concentration ratios for cities as is done for industries. For example, because of the huge returns to scale in the auto and aircraft industries, there are only a small number of very large firms. In contrast the banking and publishing industries' returns to scale are much smaller, giving rise to a large number of relatively small companies. Since the U. S. and other industrialized nations have great numbers of both large and small cities, larger cities do not appear to offer significant advantages in terms of the cost of providing public services, but instead display a variety of external costs and benefits that are difficult to give monetary values to.

Therefore, positive and negative externalities arise from two sources: larger cities and rapid population growth. But it is rarely easy to distinguish the two. For example, suburban sprawl occurs as new residents move into areas surrounding the cities, but it also occurs because city residents move to the suburbs. This causes property values in the central city to fall resulting in a rise in property tax rates, pushing more middle-class families to move out of the city, leaving behind the economically disadvantaged, AND CREATING more crime, a smaller tax base, and increased welfare payments, which in turn causes more flight to the suburbs by the upper-class, generating the common urban problem of economic segregation.

As suburban sprawl increases, congestion occurs requiring more roads, but as more roads are built to decrease congestion, this attracts more people to leave the city and move to the suburbs, which creates more traffic congestion and the necessity for more roads. The traffic congestion also creates delays which results in increased air pollution.

Therefore, air pollution increases for the same two reasons mentioned above: larger cities and rapid population growth. More than half of the US Air Quality Nonattainment Areas (where "air pollution levels persistently exceed National Ambient Air Quality Standards") are in the West and of the eight fastest growing metropolitan regions mentioned earlier, four of them are classified as Nonattainment Areas for particulates; 61 Western Metropolitan Areas are designated as nonattainment areas for particulate matter (usually dust in the Western regions); 16 areas for carbon monoxide; 14 for ozone (caused largely by automobile exhaust); and 12 for sulfur dioxide (US EPA).

Las Vegas

Las Vegas, which for several years has been the fastest growing city in the nation, can be expected to face the most serious problems associated with Western growth. By taking a look at the current problems facing this city, some insights can be gained about the problems that can be expected for other Western cities in the future. Over the last ten years, Las Vegas has doubled in size, and currently has 1.2 million residents (including the surrounding suburbs). Every month it adds between 6,000 and 8,000 new residents.

Las Vegas has numerous attractions. The weather is mild and snow is a rare event. It is near major recreation sites, like Lake Mead, which is located behind Hoover Dam, and the Grand Canyon, which is within a few hours drive. Mt. Charleston is less than an hour's drive away and attracts hikers and picnickers in the summer and skiers in the winter. There are no personal or corporate income taxes and the possibility of jobs attracts numerous people to the area. The lack of a corporate tax may have caused the Las Vegas economy to diversify, but one in every three jobs is still related to the gambling industry, which attracts almost 30 million visitors each year.

The Cold War and the development of atomic testing brought the Nevada Test Site, and the above-ground nuclear explosions could be seen from the Las Vegas casinos. When the tests moved underground, Las Vegans paid less attention to the testing, although the need for workers at the Test Site did not decrease. (My father actually made the three-hour commute from Las Vegas to the Test Site each day—which was common for most of the Test Site workers since they lived in Las Vegas.)

Growth has made Las Vegas a more unique city, even though legalized gambling in other states has made that part of its economy less of an attraction. Along with the growth has come an indoor roller coaster, a volcano that erupts on schedule, and frequent pirate battles with sinking ships. Although Las Vegas has an average rainfall of only 4 inches a year, two suburbs have been built around artificial lakes created in the desert.

But with the growth has come ozone alerts, unhealthy levels of dust, scarce water, traffic congestion, and urban sprawl. Las Vegas is currently a nonattainment area for both ozone and particulates (dust). The wetlands in the Las Vegas valley are also deteriorating as a result of population growth according to environmental scientists Phillip Cuartas and Daniel Heggem (Rogers 1B-4B). The Sierra Club Executive Director, Carl Pope, says that urban sprawl is the number one environmental problem in Las Vegas (Rogers 1B-4B).

Currently Las Vegas is facing a future of increasingly scarce water supplies, and requires an expansion of its water system to allow for continued growth. On November 3, 1998 an advisory vote was held to determine which of two methods would be used to pay for this expansion. The first option was a general increase in the sales tax for all residents, while the second option consisted of higher hookup fees for new residents and a higher water rate for all residents.

Developers spent $340,000 to convince voters to approve the sales tax because an increase in user fees (reflecting the true cost of new development) would sustantially increase the cost of a new home, causing a lower demand for new homes, and putting some developers out of work. The voters agreed and the sales tax option passed with 73% approval.

Managing Growth

Since the problems that come from high growth rates are not completely offset by the benefits, the final question to examine is: "Can anything be done to reduce the negative consequences of growth and increase the positives?"

While Western population growth will certainly continue for the next two decades, cities can choose to manage it and reduce the external costs associated with rapid population growth. While there are a vocal minority of developers that argue against regulating growth and advocate letting the market determine the outcome (i.e. laissez-faire), they may be thinking primarily about their own pocketbooks, and not about what is best for their community.

Some claim that the city is growing too quickly to make plans to manage and limit growth, but imagine how they would respond if one suggested they build a house quickly without using plans. Some also suggest that the government stay out of managing growth, but none of the developers have suggested that the government stop spending current residents' tax dollars that provide water and sewer connections for the new houses they construct, stop giving tax breaks for the home buyers, or stop building new public schools and fire stations for the new residents.

Finally, the developers appear to have only a limited understanding of economic theory. While it is true that free markets can indeed allocate resources and goods in an economically efficient manner, this outcome hinges on several crucial assumptions which do not hold for the growth of Western cities. The first assumption is that there are no external costs involved in the buying or selling of new houses, which has already been shown to be false. The second assumption is that there is complete information about the costs and benefits of growth. As has been shown, there is still a great deal of uncertainty over evaluating the net value of population growth. Finally, and perhaps most importantly, the free-market idea requires that all goods be bought and sold in free, competitive markets. However, the externalities associated with population growth are not bought and sold in any markets. Since there exist no markets for clean air, for solitude, or for the beauty of a forest, strict laissez-faire would not result in the optimal allocation of goods. Furthermore, economic theory shows that even when everyone is rational, the socially optimal outcome may not occur even if the quantities of public goods, such as government services, are determined by popular vote.

Some economists also have difficulty applying economic principles to explaining Western growth issues. According to Thomas Black, an urban development economist at the Urban Land Institute in Washington, DC, "There is a lot of argument, but economists agree that when it comes to regulating growth, prices will be driven up, housing costs will rise, wages will rise, and the cost of living will rise" (Caruso). Since this institute is funded by business, real estate, and developers, the statement comes as no surprise. But it is certainly false and rather misleading, since have difficulty agreeing on complicated issues like those involving the planning and regulation of growth.

Another problem with Black's claim is that the cost of living, by definition, includes prices and housing costs. A rise in prices *is* a rise in the cost of living. The important question is whether the real wage (the cost of living subtracted from the money wage) will rise or not. Even using Black's reasoning, many people would benefit from regulating growth if real wages rise, since a rise in real wages improves workers' real incomes, and a rise in housing costs benefits those who plan to sell their houses and move out of the area.

Unfortunately, those in favor of government regulations to control growth cannot prove that government intervention will result in an optimal or cost-effective outcome either. First, the government may also fail to allocate the goods properly, and second, the cost of government action may be higher than the benefits associated with its actions. Therefore, before any government regulations or policies are undertaken, both issues should be examined. But if the cost of government action is less than the social benefits, then social welfare can be improved by correct government intervention.

Others believe that there is an additional problem associated with the free markets, even when all the assumptions listed above hold true; namely, a free market does not necessarily allocate goods fairly. And it is true that economic theory makes no claims about what is just and fair in society, since these are moral, not economic, issues. In fact, even if 1% of the people control 99% of the wealth, that can be just as economically efficient as 50% of the people controlling 50% of the wealth. Welfare, Social Security, Medicaid and Medicare were all set up because a majority of people believed that the free-market did not allocate resources fairly and equitably to the poor and the old. Of course, the same difficulty presents itself as it did above: since government action is costly, there is no guarantee that the benefits of creating a more equitable distribution of wealth from the action will outweigh the costs.

Solutions

Regulating growth can mean many things, but a city that grows at random without any planning is impossible. Building codes, zoning ordinances, public services and infrastructure are all are required by a modern industrial city, and need to be planned and have funding allocated for them. The question now is whether there should be additional regulations applied to growth that will reduce the negative consequences. It does appear that there are many regulatory policies that can be put into place at little cost that will enhance the benefits of growth and reduce the negative effects.

Simple government policies exist that can assist the free market to work properly and allocate goods and services more efficiently. The basic economic principle to be applied is that the full cost of the good should be paid for by the people who purchase it. The reasoning behind this principle is simple. Suppose instead that a house costs less to purchase than it costs to build. A shortage of houses would likely result, and the developer who builds these houses would soon go out of business.

A similar situation exists in many cities today—the current costs of new houses and new residents are being subsidized by existing residents. For example, the external costs associated with traffic congestion, additional air and water pollution, and environmental degradation are not included in the price of a new house. And second, the costs of the additional infrastructure and public services needed by the new residents is shared with the current residents through existing tax payments. In 1991 James Nicholas estimated that a new single family home in the US required more than $20,000 of public infrastructure to support new development, but in Eugene Oregon, the city collected only $2,000 in impact fees (Fodor). Such economic conditions result in more people moving to the West than would occur if all the costs of the move were reflected in new housing prices and the taxes paid by new residents.

Therefore, the economically efficient solution is to require new residents to pay for the full cost of their houses, the additional infrastructure, and public services that are needed. Appropriate usage and impact fees are one solution. If the price of a new home reflected the true costs of the externalities it generated, then new homes would then be more expensive and less urban sprawl would result. The outcome would then be slower and more manageable growth.

Zoning laws can also prevent urban sprawl; Washington and Oregon are frequently cited examples. Portland established an urban growth boundary making it difficult and costly for new buildings to be constructed outside that boundary. Although population density increased as a result, that meant public transportation became more efficient and resulted in less air pollution. And Portland's growth rate of 2.7% is still above the national median.

New office buildings also impose negative externalities on surrounding residents, but since compensation payments to the surrounding residents would be difficult to enact, other alternatives must be examined. For instance, additional zoning laws could be developed requiring (1) additional residential developments near new office buildings, (2) offices and residences being built near transportation corridors, and (3) additional green spaces near new developments. Also it would be useful to remove zoning laws that prevent residential and commercial buildings from existing side-by-side and removing laws that favor single-family dwellings over multiple-family dwellings. Urban sprawl could also be reduced by raising taxes in the suburbs and lowering them in the cities, encouraging higher income residents to remain in the city.

The solution to traffic congestion is similar to that of urban sprawl. Since each driver imposes a negative externality on other drivers, but does not pay for it, an inefficient use of the limited resource (roads) occurs. The US Department of Transportation estimates that "Tolls, gasoline taxes, and user fees cover only 70 percent of the direct costs of building and maintaining a nation's road system" (Longman). If the external costs imposed on the economy were included, according to urban planner Reid Ewing, then a gasoline tax of $6.60 a gallon would be necessary to make drivers pay the full cost of the use of their vehicles (Longman).

In other markets, people expect to pay more when the good is scarce, but they feel that using the roads, even at rush hour, ought to be free. If instead, higher prices were charged during the peak hours, this would reduce the number of people using the roads. This reduces traffic congestion by encouraging people to use the roads at other times and causing more people to car pool, use public transportation, or find alternate means of transportation.

Several problems may arise. Toll roads cause motorists to use free side roads, increasing congestion on those free roads, which are seldom designed to handle heavy traffic. Installing tollbooths slows the speed of traffic, increasing congestion; and extra costs are involved with collecting the fee. However, technological solutions, such as electronic tags, have been developed that overcome both problems and are being used in 20 different countries. Singapore has been using such devices for 22 years and Europe has been using a road-pricing for more than five years (*The Economist*).

Electronic tags are purchased by motorists and electronic monitors installed in the road which allow cars to drive over them at speeds up to 100 mph (similar tags are being used in Maryland, Virginia, and Illinois for electronic payment of tolls). In order to legally use certain toll roads, cars must have the tag installed. The cost of a trip is then calculated based on the time and distance driven and is automatically deducted from the value encoded electronic tag.

In the West, water scarcity is becoming a growing problem because the pricing of water does not reflect its scarcity and the cost of delivering it. Many Western states actually subsidize the price of water to farmers, who therefore have little incentive to conserve it. Projections of future shortages are causing questions to be raised about where additional water will come from. Las Vegas is now pursuing distant water supplies in neighboring counties, and some new suburbs near Denver are projected to run out of water within a decade (Egan).

Increases in hook-up fees and higher water rates would help ease the impact of new residents in growing cities, but harnessing the political will necessary to increase such fees is difficult. For example, as discussed earlier, the current residents of Las Vegas voted to subsidize new development in the metropolitan area by choosing an increase in the general sales tax, rather than raising water rates and hook-up fees to equal the true costs of providing these services.

The Urban and Economic Development Division at the US Environmental Protection Agency has developed "Smart Growth": a set of policies and design alternatives to reduce urban sprawl. The Smart Growth Network (www.smartgrowth. org) emphasizes how developers, business groups, citizens, and government officials need to work together to manage growth so that it benefits everyone. For example, clustered development, compared to traditional detached housing, reduces farmland and forest losses by 70%; stormwater runoff and water pollution is reduced by 50%; infiltration and recharge of groundwater is increased by 50%; the fuel required for space heating is reduced by 25%; air pollution from space heating is reduced by 25%; and the cost of installing and maintaining utility lines is reduced by 50% (Nebel and Wright 619).

The remaining question is whether existing residents should equitably share the burden of growth with the new residents, or should the new residents pay more so that free-market principles are brought into play. Unfortunately, the market only works when goods are freely bought and sold in a competitive market and the goods that are truly valuable to us have no price. Can the political system overcome these problems and bring about a more efficient and equitable system? The chances for that appear to be small.

Political Obstacles

While the economic solutions needed to achieve a more optimal level of population growth are straightforward, getting
them onto the books is a more difficult matter. In the fastest
growing city, Las Vegas, one rarely hears about the negative
elements associated with growth. The most vocal groups are
those that benefit from growth and have strong incentives to
keep growth rates high. This can result in policies that favor
the few over the many, yet this outcome is both logical and
rational.

The difficulty is that since the external costs of population growth are spread widely, but the benefits from population growth occur to only a few, the few have strong incentives to organize and lobby to prevent managed growth. In
other words, while the total benefits of slowing growth can be
substantial, since these benefits are spread so widely, few
people have any rational reason to band together and oppose
growth.

This is why special interest groups dominate politics at
both the local and national levels. Suppose a project that was
needed to insure continued growth, such as a new water system, would cost a city $500,000 paid for by an increase in
taxes. If the city has 1,000,000 people that would mean a tax
increase of 50 cents. Thus, preventing a 50 cent rise in taxes
would probably not be worth the cost of writing and sending
a letter. However, suppose that the project would benefit 50
contractors giving each an average benefit of $10,000. The
contractors have a much stronger incentive than the taxpayers to write letters, lobby the legislature, and donate money
to the candidates. This behavior leads to what economists
call "rent seeking," which causes resources to be used by
special interest groups so that those special interest groups
are given a larger piece of the government pie, which of course
causes the groups (and citizens) who lose to get a smaller
piece.

Rent seeking results in policies where the benefits are
distributed narrowly, and the costs are distributed widely.
Consumers suffer two losses: the first loss results from higher
taxes, while the second results from the higher prices imposed by the contractors to pay for their lobbying activity.
After the policy is passed, resources are then devoted to keep-

ing the policy on the books. Again, the individual consumer doesn't have a strong enough incentive to lobby the legislature to remove the policy. This explains why so many outdated policies still exist at the national, state, and local levels.

Those who benefit from growth, therefore, have strong incentives to support continued unregulated growth and mention only the positive aspects of growth and downplay the negatives. However, this may work only in the short run, since if the external costs begin to predominate, growth will slow down and may even stop, causing the benefits for the developers to end. Although developers may realize that high growth rates cannot continue forever, they have no rational incentive to do anything about it by themselves, since individual action is costly and will reduce their current profits. Likewise, current residents also do not have a strong enough incentive to take action on their own, and of course neither do the new residents or government officials.

Therefore, while a greater level of social benefits can be achieved for the West simply by applying the basic economic policies of stopping subsidies for development and requiring developers and new residents to pay the full costs, getting past the political obstacles to bring about smart, managed growth in the West will be difficult.

There is still a reason for optimism however. As the external costs associated with growth increase, more people will be affected by them and will have stronger incentives to take action, form interest groups, and vote. And even though economic theory shows that the cost of voting is always higher than the benefits one obtains from it, many people, including economists, pay no attention to this theory and vote anyway.

REFERENCES

21st Century Commission— PA Department of Environmental Protection. "Promoting Responsible Land Use." *Report of the 21st century Environmental Commission.* <http://www.21stcentury. state.pa.us/2001/i_promoting_responsible_land_use.html>, 15 Sept. 1998 (Accessed 3 Nov. 1998).
Caruso, Monica. "Push to Slow Las Vegas Growth Sparks Economic Debate." *Las Vegas Review Journal Growth Series.* <http:// www.lvrj_home/in-depth/package/growth>. 6 Apr. 1997 (Accessed: 21 Oct. 1998).

"Cities of the US" *The World Almanac and Book of Facts 1998*. Ed. Robet Famighetti. Mahwah, NJ: K-III Reference Corporation, 1998.

Egan, Timothy. "Urban Sprawl Strains Western States." <http:hannahsmac.magnet.fsu.edu/curg/UrbanSprawlinWesternUS.html>, 29 December 1996 (accessed 9 Nov. 1998).

Federation of Tax Administrators. "1997 State Tax Revenue." *1997 State Tax Burdens.* <http://www.taxadmin.org/fta/rate/97taxbur.html> (22 Oct. 1998).

Federation of Tax Administrators. "1994 State & Local Revenue as a Percentage of Personal Income." *1994 State and Local Revenue Percentage of Income. <http://www.taxadmin.org/fta/rate/95stlrev.html>* (accessed 22 October 1998).

Fodor, Eben. "The Three Myths of Growth." <http://www.plannersweb.com/articles /fod101.html> (accessed 9 Nov. 1998).

Hsing, Yu. "A Note on Interstate Migration and Tax Burdens: New Evidence." *Journal of Applied Business Research* 12 (1995-1996): 12-14.

Ladd, Helen. "Effects of Population Growth on Local Spending and Taxes" *Research in Urban Economics*, 9 (1993): 181-223.

———. "Fiscal Impacts of Local Populatin Growth: A Conceptual and Empirical Analysis." *Regional Science and Urban Economics*, 24 (1994): 661-686.

"Living with the Car." *The Economist*, 345 (6 Dec. 1997): 21-23.

Longman, Phillip J. "Who Pays for Sprawl? Hidden Subsidies Fuel the Growth of the Suburban Fringe. <http://www.usnews.com/usnews/issue/980427/27spra.htm>. 27 Apr. 1998 (accessed 9 Nov. 1998).

Molotch, Harvey. "The City as a Growth Machine: Toward a Political Economy of Place." *American Journal of Sociology* 82-2 (Sept. 1976): 309-332.

Nebel, Bernard, and Richard Wright. *Environmental Science*, 6th ed. Upper Saddle River, NJ: Simon & Schuster, 1998.

Nelson, Michael. "Taxation of Natural Resources and State Economic Growth." *Growth and Change* 20 (Fall 1989): 13-30.

Nevada Taxpayers Association. "The Question Revisited: Does Growth Pay for Itself." *Taxtopics* (Jan. 1997): 1-3.

Nicholas, James C. *A Practitioner's Guide to Development Impact Fees.* American Planning Association Press, 1991.

Rogers, Keith. "Waning Wetlands." *Las Vegas Review Journal*, (19 October 1998): 1B-4B.

Tax Foundation. "Total Taxes per Capita and as a Percent of Income, 1998, by State." <http://www.taxfoundation.org/totaltaxburden.html> (accessed 22 Oct. 1998).

Tiebout, Charles. "A Pure Theory of Local Expenditures." *Journal of*

Political Economy, 64 (Oct. 1956): 416-24.

United States Bureau of the Census. "Metropolitan Area Rankings." <http://www.census.gov/Press-Release/metro04.prn>, 21 Jul. 1998 (accessed: 20 October 1998).

United States Bureau of the Census. "Population Projections for States by Age, Sex, Race, and Hispanic Origin: 1995 to 2025." *State Population Projections.* http://www.census.gov/population/www /projections/ppl47.html#moredata>, Oct. 1996 (accessed: 19 Oct. 1998).

United States Environmental Protection Agency. "National Air Quality and Emissions Trends Report, 1996. <http://www.epa.gov/oar/aqtrnd96/> (accessed 27 Oct. 1998).

United States Environmental Protection Agency. "USA Air Quality Nonattainment Areas." <http://www.epa.gov/airs/nonattn.html> (accessed 27 October 1998).

THE FUTURE OF WORK AND THE WORKER
Peter Drucker's Search for Community

DARYL WENNEMANN

> *Technological optimists think that computers will reverse some of this social atomization, touting virtual experience and virtual community as ways for people to widen their horizons. But is it really sensible to suggest that the way to revitalize community is to sit alone in our room, typing at our networked computers and filling our lives with virtual friends?*
> —Sherry Turkle 235

Peter Drucker is widely known for his work in management theory. His many publications in this area are well known to business students around the world. Some of his most prominent works in management theory include *The Practice of Management, Managing for Results, The Effective Executive, Management: Tasks, Responsibilities, Practices, Managing in Turbulent Times, The Frontiers of Management*, and *Managing for the Future*. These works and others have certainly placed Peter Drucker at the forefront of the study of management theory. But there is, in addition to these works, a wide range of works that may not be as widely known by those who read Drucker for the insight he brings to the practice of management. Among his nearly thirty books are works deal-

Daryl J. Wennemann is currently an assistant professor in philosophy at Fontbonne College in St. Louis. He has co-authored a book in applied ethics, Applied Professional Ethics, *and has published a number of articles in the philosophy of technology in* Research in Philosophy and Technology *as well as articles in* Philosophy and Theology *and* The Modern Schoolman.

ing with economics, politics, and social theory, as well as two novels and an autobiography under the title, *Adventures of a Bystander.* In this study, I will focus on the theme of community in Drucker's social thought. This theme, I believe, is one that runs through many of Drucker's books and may provide a central organizing theme for understanding his social thought.

In a recent work, *Post-Capitalist Society,* Peter Drucker describes a felt sense of community as being an important benefit associated with voluntary work, and the work experience associated with nonprofit organizations. Drucker's argument is that this sense of community is vital to our post-capitalist society, a society that is dominated by the demands of information. In my view, this concern to establish a basis for community in the economic lives of persons is a constant theme of Drucker's reflections on the role of management in modern societies. The roots of Drucker's notion of community can be traced to a very early work, *The End of Economic Man,* in 1939. In this book, Drucker introduced the notion of status, which is a basic value that accrues to all persons who are members of a community, including workers. The status of the worker implies that workers should be treated as free persons and not merely as means of production. This may be seen as a precursor to contemporary theories of participatory management which recognize the right of workers to participate in decision making because they are members of a moral community or simply because they are enfranchised in some way.

As we shall see, Drucker's search for community in the economic life of modern societies was frustrated by the bifurcation of the decision-making function between management and labor. His recent reflections have led him to locate community in the post-modern economy that has developed on the basis of a knowledge economy.

The significance of this theme can be seen in a study by Robert Nisbet, *The Quest for Community.* Nisbet has argued that much of modern thought revolves around the experience of a loss of community and a concomitant search for community. His study is an important point of departure for any study of community. This is certainly true of our analysis of Drucker's work. The loss of community and the search for community is a significant theme in his thought that has not been recognized and given the significance it deserves. I hope to point to this significant theme and show how Drucker's thought itself illustrates a loss of community and a subsequent search for community.

The Quest for Community

In *The Quest for Community,* Nisbet argues that the development of modern culture is characterized by a felt loss of community and a concomitant search for community. The loss of community in modern societies has resulted, in Nisbet's view, from the rise of the modern nation-state. The modern state has taken on many of the functions of the intermediate social groups, like the family, church, guild, and other local associations, that have traditionally mediated between the individual and the state. Having lost any significant social function, these traditional associations have atrophied, leaving the individual standing alone facing the power of the modern state. This, in turn has given rise to the peculiar condition of alienation of the modern individual. The incoherence of social existence is correlated with the individual's sense of powerlessness in the face of the unlimited power of the state. As Nisbet has written,

> I believe . . . that the single most impressive fact of the twentieth century in Western society is the fateful combination of widespread quest for community—in whatever form, moral, social, political—and the apparatus of political power that has become so vast in contemporary democratic states. That combination of search for community and existing political power seems to me today, just as it did twenty years ago, a very dangerous combination. For, . . . the expansion of power feeds on the quest for community. All too often power comes to resemble community, especially in times of convulsive social change and of widespread preoccupation with personal identity, moral certainty, and social meaning. This is . . . the essential tragedy of modern man's quest for community . . . . The structure of political power which came into being three centuries ago on the basis of its eradication of medieval forms of community has remained—has indeed

become ever more—destructive of new forms of community. (vii-viii)

Nisbet argues that human freedom is ultimately grounded in human community and the development of community in the modern age requires the development of new forms of intermediate social groups that can mediate between the individual and the state. This is the real significance of Peter Drucker's attempt to locate community in the economic sphere. Drucker's insight is that the modern corporation may provide a social function beyond that of merely producing goods and services within a market that is made up of atomic individuals. Rather, it may provide a context for community among individuals as they carry out their economic tasks. As Drucker notes in *Technology, Management, and Society,*

> It is the organization which is today our most visible social environment. The family is "private" rather than "community"—not that this makes it any less important. The "community" is increasingly in the organization, and especially in the one in which the individual finds his livelihood and through which he gains access to function, achievement, and social status. (35)

The Status of the Individual

In 1939 Drucker wrote the first of a series of works that attempted to define the newly emerging economic environment associated with modern management. In *The End of Economic Man* (1939), Drucker analyzed fascist economies, especially those of Germany and Italy, in order to ascertain how they operated and how they differed from the economies of the Western democracies. It is interesting to note that fascism arose, according Drucker, as a result of the collapse of the Western ideal of human nature as "Economic Man." According to this ideal, the economic sphere of human activity is of the highest significance, inasmuch as it was supposed to produce both freedom and equality. It was only when the ideal failed to produce these expected results that Western people turned to fascism with the hope that it would provide equality and security, if not freedom. According to Drucker,

Through the collapse of Economic Man the individual is deprived of his social order, and his world of its rational existence. He can no longer explain or understand his existence as rationally correlated and co-ordinated to the world in which he lives; nor can he co-ordinate the world and the social reality to his existence. The function of the individual in society has become entirely irrational and senseless. Man is isolated within a tremendous machine, the purpose and meaning of which he does not accept and cannot translate into terms of his experience. Society ceases to be a community of individuals bound together by a common purpose, and becomes a chaotic hubbub of purposeless isolated monads. (55)

The similarity of this analysis with that of Nisbet is obvious. The difference lies in the fact that Nisbet focused on the relation of the individual to the political order i.e., the state while Drucker sees the economic order as having taken priority over other social spheres in the age of Economic Man.

Drucker's study of fascism is significant because, according to his interpretation, the Second World War represented a historical test or experiment that would determine if the worker has status and is thus a member of a free community, or is merely a factor of production or industrial slave. Fascist societies were really non-economic societies in the sense that economic activity, like investment and gaining profit, were subordinated to non-economic goals. In particular, the goal of fascist economies was a condition of full employment. As such, a basic lesson of the Great Depression, according to Drucker, is that economic security is a social goal that is more important to people than other economic goals. The task of the post-war Western societies would thus be to develop a new non-economic society that is able to structure human life in such a way that freedom and equality are experienced in concrete terms in the economic activities of individuals. As Drucker asserts in the *The End of Economic Man*,

The next decade will decide whether Europe can find such forces which would lead her out of the impasse into which the collapse of Economic Man has maneuvered her, or whether she has to grope her way through the darkness of totalitarian fascism before she finds a new, positive non-economic concept of Free and Equal Man. (268)

Drucker holds that the new non-economic society would be an industrial society that is characterized by a new system of management that would produce a level of rationality that was undreamed of in the economic society of the eighteenth and nineteenth centuries. In *The Future of Industrial Man* (1942), Drucker extends the analysis of the previous study, arguing that Nazism represents a challenge to the Western industrial culture:

> Unless we realize that the essence of Nazism is the attempt to solve a universal problem of Western civilization—that of the industrial society—and that the basic principles on which the Nazis base this attempt are also in no way confined to Germany, we do not know what we fight for or what we fight against. We must know that we fight against an attempt to develop a functioning industrial society on the basis of slavery and conquest. Otherwise we would have no basis for our own attempt to develop not only a functioning but a free and peaceful industrial society. (19)

It is clear that the non-economic values that are to guide policy making in an industrial society are, for Drucker, freedom and equality. But this means that workers must be treated as free persons having status. And this implies, in turn, that workers must somehow participate in the decision making process within the industrial order. In other words, an industrial order that is both functional and free must be conceived as being an industrial community. Such a social order must balance the demand of the individual to be recognized as having value within the group and the demand of the group that the needs of the individual should be aligned with its requirement to function effectively. The categories of status and function can only be coordinated by establishing the citizenship of the worker within the industrial order. Drucker developed this problematic to a high degree in *The New Society:*

"Status" defines man's existence as related in mutual necessity to the organized group. "Function" ties his work, his aspirations and ambitions to the power and purposes of the organized group in a bond that satisfies both individual and society. . . . Together status and function resolve the apparently irresolvable conflict between the absolute claim of the group—before which any man is nothing in himself and only a member of the species—and the absolute claim of the individual, to whom the group is only a means and a tool for the achievement of his own private purpose. Status and function overcome this conflict by giving citizenship to the individual.

Man must have status and function in his society in order to be a person. . . . But the group's own cohesion and survival also depend on the individual's status and function; without it the group is a mere herd, never a society. And only a society that gives status and function to its members can expect their allegiance. Status and function of the individual member are requirements of individual and social life. (151)

The concrete society of the West has to demand of the industrial enterprise that it fulfill that promise of status we call Justice, which is expressed by the slogan of *equal opportunities*; and that it organize function according to the belief in the Dignity of Man as it is expressed in the responsible participation of citizenship. (154)

Such a social order can be seen clearly by contrast with the Nazi social order that is founded on slavery. Even after the war against fascism was won, Drucker found that there remained the task of building an industrial civilization. Such a civilization would recognize the value of the individual worker in a concrete way within the organization of the industrial enterprise, just as the political state recognized the value of the individual citizen. Even within a democratic political order individual workers could very well find themselves as industrial slaves if their only role was that of a cog in the machinery of the industrial plant. In *The Future of Industrial Man*, Drucker saw that the end of the Second World War would give rise to a need for a new industrial civilization:

> WE DO [sic] not today have a functioning industrial society. We have a magnificent technical machine for industrial production, built and run by engineers, chemists, and skilled mechanics. We have a considerably weaker but still very impressive economic machine for the distribution of industrial goods. Politically and socially, however, we have no industrial civilization, no industrial community life, no industrial order or organization. It is this absence of a functioning industrial society, able to integrate our industrial reality, which underlies the crisis of our times. (21)

Drucker's goal, then, was to develop a legitimate industrial social order. Just as the power of the state in a free society must be legitimate, inasmuch as it flows from the consent of the people, Drucker holds that the power of the corporation must be legitimate. And the legitimacy of the power of the corporation depends upon the recognition of the status of the worker as a sort of citizen within the economy, having rights that limit the power of the corporation:

> If the individual is not given social status and function, there can be no society but only a mass of social atoms flying through space without aim or purpose. And unless power is legitimate there can be no social fabric; there is only a social vacuum held together by mere slavery or inertia. (25-26).

The status and function of the individual integrates the individual into the group and makes the actions of the individual cohere with those of the group. Status and function provide for the social cohesion of modern societies that tend to lack any of the traditional social bonds of pre-industrial societies.

In *The New Society* (1949), Drucker posits status and function as values that can lead to a free and equal society in an industrial form of federal republic. It is significant, in this regard, that Drucker has written of the plant community in order to establish a social context within which the status and function of the individual can be expressed. This represents a response on Drucker's part to the dangers inherent in the industrial mode of social production and thus organization. As Drucker notes, "Research and analysis . . . indicate *that the individual can be given status and function in the industrial enterprise.* They disprove the popular belief that the industrial system is by its very nature destructive of human community and individual dignity"(165).

One of the dangers associated with mass production is that the worker invariably becomes divorced from the means of production. For, as Drucker asserts, "It is the organization rather than the individual which is productive in an industrial system"(6). This, in turn, threatens the status and prestige system of traditional groups and tends to dissolve the traditional community, uprooting the individual in the process. The plant community is supposed to make up for this loss.

Another danger associated with mass production is the concentration of power with the concomitant loss of individual liberty. The individual becomes subject to the impersonal forces of the market which might leave her unemployed and thus separated from one of the primary sources of social contact. Anyone who has been caught in the wave of downsizing in recent years can undoubtedly identify with these dangers. Drucker argues that the most significant long-term effect of unemployment is psychological rather than physical. It can produce a loss of self-respect, loss of initiative, and even lead to suicide. While Drucker's analysis in *The New Society* is focused on the Great Depression, it seems to apply very well to the current environment of downsizing or rightsizing. The effect on the individual is the same no matter what it is called. According to Drucker,

> Denied access to the organization without which, in an industrial society, nobody can be productive, the unemployed becomes an outcast whose very membership in society has been suspended. It is no accident that the "depression shock" was by no means confined to those who actually suffered long-term unemployment, but hit fully as hard the men who never, during the Depression, were out of a job, and who

may never have been in real danger of losing their job. For a decade they lived in the constant fear of being fired the next payday; to become actually unemployed may well have been more bearable than to go on living in constant terror. (8)

Within an industrial order the individual seems to face impersonal market forces that are as irrational as the individual who lives in a dictatorship. One is powerless before the whims of a distant ruler who determines one's fate. According to Drucker's analysis, this situation is really unbearable for the individual and threatens to undermine the functioning of an industrial society. As Drucker states in *The New Society*,

> The citizen can neither control nor understand the forces that threaten to cast him out from society and deprive him of his effective citizenship. Unless modern industrial society can banish these forces, it will not be acceptable or rational to its members. It must become instead meaningless, insane and demon-ridden, and turn into an obsessive nightmare. (8)

These dangers arise in an industrial society when purely economic goals come to predominate in our decision making. Drucker argues that the social goals of freedom and equality must lead to a decentralization of power within the economy, and within the corporation in particular. Since the large enterprise is the organizing principle of our society, it is the real locus of freedom and equality. And so, the decision making process of large enterprises must not be swallowed up into the state. Local self-government within the economic sphere is essential in an industrial society. The difficulty we continually face is that it seems that we must sacrifice freedom for function or function for freedom. By describing the modern corporation as a plant community Drucker hoped to develop a mode of organization that is both functional and free.

According to Drucker, the enterprise today is both an economic and governmental institution. As a plant community, the enterprise discharges social functions, not just economic ones. The members of the plant community are, in a sense, citizens having the rights and obligations associated with citizenship within the state. In Drucker's words, "[T]he plant community is a real community, indeed . . . it is the community which appears to the member of the enterprise as the representative and decisive one for the fulfillment of his social aspirations and beliefs" (49). In this regard, Drucker notes that all members of the plant community must have a managerial attitude toward their work and toward the enterprise. For, the modern enterprise requires the active participation of every member to efficiently accomplish its task. "The major incentives to productivity and efficiency are social and moral rather than financial"(49).

Unfortunately, the need for workers to adopt a managerial attitude does not close the rift between management and labor. The central conflict of the modern industrial enterprise is the functional requirement to count the labor of workers as a cost of production, a factor of production. And this seems to be inconsistent with the status of the individual.

> [T]he real point is that *the enterprise must regard "labor" as a commodity which is bought according to the current level of production and priced according to the current price level. . . .*

> To lay off a worker in slack times implies no personal criticism but is forced upon the enterprise by imper-sonal, economic forces over which it has no control. But it is precisely this subordination of the worker's citizenship and personality to an impersonal force which is the trouble . . . To consider labor a commodity goes, therefore, against the economic needs of the worker as well as against his social and political needs. (77-78)

While Drucker holds that every individual in a firm must have a managerial attitude, his study, *Concept of the Corporation* indicates that it is a functional or structural requirement of the modern enterprise to restrict the decision making power of workers to their own particular sphere of activity.

> [D]ecentralization as a principle of industrial order can be applied only where there is at least a rudiment of

genuine executive functions. It cannot possibly be the basis for an integration of the worker into industrial society; for it is almost in the definition of the industrial worker that he does not direct but is directed. (149)

There is thus a split between management and labor which seems to undermine the sense of community Drucker wants. This is a recurring problem in Drucker's thought that all but undermines his effort at developing a living plant community that fosters freedom and equality. In *The New Society*, Drucker suggests that the worker is only able to exercise a managerial function within the social sphere of the plant community, not in the economic sphere: "[T]he worker by virtue of his position and function cannot be given managerial responsibility and experience in the sphere of economics and can obtain it only in the social sphere"(287). But the economic sphere of the plant community would seem to be decisive. It does not seem that the social aspect of the person's experience in the plant community can or should be divorced from the economic aspect of that experience. Drucker, however, sees such a divorce as a structural requirement of the modern industrial organization. In the end, Drucker sees the managerial attitude as being necessary to reconcile the individual to the impersonal economic necessities that drive decision making within the plant community. Again, in *The New Society* Drucker describes this functional role of the managerial attitude:

> The self-government of the plant community—subordinate to, and limited by, the enterprise's need for economic performance, but autonomous within its limits—is the answer to the enterprise's demand for a "managerial attitude" of its members, and for acceptance on their part of the economic rationale of the enterprise. It satisfies the member's needs for citizenship, recognition and opportunities; it alone can solve the problem of the "split allegiance" between enterprise and union, as well as the problems of union function, union cohesion, and union leadership. (288)

The market economy thus gives rise to certain economic demands that appear to be inimical to community. Do temporary and part-time employees have status within the economy? Or, are they merely disposable factors of production? As long as Drucker dealt with the problems of the market economy, there seemed to be no way for him to find a real community within the confines of the economic laws that drive economic decisions. Within the economic sphere of the plant community, the worker is not to direct but only be directed.

On the other hand, what is the basis of the power of the managerial elite? Within an industrial civilization the power of management must be seen as legitimate, just as the power of the political elite is legitimate. Since the famous study of Berle and Means in 1932, *The Modern Corporation and Private Property*, we have known that the traditional foundation for the legitimacy of management power (i.e., ownership) is no longer valid. Do the high executive salaries we see in contemporary corporations represent a commitment to community life, especially in light of the concomitant tendency to downsize companies for the sake of short-term profitability? Here Drucker suggests that a profit-sharing plan for workers must be instituted alongside a profit-sharing plan for executives. Understood as a community, the industrial plant must make sure that the workers see themselves as being engaged in a shared undertaking with management. Thus, Drucker notes in *The New Society*, "This would limit fixed incomes to a sum which, while significantly higher than the worker's income, is still within reach of his imagination" (252).

It is significant that in 1949 Drucker saw that in the new society it is the skills of the worker that represent the primary resource of modern industrial firms. This is a common insight in today's knowledge economy, and it may point to a significant development in the social status of individuals. In *The New Society* Drucker suggested, "The approach to a solution . . . is to consider wage both as a current cost and as future cost, that is, as an investment in the major productive resource of any enterprise, its labor force"(87).

Community in Post-Capitalist Society

I have said that the pressures of the market economy introduced a seemingly irreconcilable split in the modern indus-

trial plant that tended to undermine Drucker's effort to develop a sense of community within the economic sphere. In
Drucker's recent books we can see a new effort to promote
the importance of community within the economic lives of
persons within the newly emergent world economy. It is significant that Drucker has turned to the nonprofit sector of
the economy to find a role for the modern manager in building community life. In *Post-Capitalist Society* (1993), Drucker
observes how significant the nonprofit sector has become in
the present knowledge economy. In such an economy, of
course, the skills of the worker become of primary importance to economic performance. Indeed, Drucker wants to
rethink all of the economic categories like investment, sav-
ings, profit, productivity, etc., in terms of knowledge rather
than the traditional notion of capital. But he also wants to
promote the possibility of community within the post-capitalist enterprise:

> In the West, the plant community never took root. I
> still strongly maintain that the employee has to be
> given the maximum responsibility and self-control—
> the idea that underlay my advocacy of the plant com-
> munity. The knowledge-based organization has to be-
> come a responsibility-based organization. . . .

> But individuals, and especially knowledge workers,
> need an additional sphere of social life, of personal
> relationships, and of contribution outside and beyond
> the job, outside and beyond the organization, indeed,
> outside and beyond their own specialized knowledge
> area. (174)

Drucker sees the primary locus for community in post-
capitalist society as lying in the many voluntary efforts of
individuals who build community not on the basis of economic necessity but on the initiative of persons actively re-
sponding to both the needs of their society and their own
need for commitment and a sense of belonging.

> [E]very developed country needs an autonomous, self-
> governing social sector of community organizations—
> to provide the requisite community services, but above

all to restore the bonds of community and a sense of active citizenship. Historically, community was fate. In post-capitalist society and polity, community has to become commitment. (178)

The ultimate significance of the post-capitalist knowledge society is, according to Drucker, that it "puts the person in the center" (210), in the sense that, "The educated person now matters" (211). The educated person now matters in post-capitalist society because it is a knowledge society. As such, the educated person must carry out two roles. One is that of an intellectual (having specialized skills) and the other that of a manager, "who focuses on people and work." (215)

Of course, from a moral perspective, all persons matter because they have the status of a person who is a member of a moral community. The management perspective that Drucker has consistently adopted tends to recognize the status of persons who have a managerial function. Thus, Drucker tried to extend the managerial function to non-managers, the common workers of the so-called plant community. Still, he could never overcome the division between the functional economic needs of the organization and the human needs of the worker. This can be clearly seen in *The New Society*,

We need a principle that expresses the fact that the interests of the enterprise and of its members are different interests. They differ in character: the one is exclusively economic; the other is a mixture of the political, the economic and the social, with the social predominating. They also differ in direction: the one looks to the production of goods, the other largely to the production of status and the function of citizenship. (282)

This is why Drucker eventually turned to the nonprofit sector of the economy in order to find an organization whose functional economic requirements are not in conflict with the social needs of its workers. My view is that there is a moral imperative to recognize the status of all persons within or without the market economy, even those who are merely part-time employees, or temporary employees, or unemployed persons.

One danger of the new knowledge society is the one that Sherry Turkle described. We may tend to shut ourselves up in our own rooms and restrict our experience of community with others to the virtual relationships of the internet. Another danger is that we may tend to shut out those who do not enjoy the franchise of knowledge necessary to participate in the post-capitalist society.

However we experience community in the next millennium we can, I believe, find a broad and deep reflection on the problems of community in the thought of Peter Drucker. His notion of the status and function of the worker as a basis for community within the economic sphere introduces a challenge to us: can we develop a real concrete community life that has as its goals values that are worthy of our Western heritage, i.e., the freedom and equality of persons?

REFERENCES

Drucker, Peter, *The End of Economic Man*. New York: The John Day Company, 1939.
———.*The Future of Industrial Man*. New York: The John Day Company, 1942.
———. *Concept of the Corporation*, New York: Mentor Books, 1972.
———. *The New Society*. New York: Harper & Row, 1962.
———. *Post-Capitalist Society*. New York, HarperBusiness, 1993.
———. *Technology, Management, and Society*. New York: Harper & Row, 1970.
Nisbet, Robert. *The Quest for Community*. New York: Oxford University Press, 1977.
Turkle, Sherry. *Life on the Screen*. New York: Simon & Schuster, 1995.

LITERATURE AND LANDSCAPE

In "Humanities and Science" Lewis Thomas builds a bridge between the education of scientists and humanists and tells us the future rests on the shoulders of poets. Thomas's ideas can serve us well as we consider the place of the humanities in the future:

> We have a wilderness of mystery to make our way through in the centuries ahead, and we will need science for this but not science alone. Science will, in its own time, produce the data and some of the meaning in the data, but never the full meaning. For getting a full grasp, for perceiving real significance when significance is at hand, we shall need minds at work from all sorts of brains outside the fields of science, most of all the brains of poets, of course, but also those of artists, musicians, philosophers, historians, writers in general. (63)

While science and technology may provide the vehicle that hurls us into the future, the humanities will give us the means to appreciate what we encounter there. This section opens with a look at a modern western, Cormac McCarthy's *All the Pretty Horses*; Andrew Spencer asks us to confront our notions of the Old West and its mythic cowboy "who has no place in a modern world." In "A Cowboy Looks at Reality." Paul Lindholt proposes the canon of environmental literature be extended to include writings of the wise use movement in order for us to understand its motivations and purposes in "Considering the Canon." In "The Quest for Official English," Steve Hecox explores whether language is a bond that ties us together as Americans or a barrier that perpetuates cultural separation.

REFERENCES

Thomas, Lewis. "Humanities and Science." *Late Night Thoughts on Listening to Mahler's Ninth.* New York: Viking Press, 1984.

A Cowboy Looks at Reality
The Death of the American Frontier and the Illumination of the Cowboy Myth in Cormac McCarthy's *All the Pretty Horses*

ANDREW BLAIR SPENCER

> *Mother, Mother Ocean*
> *after all the years I've found*
> *my occupational hazard to be*
> *that my occupation's just not around.*
> Jimmy Buffett
> "A Pirate Looks at Forty"

Tom Pilkington writes of Cormac McCarthy's, *All the Pretty Horses,* that it is, "on one level, a coming-of-age story" (320). The novel is the story of a young man, John Grady Cole, and his friend Lacey Rawlins, who leave their homes in West Texas and cross the border into Mexico seeking work and adventure. While there, the two live lives that seem to be taken straight from stories of the Old West. However, the romantic images the boys had of their would-be lives in Mexico soon fade into reality, as they are confined to a Mexican prison for supposed involvement with horse thievery and murder. After fighting for their own lives and seeing a friend murdered, the boys are eventually released from prison to return to their homes. Lacey returns to Texas, while John Grady attempts to win the heart of the Mexican girl with whom he has fallen in love. She agrees to see him, against her grandaunt's wishes,

Andrew Spencer is a graduate student in English. His literary interests focus on twentieth century writing of the American West. He wishes to express his sincere thanks to Dr. Don Graham of the University of Texas for teaching him about the myths of the American West and to his wife, Portia, for her love, patience, and support.

but refuses to stay with him. So John Grady returns to Texas, filled with disillusionment about the life that he so desperately wanted to live.

This basic synopsis, which Pilkington calls "the surface plot" that is simply "a variation on a story that has been told often in Western literature" (317), merely illustrates the novel's theme of the loss of innocence. On a deeper thematic level, though, McCarthy uses Lacey Rawlins and John Grady Cole as vehicles both to mourn the passing of the American frontier, as well as to tell a reality that debunks the popular myths regarding the Old West, namely the myths of the American cowboy.

On July 12, 1893, Frederick Jackson Turner read a paper entitled "The Significance of the Frontier in American History" at the American Historical Association meeting in Chicago. He opens this paper with a quote from the 1890 Census:

> Up to and including 1880 the country had a frontier of settlement, but at present the unsettled area has been so broken into by isolated bodies of settlement that there can hardly be said to be a frontier line. In the discussion of its extent, its westward movement, etc., it can not [sic], therefore, any longer have a place in the census reports (Turner 1).

Turner says of this statement that it "marks the closing of a great historic movement" (1). Thus, according to the Census Bureau, the frontier was dead, and with it, so argues Turner, the frontier spirit.

Turner defined the frontier as "the outer edge of the wave [of advancement]—the meeting point between savagery and civilization" (3). For many people, the frontier was the embodiment of the "American Spirit." The frontier was a place where rugged individuals carved lives out of the untamed wilderness. When these rugged individuals reached the Pacific Ocean, there was no need to search further; they had reached the boundary of the frontier. Once this boundary had been reached, those who sought the frontier lifestyle were forced to search elsewhere, for new frontiers. In McCarthy's novel, this search for new frontiers takes John Grady and Lacey to Mexico, to a ranch where their boyhood fantasies about the

West and about the American frontier can come true. It is only in this mythical place that these fantasies can become reality, because that frontier that Turner mourned and longed for no longer exists anywhere in the world.

E. Douglas Branch points out that "the end of the open range was the end of the Texas trail" (570). He also says that the "distinctive craftsman" that is the American cowboy has been "magnified . . . into a legend" by "romancers" (570). This romantic view of the familiar image "was, in his avatar, a Texan" (570). Among the articles of clothing that defined his costume, Branch includes a Stetson hat, a flannel shirt, a bandanna around his neck, high-heeled boots, a vest, leather gloves, and leather chaps. Among the characteristic traits of the cowboy, he includes skill in horsemanship, and says that the cowboy was "damned fond of his horses" (570-71). Most people are familiar with this image of the cowboy. Young boys still dress up and play "cowboys and Indians," and "good guys" wear white hats and "bad guys" wear black hats. As a way of illustrating this specific idea, Lacey Rawlins tells John Grady at one point that his new black boots are "the shits," because he "always wanted to be a badman" (McCarthy 121). It is this image that Branch describes that I shall incorporate into my discussion as the image accepted in modern culture of what the "true" American cowboy was.

William Savage, Jr., writes that the American cowboy "in various guises is popularly accepted by Americans as a symbol, indicative of his stature as myth" (3). The truth in modern culture, though, is that this myth has become accepted as reality. Regarding Western novels, Savage writes that the presence of the romanticized cowboy figure "is mandatory because readers steeped in his myth expect to find him there" (4). McCarthy seems to be, on the surface, writing to this group that "expects" to find the "true" cowboy figure in novels about the American West. However, that picture of the American cowboy is the target of McCarthy's writing in addition to being the subject of it. Cormac McCarthy himself has said, "There isn't a place in the world you can go where they don't know about cowboys and Indians and the myth of the West" (Pilkington 312). McCarthy's motives in *All the Pretty Horses*, then, appear to be two-fold. First, McCarthy illuminates the fact that this myth of the American cowboy, that myth known the world over, does not exist in the same way that many readers feel it does. Secondly, he shows his readers that the American frontier is dead, and that those seeking it must look elsewhere, specifically in their imaginations. So, rather than calling *All the Pretty Horses* a romantic novel about the American West, I would refer to it as a sort of educational tool for readers "steeped" in the Western myth.

One of the first scenes in the novel immediately follows the funeral of John Grady's grandfather. John Grady Cole rides his horse along his family's ranch in the evening, riding west, and is described as looking "like a man come to the end of something" (McCarthy 5). The unnamed "something" that John Grady has come to the end of is his illusions. He realizes that the frontier of his ancestors no longer exists, and the figure he creates, the lone cowboy out riding the range, looks almost comical. As if to punctuate this idea, John Grady picks up the skull of a long-dead horse: "Frail and brittle. Bleached paper white . . . the comicbook teeth loose in their sockets" (6). This skull is a tangible image of the death of the frontier, brought about by the infiltration of modern advances into the world of the frontier.

John Grady and Lacey are out riding the next night, and McCarthy again drives home the point that these boys are living a myth. The boys unsaddle their horses, and they "hear the trucks out on the highway" (McCarthy 10). The image of these two young "cowboys" lying out under the stars is juxtaposed with the image of the modern highway, crawling with eighteen-wheelers hauling their loads in the modern world. The noise created by these trucks is another blow to the frontier image, as it furthers the idea that the frontier no longer exists. Vereen Bell writes, "The ruling desire of McCarthy's strongest characters . . . is to live in some place that is not yet touched by the complications of the modern world. . . . In practice this means that they want to not so much reverse history as to transcend it" (925). John Grady Cole and Lacey Rawlins fit this description quite well, as they are in search of a place that is literally untouched by history's advancements, a place where cowboy fantasies can still be realized.

I wish to shift the focus now to the driving force behind John Grady's departure for Mexico. Early in the first section of the novel, the reader is introduced to the conflict between John Grady and his mother. John Grady, at age sixteen, feels that he should be running the family ranch because his father, traumatized by his experiences in the war, is in no condition to do so. His mother tells John Grady that his idea is ludicrous, as he is still only a young boy. John Grady sets out, then, to find a place where he can run a ranch, where cowboys are the cowboys of the Western myth, and where the frontier really exists as it did in the days before modernization. He and Lacey sneak out of their houses and head for Mexico to follow their dreams. Again highlighting the fact that cowboys are out of place in this world, Lacey, after being hindered by a barbed wire fence, asks John Grady, "How the hell do they expect a man to ride a horse in this country?" (31). John Grady's response is simple and true: "They don't" (31).

By noon of the following day, it is clear that the boys are out of range of being discovered, and an almost childlike exuberance fills them, as Lacey grins and says, "We done it, didn't we?" (McCarthy 31). The boys are living out their dreams of running away from home and living the life of cowboys on the open range. They are still living in a world of reality, though, where they are nothing more than children, a fact pointed out to them by the proprietor of a café, who refers to them as "boys" (33), a comment which meets with no argument from either John Grady or Lacey.

After eating, the boys look at a map, trying to decide where it is they are going, but it does not seem to be of much help: "There were roads and rivers and towns on the American side of the map as far south as the Rio Grande and beyond that all was white" (McCarthy 34). In this description, south of the Rio Grande is unsettled frontier land that has not been surveyed by any mapmaker; this land appears to be the paradise John Grady and Lacey have been dreaming of.

The boys soon meet up with a traveling companion, Jimmy Blevins, who is also headed to Mexico, and the three boys head south for the border. Upon crossing into Mexico, the boys ride up into the foreign land, and, upon their initial realization of their achievement, are immediately silent. This moment of profound silence is an indicator that some major change has taken place, and, in fact, just such a change has taken place. The boys have literally been transported back in time, to a world where the romantic visions of the American West and the cowboy myth are reality, and they have accomplished their goal of leaving the United States and traveling to Mexico. Now the quest for a "true" cowboy job can commence.

Alan Cheuse says of the description of the landscape in *All the Pretty Horses* that it is "almost a 'character' in itself" (140), and the boys' first impression of Mexico is one of a sort of long-lost character, a character stuck in the past: "The mud huts. The dusty agave and the barren gravel hills beyond. A thin blue rivulet of drainwater ran down the clay gully in front of the store and a goat stood in the rutted road looking at the horses" (McCarthy 51). Clearly the boys are in a land that is not only foreign to them in terms of their geographic origin, but also foreign in the sense that they are completely ignorant as to the existence of such a place.

After riding for several days, Lacey mentions that there "damn sure is a bunch" of land stretched out before them (McCarthy 59). The fact that there is so much land to be explored is indicative of the ideal frontier, that which they so desperately sought, although in vain, in Texas. This point is emphasized when the boys pitch their camp for the night, and they hear "three long howls to the southwest" (60), howls that the boys determine to be from a wolf, an animal that they have had no contact with before. This eerie howl is emblematic of the frontier, and the fact that the boys have never heard it before suggests that they have never truly been on a frontier before. When it seems that the boys will fulfill their fantasies of living out the cowboy dream, another Western emblem—the bandit—thrusts itself into their world, and sets off a series of events that drastically changes the course of the boys' lives.

Jimmy Blevins' horse runs off one night during a rainstorm, and the boys find him in a small town. Despite John Grady and Lacey's objections, Jimmy is determined to recover his horse. Jimmy is sure they won't give it back to him without a fight, so he steals it, and the boys flee the town, with the authorities in pursuit. During the chase, the boys decide to split up, because they feel that it is Blevins and his horse that the pursuers are after.

While traveling the next day, John Grady and Lacey scare a deer out of its hiding place, and Lacey takes a shot at it: "In the evening passing through a saddle in the low hills they jumped a spikehorn buck out of a stand of juniper and Rawlins shucked the rifle backward out of the bootleg scabbard and raised and cocked it and fired" (89). Lacey Rawlins here accomplishes what, in reality, seems impossible: he pulls a gun out of a scabbard backwards, cocks it, aims it, and pulls the trigger, all of this while astride a moving horse. Despite the initial shock associated with a surprise such as this, and despite the fact that the deer is scared and running and the sun is setting, Lacey manages to shoot with pin-point accuracy in the dying light, hitting the deer perfectly in the base of the skull. Lacey acknowledges that his success was a result of "blind dumb-ass luck" (90), but this incident works in a manner of foreshadowing for what is to come. McCarthy is giving the reader the sense that these boys are capable of accomplishing things that, up to this point, would have been otherwise impossible. This idea comes up again when the boys begin their work on the La Purisima Ranch.

The boys, upon being hired as ranch hands, are suddenly thrust into a world of unknown pleasures and joys. The ranch is in some mystical location, and McCarthy gives it the air of a fantastical place: "In the lakes and in the streams were species of fish not known elsewhere on earth and birds and lizards and other forms of life as well all long relict here for the desert stretched away on every side" (97). In this mirage-like oasis, the boys are encountering animals that they never knew existed, representative of the fact that the boys have entered a world that, in reality, does not exist. In this world, suddenly, the boys are transformed from young teenagers to experienced ranch hands, another by-product of the fantastical, mythical qualities of the ranch itself. The boys are changed into the romantic image of cowboys, and begin to live the myth.

The first "cowboy job" the boys take on is the breaking of a group of wild horses that the ranch *vaqueros* have brought in. Rawlins' first impression of these horses is "That's as spooky a bunch of horses as I ever saw" (McCarthy 98). However, John Grady is sure that they can break all sixteen of the horses in four days, and he approaches their boss. John Grady explains to the *gerente* what they want to do, and then informs Lacey of the *gerente's* response: "He said we were full of shit. But in a nice way" (102). The situation seems an impossible one, and the words of the *gerente* reflect that idea. However, the boys are living in that mythical world where unknown species of animals exist, as do tangible manifestations of the cowboy myth. Things happen here that might seem impossible elsewhere.

The boys begin their work early the next morning. They devise a sort of trap for the horses, in which they hope to keep them while they put saddles on them. Their work draws a constantly growing group of admiring followers which continues to grow as the day progresses. The horses "looked like animals trussed up by children for fun," and they had "the voice of the breaker still running in their brains like the voice of some god come to inhabit them" (105). John Grady and Lacey are, in fact, "children," and these horses have been "trussed up" by them. However, the fact that these children are seen as gods in the eyes of the horses is further support for the idea that John Grady and Lacey are accomplishing things well beyond their true abilities.

The breaking process continues, and the gallery of onlookers grows. By the end of the day the boys have attracted a huge gathering: "By dark . . . there were something like a hundred people gathered, some come from the pueblo of La Vega six miles to the south, some from farther" (107). The result of the boys' incredible display of ability is apparent, as the men in the bunkhouse "seemed to treat them with a certain deference" (105), and, when the boys leave the corral for the night, "[t]hree separate strangers offered them a drink from bottles of mescal before they were clear of the crowd" (107).

The boys have achieved celebrity status as a result of their abilities. They have evolved into incredibly skilled cowboys, and are suddenly, magically, able to break horses better than the most seasoned hands on the ranch. This is yet another indication that the boys have become something beyond reality, much like the cowboy myth that they are living. The fact that the boys have to travel to a mythical land to achieve this super-human status, though, again speaks to the fact that the American frontier is dead, the cowboy image is based on a myth, and that the boys have no true place on a ranch in the real world.

The *hacendado* of the ranch is sufficiently impressed with John Grady's abilities. So much so that he invites John Grady to accept the role of his personal assistant, and, after conferring with Lacey, John Grady accepts the position. With his new authority, John Grady enters yet another world, the world of the ranch elite. He is invited in to play chess with *señorita* Alfonsa, the grandaunt and Godmother of Alejandra. Alfonsa has great authority on the ranch, as it is said that "her life at the hacienda invested it with oldworld ties and with antiquity and tradition" (McCarthy 132). One of her passions is chess. She invites John Grady to play, and he beats her twice in a row. Thus, John Grady, in addition to suddenly possessing super-human ability in the field of horse-breaking, is also an expert at chess, a combination not often associated with young boys from West Texas. John Grady is living a life that he could not lead in his real world existence, yet another statement regarding the myth of the American West.

While John Grady and Lacey are "playing cowboy," Jimmy Blevins returns to Encantada to recover his horse, and kills a man in the process. The police arrest John Grady and Lacey as his accomplices, and take them to jail. Initially, the boys relish their new celebrity status, as they tell a group of young girls that they are "*Ladrones muy famosos. Bandoleros*" (McCarthy 156). The reality of the situation, though, soon sets in, and the boys are taken to a police interrogation center that seems to come straight from a Western novel, with walls of "mud brick" with "[s]cales of old painted plaster" still stuck to them. The windows are missing the glass in places, and the vacancies are filled by "squares of tin all cut from the same large sign" (156-157). The boys are beaten into confessing, and are sent to a Mexican prison, also straight out of a Western novel, with all the typical stereotypes intact.

Upon arriving at the prison, the boys are told by the captain, "You stay here you going to die. Then come other problems. Papers is lost. Peoples cannot be found. Some peoples come here to look for some man but he is no here. No one can find these papers. Something like that" (McCarthy 180). Many a young boy who has ever ventured "south of the border" in search of fun and enjoyment has been warned by his elders of the dangers of Mexican prisons, from where people seldom return. This idea, much like the myth of the cowboy, has become so engrained in the minds of people that it is as much a part of the legend of Mexico as the cowboy is of the American West. McCarthy uses this well-known legend to place the boys in another situation in which they are able to exhibit powers and abilities that they would not have in any sort of real world existence.

The first day the boys spend in prison is one composed of a fight for survival, during which both boys are badly beaten and Lacey has his nose broken. Here again McCarthy is playing on the popular images of Mexican prisons, where the rule of "survival of the fittest" is the only rule, and only the strong survive to fight another day. The boys continue their struggle, and it is during this experience that the reality of life comes to Lacey Rawlins. He is the first to realize that the image of the cowboy is based on a myth, as he says to John Grady, "We think we're a couple of pretty tough cowboys. . . . They could kill us any time" (McCarthy 186). Lacey here expresses the initial signs of disillusionment regarding this adventure. He is beginning to realize that there is no "true" cowboy, at least not in so far as he understands. He is scared and he wants to go home, both very un-cowboy-like characteristics. Lacey is badly wounded in a fight soon after, and is not heard from again until the boys are released from prison. His purpose, as far as McCarthy's theme is concerned, is done, and he is sent off, so as to allow John Grady to learn for himself what Lacey has already learned. This lesson is a difficult one for John Grady to learn, and he will have to continue to fight for his life as long as he stays in the prison and maintains his beliefs regarding how a "real" cowboy should act.

After Lacey is sent to the hospital, John Grady is left to fight alone, and he buys a knife from a prison acquaintance. The purchase turns out to be very timely, as soon after buying it, he is attacked by a hired killer. After exchanging repeated blows, John Grady slumps down, and acts as if he is dead, only to lunge on his attacker, thereby outsmarting a professional killer. In short, he beats the *cuchillero* at his own game.

John Grady has managed to stay alive in a Mexican prison full of vicious murderers, most of whom seem to want him dead, and he has managed to kill a professional killer by fooling him. He has accomplished things that no sixteen-year-old boy could accomplish, but things that compose many a young boy's fantasy. He has lived the life of a "true" cowboy, and he has now lived the life of a fugitive fighting for his life. After surviving this test of endurance and survival, John Grady and Lacey learn that their ransom has been paid, and that they are free to leave the prison.

Lacey, having given up on the idea of "playing cowboy," returns home to Texas, but John Grady returns to the La Purisima Ranch to see Alejandra, and while there, he completes his education, compliments of *señorita* Alfonsa, the person to whom he owes his release from prison. This woman, with her age and experience, completes John Grady's disillusionment about this life he thinks he wants to lead. She encourages John Grady to abandon his dreams of living in a mythical world and to face reality: "In the end we will all come to be cured of our sentiments. Those whom life does not cure death will. The world is quite ruthless in selecting between the dream and the reality, even where we will not. Between the wish and the thing the world lies waiting" (McCarthy 238). John Grady leaves, determined to see Alejandra again.

After leaving the ranch, he meets some Mexican children who inquire as to his plight, and he tells them, in a brief abstract, of his tale. It reads like the cover synopsis to the typical Western novel. He describes his adventure, telling them how he traveled from Texas to Mexico, traveling with a fellow "horseman." He tells how they met up with a third companion, who rode a "wonderful horse" that had been taken from him unfairly, and then how they had attempted to right this injustice done to them. He finishes by lamenting the fact that he is now unable to see his lady love because her grandaunt had forbidden her from seeing him again (McCarthy 244).

Alejandra grudgingly agrees to see John Grady again despite her grandaunt's prohibition, and he makes his final plea to her for her love. She tells him that she loves him, but that she cannot go against the promise that she made to her grandaunt, and John Grady feels "something cold and soulless enter him," and he suddenly knows that this feeling will never leave him (McCarthy 254). This feeling that is infiltrating John Grady's being is the knowledge that he has been living a myth, and that he must return to reality.

John Grady, though, still has some semblance of the "cowboy code," and he feels compelled to avenge the wrong that was done to him. It is almost as if John Grady is bitter about learning the truth regarding the Western myth, and, in the same spirit as his final plea to Alejandra, he makes one final, futile attempt at living the myth. He takes the police captain of Encantada captive, and uses him as a hostage to secure the release of the horses that formerly belonged to Jimmy

Blevins and Lacey Rawlins. During the recovery of the horses, John Grady is shot in the leg, but still manages to ride his horse and control the captain in a heroic way. Later, he dismantles his pistol, puts the barrel in the fire, and sticks the red-hot metal into his wound to cauterize it. Despite the blinding pain, he remains conscious and coherent enough to wade out into a pond to cool the burning flesh. The strength he exhibits is truly super-human, and further evidence of his remarkable deeds while on his journey, and he even exhibits medical expertise, as he skillfully sets the captain's dislocated shoulder.

As John Grady starts the final leg of his journey home, the modern world of reality starts to gradually seep in. He hears in the distance "a steady hammering of metal as of someone at a forge" (McCarthy 279), a sound, perhaps, of modern industry. He finally arrives at the border town of Los Picos, where he sees a Mexican wedding party exiting a church. The scene is described as one of discomfort for both the bride and the groom. John Grady notices that, as the two pose for pictures outside the church, "they already had the look of old photos. In the sepia monochrome of a rainy day in that lost village they'd grown old instantly" (284). This newlywed couple represents the final stage in John Grady's education. He has learned, at this point, that the past is irrecoverable, and this scene looks completely alien in a modern world.

When John Grady finally crosses the border back into Texas, he is suddenly thrust back into the world of reality where there is no frontier, where there are no mythical cowboys, and where he is once again a young boy. When he rides across the border, he is described as being "pale and shivering" (McCarthy 286), in stark contrast to the tough cowboy image he had exhibited previously. He sees a pickup truck parked on the side of the road, and the two men working under the hood stop what they are doing and look at John Grady, who "must have appeared to them some apparition out of the vanished past" (287). He is truly representative of something of the vanished past: the frontier-riding cowboy figure that no longer exists in the modern world.

John Grady goes to see Lacey, who suggests that John Grady get a job working on the Texas oil rigs, symbols of industry and modernity in Texas, but John Grady says that this "ain't [his] country" (McCarthy 299). Lacey asks him specifically where his country is, and John Grady replies, "I dont know where it is" (299). He does not know because it does not exist.

John Grady goes out riding again, in search of something he will never find, and a group of Indians watch him ride past: "They stood and watched him pass and watched him vanish upon that landscape solely because he was passing. Solely because he would vanish" (McCarthy 301). The Indians, like John Grady, know that he is riding off in search of a myth. He rides along a highway, a symbol of all that is lost, and the novel ends with the simple phrase: "Passed and paled into the darkening land, the world to come" (302). John Grady is, in short, fulfilling his role as, to use Vereen Bell's words, "an unaccommodated visionary" (927), who knows that what he perceives as his true calling, the life of a cowboy, is based on nothing more than a myth.

Why did McCarthy choose to have three boys as the vehicles for his message? I would like to suggest there is a triad theme at work here: John Grady represents the myth of the American cowboy, who has no place in a modern world, and does not know where his "country" is; Jimmy Blevins represents the frontier, and his death represents the death of the American frontier; Lacey represents the truth about the West, returning to reality at the first opportunity. This "Anti-Western Trinity" works to debunk the popular myths of the American West.

Aristotle wrote in his *Poetics* that a tragedy should have a beginning, a middle, and an end, and it is a frequent custom of tragedians to write tragedy in the structure of five acts. Cormac McCarthy, though, chooses to write his novel, his tragedy, in four "acts" and never provides a feeling of ending for the novel. He simply leaves off the action, with John Grady still riding his horse, still searching. *All the Pretty Horses* is the first part of McCarthy's larger "Border Trilogy," but in this discussion, I wish to focus on it as a single entity, distinct and separate from the larger whole. As a single work this novel mourns the passing of the American frontier, and highlights the myth of the American cowboy. In a manner of speaking, John Grady is faced with a sort of identity crisis, as he searches to find his occupation in the twentieth century, much like the pirate in the Jimmy Buffett song cited at the beginning of this essay. In terms of this identity crisis, I feel that John Grady mirrors the American West, as that region faces the dawn of the twenty-first century.

Modern culture's view of the American West and the identity which the West has ascribed itself are both based on the American frontier and the cowboy image. This idea is evident in the fact that there is an entire literary genre based on the "true West" that is, in fact, based on these myths. Regardless of the validity of this image's origin, the fact is that the frontier is dead. With the beginning of the twentieth century, there was still some semblance of the American frontier, so the West's image was based, to a certain extent, on fact. However, the American West of today is nothing like it was in 1900. The year 2000 will begin with the American West as a progressive region, spawning everything from computer technology to alternative music. What, then, is the West to do regarding its image? Is it to stay stuck in the past, living a myth like John Grady Cole, or is it to jump forward into reality like Lacey Rawlins? Or, possibly, is the image itself going to die, like Jimmy Blevins, and be subverted to a distant, fond memory?

These issues of the future of the West's self-image are what compose the missing fifth act of this single work, and will ultimately provide the missing Aristotelian ending. John Grady rides off into the sunset, into "the world to come." The question, though, is what is this world to come? The fifth act is not written, I feel, because there is no fifth act, or true ending, as of yet. The fifth act is embodied in the future, and McCarthy left his novel, symbolically, without an ending on purpose, because the West is truly faced with an identity crisis which is not yet resolved. It is our duty to reconcile the past with the present, and to ascribe to the West an image that fits not only the region itself, but also reality. McCarthy has bestowed this duty upon his readers, as it is they who will determine the identity of the American West in the twenty-first century.

REFERENCES

Bell, Vereen. "'Between the Wish and the Thing Lies the World Waiting.'" *The Southern Review*, 28.4 (1992): 920-27.
Branch, E. Douglas. *Westward: The Romance of the American Frontier.* New York: D. Appleton and Company, 1970.
Cheuse, Alan. "A Note on Landscape in *All The Pretty Horses*." *The*

Southern Quarterly 30.4 (1992): 140-43.

McCarthy, Cormac. *All the Pretty Horses.* New York: Alfred A. Knopf, 1993.

Pilkington, Tom. "Fate and Free Will on the American Frontier: Cormac McCarthy's Western Fiction." *Western American Literature* 27.4 (1993): 311-22.

Savage, William W., Jr. *The Cowboy Hero: His Image in American History & Culture.* Norman: U of Oklahoma P, 1979.

Turner, Frederick Jackson. *The Frontier in American History.* New York: Henry Holt and Company, 1920.

Considering the Canon
American Nature Writing and the Wise Use Movement

PAUL LINDHOLDT

The counter-environmental wise use movement not only impedes the conservation of species and ecosystems, as a spate of new books attests, but it obliges us also to modify our definitions of nature writing. Traditional nature writers, as Scott Slovic has noticed, vacillate "between rhapsody and detachment, between aesthetic celebration and scientific explanation" (4). Yet some nature writing can be quite militant, like the Edward Abbey best sellers *Desert Solitaire* and *The Monkey Wrench Gang,* which cultivate indignation and outrage using scientific evidence. And all forms of environmental writing construct nature, as Neil Evernden has demonstrated, by constructing our perceptions of it.[1] So it is with the burgeoning literature of the environmental backlash, a literature that sets out to correct a perceived disparity between economic growth and nature, human rights and nature's rights. When nature advocates use the science of ecology, as Abbey and other activist writers often do, they effectively contest American industry and technocracy whose profits hang in the balance. They challenge the status quo. The rise of wise use literature is industry's answer to the assertions of ecology, to the growing popularity of nature writing, and to a series of scientific conclusions that stymie industrial progress. To say it another way, the counter-environmental wise use movement offers antitheses to the various theses that drive nature writing and environmentalism. What I call wise use "counterscience"— non-consensus scientific judgments promulgated by organizations whose goals are political, ideological or industrial—

Paul Lindholdt specializes in American literature and culture with a primary emphasis on environmental literature at Eastern Washington University. Thanks to colleagues Anthony Flinn and Paul Metzner for incisive comments on this essay.

challenges the legitimacy of scientists and nature writers alike ("Counterscience" 64). Like their rivals in the environmental movement, wise use writers socially create nature.

The canon of American nature writing and environmental literature is broader than our conventional wisdom allows. It encompasses more than scientific assessments and rhapsodic passages. It also typically entails an implicit or explicit culture criticism. Indulge me in a brief example of this culture criticism via a non-fiction classic of American nature writing, Mary Austin's 1903 book, *The Land of Little Rain*, widely supposed to be rhapsodic chiefly. Set in California's Owens River Valley, the book profiles a land and its humans, including "The Pocket Hunter," an itinerant miner who strikes gold and heads to London to spend it, where "the English middle class, with just enough gentility above to aspire to, and sufficient smaller fry to bully and patronize, appealed to his imagination, though of course he did not put it so crudely as that" (24). What do class issues have to do with nature? The land, Austin suggests, attracted the man and gave rise to his austerity of character; for dry landscapes ordain certain behaviors.[2] This intersection of culture and landscape is more overt where Austin issues religion an ecological reality check: "'Come,' say the churches of the valleys, after a season of dry years, 'let us pray for rain.' They would do better to plant more trees" (52). Along with class commentary and religious commentary, Austin's book implicitly reproaches sheep and cattle ranchers, too: "Now and then some [pine] seedling escapes the devastating sheep a rod or two downstream" (37).

Critiques of our cherished cultural institutions, combined with fresh environmental observations, lie at the heart of most American nature writing. Rhapsody is correctly an accouterment, not a central feature. Even Annie Dillard, probably the most rhapsodic of contemporary nature writers, criticizes our (and her own) obliviousness to creation's wonders, a criticism that lies at the center of her Pulitzer Prize-winning *Pilgrim at Tinker Creek*. Moreover, backlash literature produced by the wise use movement satisfies the twin prongs of my revised definition of nature writing: It builds a cultural criticism, and it focuses predictably on nature as the site of that criticism. The following discussion aims to expand the canon so students of American civilization can confront the burgeoning anti-environmental movement with greater intelligence and care.

I.

At the University of Idaho in 1993 I was moonlighting as the coordinator of a business communication laboratory while at the same time teaching a full load of literature courses and dreaming about designing a new class that would explore the nexus between ecology and culture. In that College of Business I was a rare bird who liked to read poetry and stories, so the business professors and dean engaged me in ideological debates. They endeavored to pick my brain, puncture my pretensions, see what made me tick. One day I was toting around a book, British critic Jonathan Bate's groundbreaking study that had just come out that year, *Romantic Ecology: Wordsworth and the Environmental Tradition*, and a professor of management asked me about it. In terms that I recognize now as dangerously simpleminded, I summarized the book's thesis: The poet Wordsworth began as a socialist who cared for the common folk; as he matured, his circle of concerns grew to encompass other species. The socialist became an environmentalist. "Socialists and environmentalists!" that Idaho management professor thundered back my words. "Not a lot of difference in my mind between the two. Both of them try to tell me what to do with my private property."

Especially in reactionary states like Idaho, where I spent seven years teaching at three institutions, *socialist* and *environmentalist* prove to be hot-button terms. Swiftly I began to appreciate how people confederate them mentally. Members of the "wise-use" movement (as they denominate themselves) call such confederated demons "watermelons" (i.e., green on the outside and red within). Like Native Americans who've forgotten their heritage (critics call them "apples") and over-assimilated African Americans ("Oreos"), environmentalists who hide their socialism are construed as fruits who disguise their true hues. Many American leaders of business and industry, along with Republican senators and county commissioners in my particular region (e.g., Idaho's Representative Helen Chenoweth and Senator Dirk Kempthorne, the former a pioneering Sagebrush Rebel, the latter an author of Endangered Species Act "reform" legislation), represent environmentalism as deadly subterfuge for the real agenda of grabbing hard-won wealth. And Christian patriots fear environmental ideologies as covertly encoded paganism designed to brainwash children into worshipping nature. To stake out parameters in these culture clashes, to see how they bear on the environment, allow me to survey some beliefs environmentalists share.

Legally and philosophically most greens agree that the natural rights assured by the Magna Carta and Declaration of Independence should be extended to certain parts of nature. Indeed, some of our laws already do. We can't beat or starve or mutilate a domestic animal without fear of legal reprisal, for instance; can't drive motor vehicles into wilderness areas since the passage of the Wilderness Act of 1964; can't legally harm threatened creatures, not since Richard M. Nixon signed the Endangered Species Act into law in 1973. Such laws were made to protect nature, to extend it decided rights; we depend on nature, the argument often goes, and when we do it harm we threaten ourselves. Peregrine falcons are recovering nicely since we stopped shooting them and spraying their habitat with DDT. A proverbial canary in a coal mine, the peregrine warned us that part of our planet was imperiled. All aside from selfish motives and grounds, visionaries as diverse as Saint Francis and Albert Schweitzer have argued it's ethically wrong to base nature's worth on our own needs. For my present purposes, ethics are "extended sympathies" (Nash 45). Extending sympathies to nature helps create the "expanded community on which environmental ethics rests" (20). In short, ethical standing does not begin and end with human beings, just as it's no longer restricted to propertied white Christian males. We look back with amazement to a time when that was so. In a few generations we might look back with as much amazement to a time when we excluded rivers, oceans, and other species from our ethical regard. Meantime, clashes are taking place. As we extend rights to nature, human "custom and culture" suffers; so the wise use argument goes. Environmentalism becomes politicized and occasions a backlash, much of it dedicated to arguments that our "uses" are sustainable and nature is in no danger.

Views on the rights of nature need to be further excavated; because they have faced a hostile climate of opinion for centuries, they "took what shelter they could find in the humanities, in religion, and in the so-called counter-culture" (Nash 73-4), a remark that supports a revisionist definition of nature writing to embody a culture criticism. To read literature ecocritically, from an ecological perspective, is to excavate ideas that found little acceptance in our ethics, politics, and laws until the late twentieth century. Another reason readers need to discover nature writing is to reclaim regionalism. Some of the most vivid stories and poems spring from intimate familiarity with backwater locales, with the tulles and the boondocks. For generations professors have pontificated about how the best literature should be universal. Regionalism, and its retarded cousin local color, "reeked of provincialism" (Parini 60). Who wants second-best? Reading ecocritically, we now appreciate Sarah Orne Jewett more deeply for the wealth of detail she furnishes about rural Maine; we understand Lame Deer and Black Elk as culture critics with environmental messages; and we can read all Native American literature anew for its green views. Now we can discover riches in dozens of yet-to-be-remembered regional writers. I am talking here about a "placed" literature as opposed to a placeless or interior literature. Henry James's fiction, for instance, is masterfully nuance but is mostly situated outside his characters' minds—which is not to say James can not be read ecocritically. Literature of the environment asks us instead to discover, as John Elder has stated it, "some larger grammar in which the words *culture* and *wilderness* might both be spoken" (25).

In the following visual aid, comprised of three intersecting circles, I try to codify the elements of environmental literature (see Figure 1.). Traditional nature writing is the top circle, built on rhapsody and aesthetic celebration. The human endeavors of criticism and science intersect with nature as integral parts, molecules if you will, of this literature. Science is integral insofar as it is a theoretical basis of knowledge about the natural world, which in turn provides us life and a focus for our art. Criticism is a theoretical basis also, a basis for understanding human worlds. By suggesting that criticism intersects the nature-science juncture, I mean to insist again that writers of environmental literature set about delivering an implicit or explicit cultural criticism. They utilize nature as a way to critique human endeavors. Thoreau's

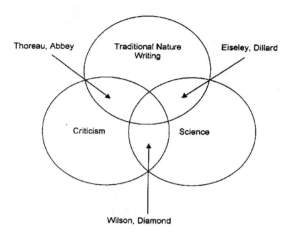

Figure 1: Elements of environmental literature

Walden, to my eyes, is not a book primarily about nature. It is a book that criticizes human foibles and institutions vis-à-vis nature. Edward Abbey and Thoreau abide in that nexus between nature and criticism. Between science and criticism, I position E.O. Wilson and Jared Diamond, Pulitzer-prize winning writers of non-fiction who wield science (in which they are trained) as a tool of criticism. Dillard and Loren Eiseley, practicing an "ecstatic science" (Elder 3), emerge from a fusion of nature and science.

My examples draw chiefly from non-fiction, which seems to be the favorite genre of nature writers—from early American natural historians, to Ralph Waldo Emerson, and forward to the nature-advocates of the present day. But plenty of novelists (e.g., Abbey, Wendell Barry, Leslie Marmon Silko, and Ursula LeGuin) and poets (e.g., Mary Oliver, Theodore Roethke, Pattiann Rogers, and Gary Snyder) also generate environmental belles lettres. Yet it is in non-fiction nature writing and environmental literature, both primary and secondary works, that our definitions need to accommodate the literature of the wise use movement.

II.

Late in 1993, Mitch Friedman and I published *Cascadia Wild: Protecting an International Ecosystem.* That book, a collection of essays we wrote along with other activists and scientists, studied the ecology of one of North America's largest contiguous wilderness areas and proposed that a Cascades International Park be established and managed jointly by the US and Canada. This proposal came about after a coalition of environmental groups on both sides of the border discovered that the piecemeal approach to conservation in the north Cascades was ineffective. Canadian Crown and US Federal lands butt against private inholdings on both sides of the border and create a bureaucratic tangle that fragments wildlife habitats. Despite this fragmentation, there is geographical integrity enough in the north Cascades to warrant a park plan. The governments of both countries wisely have set aside terrain for protection over the years. On the Washington side are the North Cascades National Park, three recreation areas, and seven wilderness areas. Other lands are semi-protected through Federal forest plans. In British Columbia there are Manning Provincial Park, Cathedral Provincial Park, and two recreation areas. All of these names on a map might give the appearance of discontinuity, but the area is a remarkably intact and contiguous ecosystem—that is, a diverse system of plants and animals living in a native environment. Is *Cascadia Wild* nature writing? We like to think so, despite its often polemical approach and our reliance on various research apparatus.

My partner in the book project, Mitch Friedman, is the founder of the Northwest Ecosystem Alliance, formerly the Greater Ecosystem Alliance, of Bellingham, Washington. The book is his brainchild. Washington state organizer for Earth First! when we met in 1988, Mitch co-edited and wrote key chapters. I contributed a single chapter on the impacts of livestock grazing on public rangelands that concluded with a case study of cattle allotments in the Okanogan National Forest. Since my interests lie chiefly in language and literature, I approached my chapter by deconstructing government reports on livestock grazing. We solicited chapters from scientists and activists, academics and independents, civil servants and conservationists. Our guiding principle in the book is conservation biology, a science designed to restore ecosystems that industry, technology, and bureaucracy have sundered.

After the book came out, it began to get some favorable press in parks and conservation magazines, but backlash by regional wise use organizers was bitter and swift. The first two critics of the park proposal, Washington State citizens Don Kehoe and Homer Bakker, toured the Northwest with a Christian patriot group called Citizens for Environmental Justice. That group distributed literature from the Militia of Montana and promoted a theory that the United Nations was poised to take over the north Cascades of Washington. Our proposed park, they claimed, was intended as part of a global plot to fragment the United States and install a one-world government. If this scheme were ever to succeed, they warned, internationals would control one-quarter of Washington State and kick out current residents! Beware, Kehoe cautioned— the borders of this compound will use electronic fortifications patrolled by the CIA (Pryne A1). Imagine our surprise, we writers and editors, to be named pawns of a one-world government. Kehoe asserted that owners of private lands in the north Cascades, after arriving at their remote cabins, were accosted by Forest Service rangers who claimed their travels had been tracked by satellite. Kehoe forgot to get the landowners' names, but he later carried his message of espionage and fear to Maltby, Washington, for a recruitment meeting for the Militia of Montana (deArmond).

Overt anxiety about government intervention into private lives, a cornerstone of right-wing ideology, looms especially large in the rural West where natural resources underpin many slumping economies. In those places wise use organizers, typically funded by polluting industries that have much to gain by relaxing environmental regulations, make greatest progress where people are least educated (Deal). Connections are tight, according to recent research, between gay rights opponents, militias, conservative think tanks, and the leaders of the powerful wise use movement who exploit irrational fears to further their economic and political agendas (Ramos 103-06; Lindholdt, "Wise" 10-13).

The rise of private American militias, whose theories of conspiracy have been well documented in the wake of the Oklahoma City bombing, is attributable in part to fear and hatred of outsiders and outside laws. American Jewish Committee hate-group specialist Kenneth Stern, in his recent book on the militia movement, devoted a chapter to the militia backlash against environmental regulations. In Stern's analysis, private militias in the mid-1990s "attracted people frustrated over environmental regulations, especially in the West" (119). The trend toward county supremacy is a consequence. County officials and private landowners claim Federal lands are actually theirs and thus now subject to their "sovereign" jurisdiction. They defend this viewpoint chiefly by using the legal argument of adverse possession, which says that a landowner who lets his land lie idle for a given time effectively surrenders claim to it. According to the custom and culture argument, which stems from these arguments of adverse possession, individuals who've grown historically accustomed to using public lands should be able to lay claim to those lands, if those lands have become indispensable to the upholding of their culture. To deny them "rights" to graze their cattle on those lands, for instance, is to deprive them of a civilization. Counties in Idaho, Nevada, and New Mexico have gotten publicity by doing their best to seize Federal lands. The Posse Comitatus, a Christian militia group whose name means "power of the county," shared such tactics. Posse Comitatus members formed common cause in the 1980s with white supremist organizations like the Order, whose members are in prison today after murdering Denver talk show host Alan Berg in 1984 (Corcoran 42). At least seventy US counties have passed county supremacy laws that challenge Federal jurisdiction on Federal lands.

The nativist beliefs of some wise users link them to white supremists. At a 1994 meeting in Whatcom County near Bellingham, Washington, citizens assembled to explore the formation of sovereign "Freedom County." Organizer John Stokes addressed the threats of the Growth Management Act passed by Washington voters in 1993 to curb urban sprawl and conserve wetlands. Stokes warned that "job allocation limits" will forbid new employment in certain areas, but wealthy counties will be able to buy out of this mandate with what he called "mitigation fees." Poorer rural counties, he reasoned, unless they can become self-governing, ultimately will become "dumping grounds" for low-income citizens, including "Haitian, Chinese, and Russian immigrants, uneducated people, people with HIV, the criminally insane, sexual predators," and others (deArmond). On the east side of the Washington Cascades, especially in Ferry and Stevens counties, wise use militants are spreading unrest about an impending "new world order." Kettle Falls resident Glenn Rowe opened a meeting in February 1995 in Colville by denouncing "commie Nazis" who have infiltrated the Federal government and are set to take over the US—"a Christian nation." A second speaker, Fred Kisman, asserted that socialist journalists, by discussing counties as "regions" instead of as autonomous political entities, are taking steps toward abolishing traditional borders. "We're being psychologically brainwashed," Kisman insisted. To prove it, he pinned up an ecosystem map entitled "Nature Has No Borders," from a conference sponsored by the University of Washington (Marie A1).

That conference, co-sponsored by Greater Ecosystem Alliance in 1994, returns us to the zealous backlash to the park proposed in *Cascadia Wild*. Don Kehoe, the Christian patriot speaker who claimed the Forest Service had been tracking private landowners in the north Cascades by satellite, spoke again on January 16, 1996, at a meeting in Bellingham, Washington, of a group called Citizens for Liberty (deArmond). A former landscaper, Kehoe served on the board of the now-defunct Snohomish County Property Rights Alliance. The topic of Kehoe's speech at the Citizens for Liberty meeting was "The CIA, Toll Roads, and Mind Control." He distributed papers from various public agencies that allegedly describe a plan to implement an Intelligent Vehicle Highway System (or IVHS). This supposed technology entails a network of highway sensors and "smart" cars.

Kehoe wove his discoveries into a conspiracy theory involving the CIA, the United Nations, and the new world order. According to Paul De Armond, who was in his audience, Kehoe claimed that IVHS technology will allow vehicles to be remotely tracked, monitored, and controlled by satellite transmissions. Ostensibly the microchips to effect this control are already in place in late-model cars. (People who followed Oklahoma City bombing research will remember suspect Timothy McVeigh's claim the US military had surgically implanted a microchip tracking device in his buttocks.) One of the links in Kehoe's sinister chain of technology is his discovery of the Cascadia Project, which he believed is participating in IVHS discussions. "Cascadia," by now a bit of marketing jargon in the Pacific Northwest, denotes everything from a bioregion to a soft drink. The Cascadia Project, however, in fact a planning effort spanning the I-5 corridor from Portland to Vancouver,

BC, seeks to accommodate present and projected trends in commerce, transportation, and urban growth.

These extremist mouthpieces of wise use don't truly represent the movement any more than the monkey wrenching Luddism of Earth First! characterizes environmentalists. It is rather in more moderate and reflective counter-environmentalism that the simultaneous threats and potential lie. I acknowledge them as "threats" because they impede the valuable and necessary work of conserving species and ecosystems, because they confuse students with counterscientific claims, and because ignoring them is perilous to perceptions of fair play. I recognize the "potential" in moderate wise use literature to expand the abilities of environmental students, writers, and activists to confront their rivals and clarify thought.

III.

The term "wise use" originated with Gifford Pinchot, US Forest Service Chief under Theodore Roosevelt. No friend of the environment, Pinchot supported a destructive dam in 1913 in the Hetch Hetchy Valley near Yosemite, a valley that now is stoppered like a bathtub to make the city of San Francisco bloom. Pinchot argued that the project was an improvement upon nature, but the dam in fact proved to be chiefly about political power. John Muir opposed the project, which sparked the founding of the Sierra Club. An earlier boondoggle that empowered the proto-movement toward wise use was the 1864 public land give-away under Abraham Lincoln known as the Northern Pacific Land Grant, the subject of a book by Derrick Jensen and George Draffan entitled *Railroads and Clearcuts*. Such historical precedents should remind Americans that, although we might be tempted to think of the wise use movement as a very recent trend, history shows that our government long has combined with industry to push through environmentally destructive projects.

So it is dangerous and wrong to see wise use as just another skirmish in what have come to be called the culture wars dividing America in recent years. The problems have been around a lot longer than that. In writing his play *An Enemy of the People* in 1882, Henrik Ibsen grappled with some of the same scientific and economic rifts that currently divide environmentalists and members of the wise use brigades. Insofar as human cultures construct nature, Ibsen's work can be considered nature writing in its broadest sense. Brothers Thomas and Peter Stockmann are clashing over the economic fate of a small Norwegian town. Peter is the wealthy magistrate and mayor, while his brother Thomas is a physician, a man of science. Together they are building a health institute from mineral springs that are reputed to have curative powers. The mineral springs are drawing sick people from far away—a nineteenth-century business trend T. Coraghessan Boyle lampooned in *Road to Wellville*. (Can Boyle's novel justifiably be called nature writing? It criticizes cultural trends that impact nature, but it is satirical not rhapsodic. Can nature writing satirize?)

Booming with enthusiasm for their health enterprise in *An Enemy of the People,* Peter Stockmann boasts, "Everything is shooting ahead—real estate going up, money changing hands every hour, business humming!" (21). The last thing he wants to hear from his scrupulous brother is that a tannery has polluted the springs. But indeed some chemicals used to tan animal hides have leached into the stream. When Thomas proves that microscopic bacteria in the water are infecting the health of patients—when he argues that costly repairs to the springs will be necessary before allowing sickly bathers to patronize the spot—Peter rallies the townspeople to discredit his whistle-blowing brother's threatening message. Ibsen's play is nature writing even though it's set in drawing rooms.

Just as the wise use movement issues denials and uses counterscience today, so the leaders of the fictional Norwegian town deny the science underlying the findings of Tom, who cries with exasperated irony, "Who am I, a mere scientist, to tell politicians where to build a health institute!" (36). Unlike the rest of the community, he has the training to discern the truth through the lens of his microscope. Exactly like the other townsfolk, though, the matter makes him passionate. To Peter's economic arguments about the "source" of the town's "most important industry," Thomas responds, "That source is poisoned, man. We are getting fat by peddling filth and corruption to innocent people!" (58). Peter follows through on threats to declare his scientist-brother an enemy of the people. The people accordingly pelt Thomas' house with stones and assault his children. Peter's rhetoric effects these ends; it makes over nature in a business paradigm. He decries Thomas's scientific report as "the mad dream of a man who is trying to blow up our way of life! It has nothing to do with reform or science or anything but pure and simple destruction!" (74-5). More than a century later, many resource-dependent communities in the rural West are echoing Peter Stockmann's cry, for they are proving to be the victims of misinformation spread by corporations that stand to gain financially from weakened laws.

Aldo Leopold, author of the classic *Sand County Almanac*, remarked upon a trend that likewise characterizes our own wise use scuffles. Leopold made his observations in a chapter entitled "The Land Ethic," which was delivered first as a paper before the American Association for the Advancement of Science in 1933. "When the private landowner is asked to perform some act for the good of the community," Leopold wrote, that landowner commonly assents "only with outstretched palm" (202). Leopold lamented that only "economic self-interest" provided impetus to the farmers of his place and time to conserve natural resources (203). Unless tempted by promises of profit or compensation, Leopold concluded, most individuals and corporations simply cannot be expected to comply with environmental codes and regulations. The truth of Leopold's assertion is evident today in the pollution credits and tax incentives our government uses to gain corporate compliance with environmental laws. Leopold's paper, delivered as a public speech, is nature writing.

Aldo Leopold lamented that economic imperatives hamstrung conservation efforts in the 1930s. So did David Brower in the 1971 book *Encounters with the Archdruid* by John McPhee. McPhee expertly chronicled the encounters between conservationist Brower and three counter-environmentalists, three wise use precursors. Brower debates the merits of mining with Charles Park, a mineral engineer who believes our economic well-being relies on extracting metals from the planet wherever they be found, including the North Cascades Park of Washington State, where the men hike together. On Cumberland Island in South Carolina, Brower encounters real estate developer Charles Fraser; and on the Colorado River he meets and confronts Floyd Dominy who impounds big rivers for a living. The book presages the terms of wise use in the US and the share movement in Canada. All three men insist that they are practicing the wisest use of the nation's natural resources.

Developer Charles Fraser echoes the Gifford Pinchot phrase by asserting that "The government has a perfect right to condemn my land here if it thinks its use is wiser than mine" (McPhee 140). Wise use leader Ron Arnold of Washington State co-opted the Pinchot phrase in 1988 and adapted it for use by the counter-environmental forces (Lewis 16). Charles Fraser practiced such co-optation—known widely as greenwashing, one modus operandi of public relations firms today—by naming his new development "the Cumberland Island Conservation Association" (McPhee 138). In studying tactics of the counter-environmental organizations, Stanford University biologists Paul and Anne Ehrlich dub such practices "aggressive mimicry" (16), that is, co-optative tactics whereby the parasite or predator adopts the colors or behaviors of its host or prey. Such cultural clashes are battles of words, of ideology, and of science. Developer Fraser decries environmentalists for the way they "worship trees and sacrifice human beings to those trees," resembling pagan druids of old (95). McPhee's book is a best-selling classic of nature writing, even though most of its matter is polemical.

IV.

Conventional wisdom on the wise use movement sees it as a collection of industry front groups. In the mid-'80s, corporations that profited from extracting natural resources hired organizers to go into rural Western communities and stir up distrust of government regulations. Honda and Suzuki have proven the financial mainstay of the Blue Ribbon Coalition, for instance, an Idaho-based wise use group that agitates to open wilderness and park lands to snowmobile and motorcycle riders (Deal 33-4). That same off-road vehicle industry also keeps lobbyists on salary to convince politicians to vote against environmental laws. Blue Ribbon was one of the original participants in a June 1988 conference that was held in Las Vegas to ally disparate wise use interests. From that conference emerged "The Top Twenty-Five Goals of the Wise Use Agenda," including watering down the Endangered Species Act, defunding the National Parks by allowing their privatization through companies like the Disney Corporation, and a host of other such reformations of nature. The Las Vegas conference has now become an annual event. And the spate of backlash books appearing since that conference is itself an emerging form of nature writing, intended for a conservative readership mindful of the culture clashes that hinge on natural resources. Ehrlich and Ehrlich dub such books part of the "brownlash," a nonce word suggesting that the backlash against the green movement will turn the planet brown, and the Ehrlichs agree that teachers of American nature writing ignore them at their peril (217).

A second segment in the wise use coalitions are conservatives and libertarians who respond with contempt to government intervention into the economy and religion. Perhaps the most visible and active is the Rev. Sun Myung Moon and his Unification Church. The Moon empire is immense, marketing everything from colas to guns. Its chief front group, the American Freedom Coalition, works to open the Alaska National Wildlife Refuge to oil exploration (Helvarg, *War* 260). Very similar in his wealth and conservatism and distrust of environmental regulations is Lyndon LaRouche, convicted tax felon and erstwhile Nazi Party leader whose followers spearhead campaigns to discredit ozone depletion theories and other forms of science that block his platforms and progress (254-58).

A third sector of support for wise use includes grassroots activists. Here the mix of ideologies and priorities gets very tricky to depict. While some grassroots activists are recruited by industry organizers, others are independent as the wind. Here the researcher can find extreme Christian fundamentalists, conspiracy theorists, tax resisters, militias, survivalists, even white supremacists. The movement, as researcher Paul deArmond has observed, is less a movement at all than a Hydra—that monster of Greek mythology that astounded with its capacity to grow two heads to replace each one cut off in battle. Just as that mythical beast was able to regenerate itself, so the extremist fringes of wise use and the militant right display the ability to resurface with redoubled energy after each defeat.

Wise use coalitions unite in the goal of repealing or watering down environmental regulations. The most prominent leaders in the Pacific Northwest are Ron Arnold, Chuck

Cushman, and Alan Gottlieb, all of whom live in Washington State, which nonetheless voted down a very stringent counter-environmental property-rights measure in November of 1995. Washington Referendum 48 would have made governments (i.e., the taxpayers) compensate landowners if zoning or environmental laws should diminish property values. Ron Arnold—the former public relations consultant to industry who gave the movement its name when he appropriated the 1907 Gifford Pinchot definition of conservation as "the wise use of resources"—openly aspires to "'systematically destroy the environmental movement,' which he believes to be 'polluted with a hatred of humans'" (Lewis 15-16).

The Sahara Club gives a taste of the sort of hate speech that President Clinton denounced in the wake of the Oklahoma City bombing. The Sahara Club began as a band of angry California dirt-bikers deprived of racing across a certain desert where tortoises were found crushed (Deal 87-8). The club's chief function was to breathe fear into the conservation movement. In 1994 it issued an "Agenda to Attack Environmentalists." "Consider this your guide book," the document begins, "to effectively battling New Age nuts, militant vegetarians, anti-gun pukes, animal rights goofballs, tree worshipers, new world order pushers, human haters, pro-socialists, doomsdayers, homosexual rights activists, militant feminists and land closure fascists!" ("Sahara Club's"). The guidebook offers dirty tricks to intimidate government officials and environmentalists, including smashing headlights at environmental gatherings with ball bearings wrapped in a sock—a weapon that many readers would have recognized as a de facto blackjack. Organizing has become more dangerous for activists and bureaucrats, especially those who perform field work. A good friend of mine has a job as rural outreach coordinator for the Idaho Conservation League that will carry him into hostile spots in North Idaho to speak to the public and to give slide shows. It might not avail him that his name is Guadalupe Flores.

Two more examples of counter-environmental intimidation should suffice. At a 1995 public hearing in Everett, Washington, Audubon Society activist Ellen Gray testified in favor of protection requirements for wildlife and wetlands. Two men approached her afterward. According to Gray, one placed a hangman's noose on a nearby chair, saying, "This is a message for you." He also distributed cards with a picture of a hangman's noose that said, "Treason = Death" on one side, and "Eco fascists go home" on the other. The other man told Gray, "We have a militia of 10,000. If we can't get you at the ballot box, we'll get you with a bullet" (Helvarg, "Anti-Enviro" 724). Similarly in the fall of 1994, Oregon activists Ric Bailey and Andy Kerr were burned in effigy in rural Joseph, Oregon. Besides such acts of random intimidation, the widespread national tactic of wise use groups is to kindle discontent regarding public and private land-use policies. Congressman Richard Pombo, a California Republican, is emerging as a wise use stalwart and vocal opponent of the Endangered Species Act with the publication of his recent book *This Land is Our Land*. But Pombo is only one of dozens of writers who have turned to literature and scholarship as useful tools to combat what they see as the excesses of mainstream environmentalism.

V.

Perhaps the most active and provocative writer in the wise use movement is Ron Arnold, a former Sierra Club member who now assails environmentalism and environmentalists. Arnold embarked on his literary career with a biography of James Watt, Interior Secretary under Ronald Reagan. In that 1982 book he not only leveled ad hominem attacks but also applied some ambitious semiotic analyses to the concept of "wilderness." He sees the social construction of wilderness as comprised of "images and emotions of profound connection to the earth, of pristine primal peace, of nature in perfect harmony, of a time and a place unmarred by the meddling hand of man" (xiv). Arnold practices environmental writing. He seldom recurs to science, and he scorns rhapsody, but he builds a culture criticism anyway via his antipathy to nature as the confused site of dangerously skewed perceptions. With equal virulence he disdains journalism, about which he writes, "Drama, the active pursuit of conflict, has become a basic convention of newswriting, and that is not likely to change. Every page of the newspaper is the drama page. Every newscast is a soap opera" (210). Arnold subsumes the life of James Watt to a critique of cultural issues surrounding him.

A frequent refrain of wise use writers generally, and of Arnold in particular, is that economic ruin ensues from environmentalism. Hence the title of a book he co-authored in 1993, *Trashing the Economy: How Runaway Environmentalism is Wrecking America* (a title that alludes to 1990 milestone of the wise use movement, *Trashing the Planet*, by former Washington State governor Dixy Lee Ray). Arnold's co-author of that book, Alan Gottlieb, chairs the Citizens Committee for the Right to Keep and Bear Arms, directs the American Conservative Union, and serves as President of the Center for the Defense of Free Enterprise. *Trashing the Economy* is self-published, which suggests that even sympathetic presses found it unsound.

Disputes over nature and natural resources in America are escalating, and writing about wise use hastens the pace. The disputes pit environmentalists, scientists, and civil servants against what Anne and Paul Ehrlich define as "representatives of extractive and polluting industries who are motivated by corporate interests as well as private property rights activists and right-wing ideologues" (15). On the contrary Congressman Pombo, in his book, centers the dispute within an "eco-federal coalition" that has given rise to "a growing body of federal, state, and local regulations and . . . open-ended Supreme Court decisions without standards or constitutional foundation" (7). Paul Ehrlich, a Stanford University biology professor and leading scholar in the environmental sciences today, is best known for his 1969 book *The Population Bomb*. Richard Pombo, a second-term California Republican who wrote his book in the first-person singular, names his nemeses "environmental zealots who believe that mankind brings only harm to his environment" (5).

The Ehrlichs' central premise is that contrarian or non-consensus science—a body of claims about the natural world that rejects "the deepening consensus among scientists" (2)—is being used "to bolster a predetermined worldview and to support a political agenda" (12). Contrarian science, enhanced by an "overall lack of scientific knowledge among United States citizens" (13), poses a grave threat insofar as it is "being adopted and used as a basis for critical policy decisions" (201). In short, politicians today are founding policies increasingly upon non-consensus scientific conclusions that arise from right-wing ideologies. Complementing the book's 848 notes are two appendices, the first of which analyzes "Brownlash Literature" like journalist Gregg Easterbrook's *A Moment on the Earth: The Coming Age of Environmental Optimism* and Stephen Budiansky's *Nature's Keepers: The New Science of Nature Management.* The second appendix, "The Scientific Consensus," names and numbers the international scientists who agree in trepidation about the dismal state of the environment today. Anne and Paul Ehrlich write well and demonstrate a gift for analogies that speak clearly to lay readers. Their ambitious book is a call to activism, a plea for scientists and other citizens to "'tithe to society'—spend 10 percent of their time trying to make the human endeavor more sustainable" (205).

Congressman Richard Pombo writes a more private response to the ongoing changes in American public policy. His book, co-authored with journalist Joseph Farah, culminates by promoting Pombo's own reform measures for the Endangered Species Act, or ESA (188-93). Pombo also recounts his family's travails when a railroad right-of-way through their ranch in California violated their perceived property rights (114-115). The 1973 ESA now is overseen by Federal thugs, Pombo charges, who wield "their own private, armed, enforcement agents" (27). Essentially an anti-ESA tract, *This Land Is Our Land* borrows from the growing wise use literature as well as from studies by the Cato Institute, opinions by Supreme Court justices Clarence Thomas and Antonin Scalia, and from the anonymously authored article "Eco-Fascism" in a paper tellingly entitled *The Freeman* (100). Other dimensions of Congressman Pombo's book include its reasoning fallacies, slipshod editing, and lack of documentation. Lake Tahoe is near "Loss Angeles" (100), while "today's miner's [sic] are very land-efficient" (108). Congressmen Murkowski, Stevens, and Young are said to hail from Arkansas not Alaska (159). Eugene Hussey—a wise use poster figure who claims to have been harassed by Federal agents when he "found" a dead wolf on his remote Idaho ranch—was said to have been both 74 and 75 years of age at the time (27, 170). In a flagrant appeal to ignorance, the authors dismiss spiraling extinction rates by noting that "some of these species may carry organisms or bacteria that could be extremely harmful to humans or other life. Maybe their extinction will save us!" (54). A false analogy arises when they ask, Sagebrush Rebel-fashion, "Are the people who give us slow mail service, low SAT scores, and the 1040 tax form best suited to control millions of acres of land?" (182). Nowhere does Congressman Pombo address the role of science in shaping public policy. Yet the center of wise use disputes is the politicization of scientific principles which ground so much public policy.

VI.

Ibsen, Leopold, and McPhee wrote classics of nature writing and its sibling-genre, environmental literature, by critically examining the interface of environment and American free enterprise. In doing so they highlighted some of the culture clashes that would occasion the later rise of wise use. But none of those books had the influence of Rachel Carson's *Silent Spring* (1962), which single-handedly effected a ban on DDT in the US (DDT still is manufactured in the US and brokered to developing nations). What Upton Sinclair's *The Jungle* (1906) did for meat safety in the US, Carson did for American nature writing and the environmental movement. Accordingly the backlash against Carson has gained a life of its own. American chemical company publicists have worked hard to malign her. That malignity, coupled with specious counterscience, can be traced back to interviews conducted and research published by the late Dr. Dixy Lee Ray—former governor of Washington State, chair of the Atomic Energy Commission, and professor of marine biology.

If Ray had a high profile as a regional leader in her time, she is more significant today for the way she lent her credibility to counterscientific ideologies when she became a spokesperson for the wise use movement. Would-be scholars like Rush Limbaugh use her work regularly as ammunition for their own counterscientific claims. Those of us who were raised in Washington State in the 1960s and '70s can recall Dr. Ray's staunch advocacy of nuclear energy and her ability to baffle common sense and scientific evidence when they contradicted her beliefs on natural resource conservation. In her books and in interviews, Ray maintained that the preservation of wetlands is a foolish error perpetrated at the behest of environmentalists who privilege dangerous pest and predator species above humans.

Recriminations against conservationists have become the stock-in-trade of the wise use movement. What set Dr. Ray's argument apart was the speciousness of her reasoning and the intricacy of her error. Wetlands protect mosquitoes, she began. Inasmuch as scientists have supported public policies that favor the protection of wetlands, mosquito populations have boomed, and the result is enormous increases in insect-borne diseases like encephalitis. Even worse, Dr. Ray claimed, "'the central valleys of California are areas of endemic malaria'" (Callahan 11). This assertion, made in 1993, reiterated the 1990 claims in her book *Trashing the Planet*, which added yellow fever to the list of hazards exacerbated by the ban on DDT and protection of US wetlands. Yet biologists, scientific research, and the bureaucrats contradict her: "Ray's alarmist claim that environmentalists are responsible for malaria epidemics is both contrived and grotesquely dishonest" (Callahan 15). The astounding feature of this hoax, perpetrated on a scientifically gullible public by an educated public servant, is that it took so long to be uncovered. Nor does the hysteria end there. The wetlands-malaria fraud continued to find sympathetic audiences at wise use conferences and credulous readers in right-wing periodicals like the conspiratorial *Executive Intelligence Review and 21st Century Science and Technology.* One writer in the latter publication claimed that *Silent Spring* was evidence of a plot to discredit pesticides and chemical producers, to elevate disease levels, ultimately to hasten death rates as part of a Malthusian scheme to roll back global human populations (Edwards 25). Thomas Malthus, you might remember, was the 19th-century English economist who prophesied that human populations would continue increasing at rates faster than available subsistence, thus causing poverty and degradation if not checked by moral restraint, disease, famine, war or other natural or human-induced disasters. His name, almost always rendered adjectivally, has become synonymous, in wise use locutions, for irrational and unfulfilled alarmism.

VII.

The backlash to the Cascades International Park we proposed in *Cascadia Wild* is evidence of a much larger movement to discredit environmentalism and environmentalists. Fueled by reactionary policies, funded by corporations that rely upon access to natural resources, the movement successfully galvanizes people in rural communities. Such people mistakenly target the environmental movement, insofar as the changes they are resisting will prove inevitable. As populations burgeon in the western states, economies in rural communities are undergoing inevitable transitions. In this process extractive industries like logging, mining, and ranching come to be supplanted by recreation, tourism, and retirement homes. Such extractive industries have relied traditionally upon Federal subsidies and land giveaways to keep them solvent, which accounts for the demonization of governments and environmentalists by wise use now. Newcomers to the West—taxpaying citizens and voters—statistically favor environmental safeguards as well as cutbacks in tax-supported public welfare.

As western economies undergo vast economic changes, the cultural constructions of nature change with them. Seen through the lenses of the wise use movement, nature is less a source of spiritual solace and emotional refuge than of material value and constitutional liberty. According to such formulations, nature comes again to recall the site of God's injunctions to Adam and Eve to "Be fruitful and multiply, and replenish the earth and subdue it: and have dominion over the fish of the sea, and over every living thing that moveth upon the earth" (Gen. 1: 28). That is, nature once more becomes a place where humankind exerts its will to extract material goods and prospers from what it has extracted. Seen this way, the wise use movement is more than a backlash against changing economic trends, more than antithesis to the bureaucrats perceived to be environmentalism's handmaidens. The wise use view alters perceptions of nature by constructing those perceptions anew. It is fitting and proper that current definitions of nature writing and the canon should shift to consider the counterscientific ideologies of wise use. By reading Ibsen, Leopold, Carson, and McPhee (if not Arnold, Pombo, and Ray) as texts that address an inchoate counterenvironmental movement, we can expand our definitions of environmental literature and appreciate the range of ways that nature continues to be socially constructed today.

NOTES

[1]Evernden's analyses are varied and subtle, but perhaps best expressed in his observation pointing to "the camouflaging tendency of the acculturated consciousness, which renders direct encounter [with nature] impossible most of the time" (122). Claire Lawrence concurs, and goes even further, when she notes that "The designation of the natural and the reading of the natural is always cultural" (165).

[2]A commonplace of nature writing. Barry Lopez agrees that "writing that takes into account the impact nature and place have on culture is one of the oldest—and perhaps most singular—threads in American writing" (1). For poetic expression of this notion, see "The Determinations of the Scene" (32-3) and "The Significance of Location" (38) by Pattiann Rogers, in the former of which the speaker traces children of the desert, forest, and seaside. for whom place constitutes "The underlying dominion unacknowledged / In [one's] approach to the cosmos" (38).

REFERENCES

Abbey, Edward. *Desert Solitaire.* New York: McGraw-Hill, 1968.
———. *The Monkey Wrench Gang.* New York: Lippincott, 1975.
Arnold, Ron. *At the Eye of the Storm: James Watt and the Environmentalists.* Chicago: Regnery Gateway, 1982.
Arnold, Ron, and Alan Gottlieb. *Trashing the Economy: How Runaway Environmentalism is Wrecking America.* Bellevue, WA: Free Enterprise, 1993.
Austin, Mary. *The Land of Little Rain.* New York: Dover, 1996.
Bate, Jonathan. *Romantic Ecology: Wordsworth and the Environmental Tradition.* London: Routledge, 1991.
Black Elk and John G. Neihardt. *Black Elk Speaks: Being the Life Story of a Holy Man of the Ogalala Sioux.* Lincoln: U of Nebraska P, 1932.
Boyle, T. Coraghessan. *Road to Wellville.* New York: Penguin, 1994.
Budiansky, Stephen. *Nature's Keepers: The New Science of Nature Management.* New York: Free, 1995.
Carson, Rachel. *Silent Spring.* Boston: Houghton Mifflin, 1962.
Callahan, Tim. "Environmentalists Cause Malaria! (And Other Myths of the 'Wise Use' Movement)." *The Humanist: The Magazine of Critical Inquiry and Social Concern* 55 (Jan./Feb. 1995): 10-15.
Corcoran, James. *Bitter Harvest: The Birth of Paramilitary Terrorism in the Heartland.* New York: Penguin, 1990.
Deal, Carl. *The Greenpeace Guide to Anti-Environmental Organiza-*

tions. Berkeley: Odonian, 1993.

deArmond, Paul (paulf@henson.cc.wwu.edu). E-mail 11 April 1996.

Diamond, Jared M. *Guns, Germs, and Steel: The Fates of Human Societies*. New York: Norton, 1997.

Dillard, Annie. *Pilgrim at Tinker Creek*. New York: Harper, 1974.

Easterbrook, Gregg. *A Moment on the Earth: The Coming Age of Environmental Optimism*. New York: Viking Penguin, 1995.

Edwards, J. Gordon. "Malaria: The Killer That Could Have Been Conquered." *21st Century Science and Technology* 6 (1993): 21-35.

Ehrlich, Paul R. *The Population Bomb*. San Francisco: Sierra Club, 1969.

Ehrlich, Paul R., and Anne H. Erlich. *Betrayal of Science and Reason: How Anti-Environmental Rhetoric Threatens Our Future*. Washington, D.C.: Island, 1996.

Elder, John. *Imagining the Earth: Poetry and the Vision of Nature*. Urbana: U of Illinois P, 1985.

Evernden, Neil. *The Social Creation of Nature*. Baltimore: Johns Hopkins UP, 1992.

Friedman, Mitch, and Paul Lindholdt, eds. *Cascadia Wild: Protecting An International Ecosystem*. Bellingham, WA: Greater Ecosystem Alliance, 1993.

Helvarg, David. "The Anti-Enviro Connection." *The Nation* 22 (May 1995): 722+.

———. *The War Against the Greens: The "Wise-Use" Movement, the New Right, and Anti-Environmental Violence*. San Francisco: Sierra Club, 1994.

Ibsen, Henrik. *An Enemy of the People*. 1882. Ed. Arthur Miller. New York: Penguin, 1951.

Jensen, Derrick, and George Draffan. *Railroads and Clearcuts: Legacy of Congress's 1864 Northern Pacific Railroad Land Grant*. Spokane, WA: Inland Empire Public Lands Council, 1995.

Jewett, Sarah Orne. *The Country of the Pointed Firs and Other Stories*. 1896. New York: Anchor-Doubleday, 1989.

Lame Deer, John (Fire), and Richard Erdoes. *Lame Deer, Seeker of Visions*. New York: Washington Square, 1972.

Lawrence, Claire. "'Getting the Desert into a Book': Nature Writing and the Problem of Representation in a Postmodern World." *Coyote in the Maze: Tracking Edward Abbey in a World of Words*. Ed. Peter Quigley. Salt Lake City: U of Utah P, 1998. 150-67.

Leopold, Aldo. *Sand County Almanac*. 1949. New York: Ballantine, 1966.

Lewis, Thomas A. "Cloaked in a Wise Disguise." *Let the People Judge: Wise Use and the Private Property Rights Movement*. Ed. John Echeverria and Raymond Booth Eby. Washington, DC: Island,

1995. 13-20.

Lindholdt, Paul J. "Counterscience and Conservation." *Skeptic* 5.1 (1997): 64-70.

———. "Wise Use Joins the Militia," *Cascadia Times* 1.3 (June 1995): 1+.

Lopez, Barry. "We are Shaped by the Sound of Wind, the Slant of the Sunlight." *High Country News* 14 Sept. 1998: 1+.

Marie, Lorraine. "'Black' Helicopters Bear "Big Brother'." *Colville Statesman-Examiner* 22 Feb. 1995: A1.

McPhee, John. *Encounters with the Archdruid.* New York: Farrar, Straus and Giroux, 1971.

Nash, Roderick Frazier. *The Rights of Nature: A History of Environmental Ethics.* Madison: U of Wisconsin P, 1989.

Parini, Jay. "Regionalism and Literary Studies." *The Chronicle of Higher Education* 17 Jan. 1997: 60.

Pombo, Richard, and Joseph Farah. *This Land is Our Land: How to End the War on Private Property.* New York: St. Martin's, 1996.

Pryne, Eric. "Park Plan Called Twisted Global Plot to Destroy Nation." *Spokane Spokesman-Review* October 23: A1.

Ray, Dixy Lee. *Environmental Overkill: Whatever Happened to Common Sense?* Washington, DC: Regnery Gateway, 1993.

———, and Lou Guzzo. *Trashing the Planet: How Science Can Help Us Deal with Acid Rain, Depletion of the Ozone, and Nuclear Waste (Among Other Things).* Washington, D.C:.: Regnery Gateway, 1990.

Ramos, Tarso. "Wise Use in the West: The Case of the Northwest Timber Industry." *Let the People Judge: Wise Use and the Private Property Rights Movement.* Ed. John Echeverria and Raymond Booth Eby. Washington, D.C.: Island, 1995. 82-118.

Rogers, Pattiann. *Firekeeper: New and Selected Poems.* Minneapolis: Milkweed, 1994.

"Sahara Club's Agenda to Attack Environmentalists." *Nature's Advocate: Newsletter of the Upper Columbia River Sierra Club* Feb. 1995: 13.

Sinclair, Upton. *The Jungle.* 1906. New York: Bantam, 1981.

Slovic, Scott. *Seeking Awareness in American Nature Writing.* Salt Lake City: U of Utah P, 1992.

Stern, Kenneth S. *A Force Upon the Plain: The American Militia Movement and the Politics of Hate.* New York: Simon & Schuster, 1996.

Thoreau, Henry David. *The Selected Works of Thoreau.* Cambridge Edition. Rev. ed. Walter Harding. Boston: Houghton Mifflin, 1975.

Wilson, E. O., *The Diversity of Life.* Cambridge, MA: Harvard UP, 1984.

The Quest for Official English

Prospects for the Millennium

STEVE HECOX

The United States of America is a land with a rich and diverse heritage. Americans take pride in the fact that their country is the product of a grand experiment, that it stands firmly upon the idea that free humans can govern themselves, that all are equal in the eyes of the law, and that the United States has offered freedom and hope to generations of souls who have left their homes in other parts of the world to make new ones on these shores. This is especially true in the West, where belief in the individual and the opportunity for each person to make his or her own mark on both the figurative and the literal landscape has always been most strong. The West has always been open to the influence of others who share such ideals and vision. Consequently, it has been a beacon of hope for a continuing influx of new arrivals, who bring with them their own customs, religions, food, and language. The purpose of this discussion is to address that issue of language, particularly efforts to make English the official language of the country, through an examination of such efforts both on a national and regional level.

On the face of it, the history of the United States is one of language tolerance. Nonetheless, since before the Revolution, English has been the national language, the predominant language of the country. Periodically, there have been those who have feared that its linguistic dominance was in jeopardy and have, therefore, made concerted efforts to save their native language from one or more allegedly threatening foreign tongues. The most famous of these defenders in colonial times was none other than Benjamin Franklin, who argued

Steve Hecox teaches English at the University of Nevada, Reno. His interests stretch from contemporary American political ideas to jazz and rock music to the literature and legacy of Sherlock Holmes.

strenuously for the official establishment of English in Pennsylvania, fearing that the growing number of German-speakers in the colony "could dictate outcomes in the political process and that they would undermine colonial government" (Perea 288). Franklin, however, was unpersuasive, as were others who argued this issue through the early days of the republic. After numerous and extensive debates, the founding fathers ultimately decided that the wisest thing to do with respect to language policy was to do nothing at all.

However, while Congress has been unwilling to declare English the official language of the Republic, it has been stead-fastly unwilling to use any other. In March, 1795, in fact, President Washington signed a bill which "approved publication of current and future federal statutes in English only" (Baron 89). While falling short of providing the language with official status, that act has stood to this day. Exceptions to this English only policy can be counted on one hand. Still, the issue has never been far away from the national agenda, and efforts to provide for non-English speakers have often been part of the national debate. For the most part, though, these efforts have been attempts to include rather than ex-clude those of other tongues. Between 1794 and 1862, Con-gress was presented with at least five major legislative pro-posals which would have provided that government documents be printed in languages other than English, one of which ac-tually passed the House before being repealed the next day (Perea 303-09). Still, it should be emphasized that while Con-gress consistently asserted the predominance of English for its own purposes, it mandated nothing, leaving the states the power to pursue their own policies. Many, including Pennsyl-vania, Kentucky, Louisiana, and California, did just that, for "as long as persons who spoke different languages consti-tuted a sufficiently powerful political force in their states, they were able to obtain state recognition of their different lan-guages in state law" (309).

If in domestic situations the Federal government has his-torically used the English language almost exclusively, it has never hesitated to print documents in other languages for citizens of other countries. In the 19th century, for instance, the United States "actively used minority languages to re-cruit settlers for its sparsely populated territories in the Mid-west and West" (Baron 14). And it was very successful in doing so, as foreign settlers came in droves. By the end of that period, Texas was heavily populated with "German-speaking Swiss, Alsatians, and Austrians, . . . Scandinavians [had] flowed into the Dakotas. . . [and] Czechs were an important factor in Nebraska" (Paul 123).

In the West, of course, English *was* the immigrant language. Until the Treaty of Guadalupe Hidalgo was signed in 1848, most of the land in the eleven western states belonged to Mexico and the vast majority of its inhabitants at the time, if they conversed in any European language, did so in Spanish. When the great wagon trains began their westward treks in 1843, those headed to California were, literally, journeying to a foreign land. Conflict between American emigrants and the established residents was inevitable and intensified with the onset of the Mexican-American war in 1846. Still, the numbers of American settlers remained relatively small until the Gold Rush began in 1849. Only then, did English begin to rise to prominence.

Perhaps nowhere was this international mix more prevalent or more celebrated than in Virginia City, Nevada, during the 1860s and 1870s, where, as the mining industry boomed, "the immigrant influence spread . . . through the whole societal structure of the Comstock. . . . Songs in English, French, German, Spanish and Italian were offered in productions at the opera house" (Elliott 148). In addition to these European influences, there were a large number of Mexicans as well as Chinese immigrants working the mines. Indeed, the census of 1870 recorded that 44.5% of those living in Nevada were, in fact, foreign born (405). The West was a polyglot of language, indeed; it was a place where everyone could call home, regardless of what language was used to utter the word.

A great change in Americans' attitudes toward foreign-language speakers occurred during the "national period, primarily from 1880 through the first quarter of the 20th century," when immigrants from southern Europe, eastern Europe, and eastern Asia began arriving in large numbers (Macias 7). It was largely at this time that Americans began both to "treasure the national language and perceive the learning of English by nonanglophone residents as a symbolic rite of passage, a declaration of faith in the United States" (Baron 61). When World War I broke out, and more importantly, at the time the United States became involved in it, German was the most widely spoken language in the United States after English. It was the patriotic reaction to the fact that American armies were leaving this continent for the first time *en masse* to become involved in what was perceived as, essentially, a European war that provoked such a strong reaction against all things "un-American" that began in and has followed that era.

A major portion of that reaction came in various assaults against "foreign" languages and the immigrant communities in which they were spoken. Fear of such reactions affected even the practice of religion. For example, due to the "pressure of the war hysteria in 1918, the Lutheran Church at Minden [Nevada] gave up conducting religious service in the German language on alternate Sundays" (Elliott 255). Various state and local governments even sought to outlaw the use of English in both public and private settings: "Fifteen states banned teaching foreign languages in public schools; some states required public school teachers to be citizens; and Oregon required all elementary school children to attend public rather than private schools" (314). In what is probably the most extreme example of linguistic restriction, the Governor of Iowa once went so far as to declare that it was illegal for foreign languages to be used "in conversations in public places or over the telephone" (Karst 314). While such legal prohibitions did not pass judicial muster, the sentiment behind them lingered and still affects debates about language in the United States.

The current controversy, of course, centers on a different group of immigrants, as the bulk of current newcomers to this country comes either from south of the border or from across the Pacific Ocean rather than the Atlantic. We are in the midst of another wave of immigration, and as always, the new immigrants are bringing their native language with them. Nowhere are these languages more visible than in the West, where not only Spanish, but Chinese, Vietnamese, Korean, and other languages seem to spring up everywhere. We see them on storefront signs that (many seem to recall) all used to be written in English; we see them on billboards that all used to be written in English; we hear them on radio and television stations, all of which used to be broadcast in English. Indeed, there is change in the air, and change is always uncomfortable. This discomfort stems largely from two sources. The first is the fear that we have lost control of our borders, and that we have lost them to a new breed of immigrants who have little respect for "traditional American ways." This sentiment manifests in the popular mind by the notion that, while in the past immigrants were expected to learn English, they now have "the right to preserve the languages which they bring" with them (Wardhaugh 247). The second is the fear that the courts have begun to interpret the Constitution as a document which extends the rights of American citizens to anyone standing on American soil, and have gone so far as to interpret laws in favor of those who are, in fact, in this country illegally.

These fears manifest what may best be described as a collectively schizophrenic attitude toward immigration. One of San Francisco's biggest tourist attractions is its Chinatown. Similarly, Japantown, Koreatown, and Olivera Street are designated and celebrated areas of Los Angeles. Certainly, this is not only a western phenomenon. There have long been sections of many, if not most, of our major cities in which a particular ethnic group and a particular culture are celebrated, but in the popular mind such sections seem to be breaking out of their quaint little quarters and spreading across the landscape at an alarming rate, to the extent that now "there are non-English enclaves within large cities which are almsot [sic] cities in their own right. In the heart of Miani [sic], Little Havana covers five square miles. Spanish Harlem in New York and the East Los Angeles barrios are equally extensive" (Mackey 182-83). In such instances, the fear of modern Americans is the same as that of Benjamin Franklin, that a particular jurisdiction can grow and that with enough growth, whole cities, perhaps whole states, could eventually choose to conduct business in another language or in many languages. If and when the day comes when mainstream Americans cannot speak with their neighbors and know that they will be understood, many intelligent people sincerely believe that, in the words of Alastair Cooke, "the American experiment will be in serious jeopardy of falling apart" (de la Peña 10).

These fears are not diminished when monolingual English-speakers read that "in the diocese of Los Angeles alone, the Catholic church celebrates Mass in 45 different languages" ("Pope" 11A). When they hear, as well, self-declared spokespersons for linguistic minorities seem to dismiss "the melting pot in favor of a 'multicultural' conception of American identity," they fear that the Balkanization of the United States could, indeed, have already begun (Citrin 98).

These are only some of the fears experienced by many Americans, nativist or not. Their fears may be rational or not. They may be based on emotion rather than any verifiable data. The fact remains that many people are concerned and "a concern remains a concern, whether it is justified or not," and, therefore, these concerns must, and will in one way or another, be addressed (Fishman 318). The question of how best to do so becomes, then, the heart of the issue.

The main force behind current official language proposals is U.S. ENGLISH, a lobbying organization begun by S. I. Hayakawa, a former US Senator from California in 1983 "as an offshoot of the restrictionist Federation for American Immigration Reform (FAIR)" (Nunberg 579). While Nunberg's assessment may give an indication of the group's origins, and the Tanton memo, written by one of the original members of the organization, which expresses his "grave concerns about Hispanic fertility and reproduction, Catholicism, and the threat that Hispanics pose to white Anglo dominance of American society," it gives reason to question the ultimate motives of the organization itself, the fact remains that even people whose motives may be questionable can have good ideas, and therefore it is imperative that anyone who examines an issue such as this must separate the message from the messenger and examine the idea upon its own merit (Perea 345).

U.S. ENGLISH provides an eloquent voice to those who fear that the country is falling apart on many fronts and that language is simply one more symptom of the divisiveness which seems to plague us constantly, and more importantly, it is a symptom which we can address. De la Peña argues that "the struggle for official bilingualism in America runs contrary to the civil rights movement of the past 40 years, which has sought to give *everyone*—black, brown, and white— the same opportunities and the same rights" (86). On the face of it, this is an argument that is hard to dispute. The problem is that arguments for language tolerance have nothing to do with a question of official bilingualism, or an official language of any sort—just the opposite, in fact.

Before going any further, it is important to understand that there are two ways in which an Official English proposal can be manifested. The first is that of an innocuous declaration, one which simply states that English is the official language and lets it go at that. The second is one which specifically states what such a declaration shall and shall not entail. Currently twenty-three states have made Official English proclamations, along with Hawaii, which is officially bilingual (English and Hawaiian). Most, by far, are of the innocuous sort.

Consider the example of Mississippi. In the state code, there appears the declaration that "The English language is the official language of the State of Mississippi." It appears between the declarations of the official beverage and the official butterfly. The important question, though, revolves around how such a declaration could be applied in practice.

As previously stated, Mississippi's state language statement follows immediately the declaration that "Milk is hereby designated the state beverage of Mississippi." Pretend for a moment that such a declaration had practical, political consequences. On the surface, I believe it would be clear that at all state functions—banquets, barbeques, fish frys, anything sponsored by the state—milk would be the beverage served and that for anyone who wished to drink, the liquid of choice would be milk. However, reality does occasionally attend such events. Not all people can drink milk. Some are allergic. Still others, for one reason or another, might simply prefer something else in their glasses. In its wisdom, the state of Mississippi has decided that none of these people need be excluded from the official table, and therefore, one can and does find numerous other beverages at its functions.

Although the rhetoric of the advocates of Official English might lead one to believe otherwise, the current situation we have now in the United States is not, to go back to our official milk analogy, a situation of beverage on demand. The state does not have to stock a full bar. The menu is still very select and very specific to any given populace. Current Official English proposals, however, would change this situation drastically. They declare, in one way or another, that if one wants liquid, one will drink milk.

A constitutional amendment, by definition, alters the very foundation upon which the United States is based. Of the thousands of amendments which have been proposed in the last 212 years, only 26 have been adopted, and the first ten of those, the 1791 Bill of Rights, were, essentially, agreed upon at the time of the original document. In the 106th Congress, a Constitutional Amendment (H. J. RES 21) has been proposed which reads as follows:

> SECTION 1. The English language shall be the official language of the United States. As the official language, the English language shall be used for all public acts including every order, resolution, vote or election, and for all records and judicial proceedings of the Government of the United States and the governments of the several States.

> SECTION 2. The Congress and the States shall enforce this article by appropriate legislation.

This is a very different amendment, in a rhetorical sense, from others that have preceded it, for it applies to what the government "shall" do, rather than what it is prohibited from doing. Save in those cases which deal with procedural matters, no other amendment with the exception of that which enacted Prohibition has used language in such a manner. There is no flexibility in this document. One of its scariest implications is that it includes all judicial proceedings under its mandate. Additionally, it applies not only to the Federal government, but to state governments as well. Under these provisions, it could easily be construed as unconstitutional for a judge, whether in federal, state or municipal court, to provide an interpreter to any person appearing before his or her bench—not for a criminal defendant, not for a witness to a crime, not even for the victim of a crime. The identical proposal was put forth in the previous Congressional session, where it was assigned to the Subcommittee on the Constitution of the House Judiciary Committee and never emerged. As of this writing, the same is true this time around. It is not hard to conclude, however, that such proposals are likely to be in the offing continually for the foreseeable future and that their chances of success could change at any time.

The push for Official English is, however, hardly confined to the national arena, and two of the most outrageous examples of English Only legislation in recent history have occurred in the West: the Arizona Official English Amendment (Article XXVIII) and California's Proposition 227, which came to life ten years later.

In 1988, the voters of Arizona passed, by 50.5-49.5%, an amendment to the state constitution which declared English to be the official "language of the ballot, the public schools and *all government functions* and actions" (my emphasis). Maria Kelly F. Yniguez worked for the State of Arizona. Being fluent in both English and Spanish, she routinely aided those with whom she came in contact in the language which she felt was most efficient. Article XXVIII would have compelled Ms. Yniguez to use only the English language while on the job. Shortly after passage of the amendment, she sued the state, claiming that this new provision of the state constitution was in variance with that of the United States. The Ninth Circuit Court of Appeals agreed with her, stating that her argument was reasonable and her conduct proper. They declared, therefore, that the Arizona amendment was unconstitutional. One of the principal voices of U.S. ENGLISH, however, puts the decision in a far different light, stating that "in Arizona, a US District Court judge upheld a ruling in favor of a state employee who wanted to use Spanish on the job" (de la Peña 105). While this may be literally true, it is horribly deceptive, for it implies that Ms. Yniguez used language in an arbitrary manner, invoking visions of English-speaking citizens asking for state services, being confronted with a monolingual Spanish-speaking agent, and consequently being made to feel like aliens in their own land. Such a rhetorical strategy only provides disinformation designed to enhance existing fears.

Although proponents of Official English revel in the fact that the decision of the Ninth Circuit was overturned by the Supreme Court, it is important to note that the reversal was not made on the merit of the argument, but simply because Ms. Yniguez had voluntarily left her job before being either threatened or fired. Therefore, her complaint was moot and the issue of constitutionality has not yet been decided.

One major focus of those who are concerned with the influx of foreign language speakers is the Bilingual Education Act of 1968, which "was the first significant federal step in the promotion of language rights" in America (Citrin 98). Reaction to such federal regulations, combined with an increasing number of immigrants to California gave rise to Proposition 227, an initiative which declared an end to the policy of bilingual education as it has evolved over the previous thirty years, replacing it with a one-year program of "Sheltered English immersion," after which all children will be placed in mainstream (read: "taught in English-only") classes. The argument of the proponents of the proposal is simple. English is the dominant language of the United States, and if immigrants wish their children to succeed in this land, to "fully participate in the American Dream of economic and social advancement," they will benefit from learning English as quickly as possible ("Proposition" 227). This is an obvious conclusion cloaked in tenderhearted language. But the problem is not that simple, and the factors underlying the strategy of the proposition's backers are not far from the surface: "Booming numbers of immigrants flooding into the Golden State have made California home to half of all non-English speaking school kids in the United States. Those 1.4 million students make up 25 percent of the Golden State's entire enrollment" (Phinney). For many, Franklin's fears have once again risen. Perhaps someday Spanish speakers might become a majority in the state and the monolingual English speakers of California might have to learn a new language, and who wants to do that? Clearly, it was an argument built upon emotion rather than logic. It was, however, very effective. The proposition passed by a 61-39 percent margin.

Proposition 227, however, is a badly written law. In the first place, it didn't provide enough time for educators to effectively comply in the best of circumstances. Presented to the voters on 2 June, the initiative mandated that its provisions be implemented within sixty days of passage, by the first of August. This gave the California State Board of Education and the 1000 local school districts throughout the state less than nine weeks to develop a new curriculum to replace the bilingual programs already in place, to adopt and purchase new textbooks which reflect that new teaching philosophy, and to train teachers in the newly adopted theory of pedagogy. Clearly, it couldn't be done. As it turned out, by early October, "many schools [in the Los Angeles School District had] not yet received books printed in English" (Colvin 32A). In other words, the proposition prescribed policies which could not possibly be implemented in the allotted time frame. It mandated the impossible.

The inevitable reaction to Proposition 227 quickly began to set in. Faced with a curricular impossibility, school boards across the state, especially those with large immigrant populations, finally began to get their message out, discovering "an unprecedented opportunity to explain to parents how they were educating children" (Bazeley 1A). And once informed, parents began to respond. One of the provisions of Proposition 227 allows parents to request that after their children have spent one month in an English immersion class, they can apply for a waiver from the new law if the "child is age 10 or older and would learn English faster through an 'alternate course' of study" (Connor). When it established its final guidelines for the districts, the Board stated that if such requests are made, they "shall be granted unless the school principal and educational staff have determined that an alternative program offered at the school would not be better suited for the overall educational development of the pupil" (California Board of Education). Backers of 227 believed that such applications would be sought by few parents. But they have been surprised:

> In Mountain View, 551 parents, representing 99 percent of limited English proficient students, asked for their children to stay in bilingual classes. . . . In the Hueneme district in Ventura County, the parents of more than 99 percent of the limited-English speakers asked for waivers. The Oxnard School district reported about 90 percent. (Bazely 1A)

In other districts, though, there seem to be few, if any, waiver requests. The difference seems to be due to two factors. First, different school districts seem to be willing and able, in the face of Proposition 227, to finally and aggressively explain their bilingual programs to the parents they serve. Second, "the hodgepodge of bilingual education programs in California schools . . . ranged from a few that were very effective to large numbers that were damagingly ineffective" ("Wave" A16). That disparity between programs is a large part of the problem. Those who have looked at the situation objectively and thoroughly agree that bilingual education, if it is done properly, does work. Students in well-conceived and adequately funded bilingual programs have higher grade point averages, lower drop-out rates, and lower retention rates than those put in "sink or swim" immersion programs (Krashen 74). The evidence seems clear, as well, that parents will support a good bilingual program and a school board which stands behind it. The important thing to remember, though, is that, to be effective, bilingual programs must be supported; they must be set in a firm pedagogical foundation; and the rationale for such programs must be made clear to the public. The latter point is most important. It is likely the most important lesson to be taken from the ongoing saga of Proposition 227.

With all this in mind, I believe that as long as its opponents remain vigilant, there is little, if any, chance that English will become the official language of the United States in the near future, principally due to the fact that the electorate itself is changing. According to Census Bureau projections, by 1 July 2000, 23.8% of the people in the eleven western states will be of Hispanic origin. That figure will rise to 33.2% in the next twenty-five years. In California, those figures are 32.7% and 43.1% respectively (US Census Bureau). In Nevada, the percentage of Hispanic students in the public schools has risen from 5.8% to 17.2% between 1982 and 1996 (Nevada Department of Education). Within the next decade, it is expected that Texas will have a majority of voters of Hispanic origin (News Hour). Consequently, the needs of immigrants are evermore likely to be positively addressed. A change is clearly in the air, and perhaps there is no better example of that change than Texas Governor George W. Bush, who professes to be "a leader who is compassionate and conservative [and who can] erase the gender gap and open the doors of the Republican Party to new faces, new voices" (Slater 1A). Those new voices are, to a large degree, Hispanic. Governor Bush conducted a significant part of his campaign of 1998 in Spanish. He reached out aggressively to his Spanish-speaking constituents, addressing their concerns in no uncertain terms, stating that "what English Only says to many Hispanics is 'me, not you'" (News Hour).

George W. Bush is not the only one. His brother, Jeb, expressed the same ideals in Florida. Still, even the Governors Bush are not alone. Politicians across the country, and especially in the West, are now openly courting the Hispanic vote in particular and the immigrant vote in general. They have good reason to do so, for as immigrant populations rise, they are clearly beginning to flex their political muscles, and politicians everywhere are beginning to take note for one very good reason: "Unlike most of the voters who care about a range of issues [newly naturalized citizens] go to the polls [specifically] to elect pro-immigrant candidates" (Bradley). Consequently, politicians of all stripes are backing away from the hard line on immigration.

Beyond the ambitions of politicians, though, it seems that voters in general have shown the ability to react to reason when it is effectively presented. As stated earlier, Proposition 227 was passed by the California electorate in June 1998 with 61% majority. Having seen that Proposition in action and having heard the arguments of those who support linguistic diversity (perhaps for the first time), voters had yet another chance five months later to comment on it when one of its authors, Gloria Tuchman, ran for the office of Superintendent of Public Instruction in November. From that post, she would have been in a position to assure a strict standard of enforcement to the Proposition. She was, however, defeated by the incumbent Superintendent, Diane Eastin, who favors a far more cautious approach.

On the face of it, therefore, it would seem that times favor those traditional Americans who see no reason for any declaration of official language. While there is a nativist fear of English losing its position of dominance, especially in light of the increasing number of Spanish-speaking immigrants entering the country, the facts do not justify that fear. According to the 1980 census,

> 10.9 percent of the population, claimed to use a language other than English at home, and that one out of every seven Americans spoke, or lived in a household with someone who spoke such a language . . . Among the members of this group: close to 82 percent of respondents indicated that they also spoke English well or very well. (Baron 3)

One can read this statement in more than one manner, but in any case, it states that only 2.0-2.6% of the population is not proficient in English. Other studies tell similar tales. Crawford cites research which shows that "70 percent of Spanish speakers who settle here before the age of ten become anglicized by adulthood and 10 percent abandon Spanish altogether" (128). In fact, by all accounts, "Hispanics are learning to speak English at a rate similar to that of past immigrant groups—that is, by the third generation many of them do so exclusively" (Zentella B3). Furthermore, in a world of mass media, where English is becoming ever more prominent on a global scale, it is only natural that immigrants will flow ever more strongly toward the dominant language. And as far as children are concerned, as long as there is MTV, they will be singing in English.

One of the biggest problems in putting forth such information is that complex ideas aren't easily put into simple slogans. However, simple ideas, such as "everyone should speak English," are. Fear must be countered by facts, and currently that is not being done in any effective fashion on a national scale. It must be done, though, for any sweeping language legislation would open a Pandora's box of potential problems, and it is sure to rise again. If English-Only legislation were ever to become law, the courts would be flooded with Constitutional challenges for years. Cases filed under the First, Fifth, and Fourteenth Amendments would abound. The Constitutional question, of course, would be overcome if the provisions of the language bills were simply transferred to the enabling legislation of a Constitutional Amendment. But even if legal problems might be overcome in that fashion, worse social problems are very likely to take their place. Some people would take such an amendment, which applies, after all, only to official government functions, as a license for blanket discrimination. It has happened in the past; for example,

> In the wake of the passage of the Official English amendment in the state of Florida, for example, a Miami Bank informed one of its mortgagees that they would no longer accept mortgage checks made out in Spanish; a Dade County assistant principal announced that students were prohibited from speaking Spanish on school grounds; and a Coral Gables supermarket clerk was suspended without pay for speaking Spanish on the job. (Nunberg 581)

Indeed, under cover of a Constitutional Amendment, perhaps even a ban on foreign language phone calls could be upheld.

Perhaps it all boils down to the simple concept that, as citizens of this country, we need to respect one another. The biggest problem with the idea of declaring English to be the official language of the nation is that language isn't really the problem. What unites us is far more important than what divides us. Robert D. King so eloquently states:

> In spite of all our racial divisions and economic un-fairness, we have the frontier tradition, respect for the individual, and opportunity; we have our love affair with the automobile; we have in our history a civil war that freed the slaves and was fought with valor; and we have sports, hot dogs, hamburgers, and milk shakes—things big and small, noble and petty, im-portant and trifling. "We are Americans; we are differ-ent." (King 64)

To reflect upon the wisdom of the founding fathers, to reflect upon the appeal of the West, it is those things which bring us together in this land which are most important. We are here for a reason, all of us, and as we greet the new mil-lennium, it might be good for all of us to take a step back and look at those things which unite us and revel in our good fortune.

As to the future, I firmly believe that those who cherish the idea that all are welcome in this country and that it is a land of opportunity need to be wary of challenges to that op-portunity. We can't blame those who are motivated by fear, for fear is a powerful emotion, but fears must be actively ad-dressed. If we have problems—which, of course, we do—we must deal with them in a rational manner. The remedy of Official English, however, does nothing to address any of the nation's underlying problems. It is my belief that extreme and divisive measures, such as those proposed by the advocates of Official English, have little chance of being adopted any-time in the near future. And it is my hope that those of us—educators, politicians, and anyone with a commitment to the community of America—will adhere to the original vision of this country and continually remind our neighbors and ourselves that "liberty and justice for all" is, ultimately, what this country is all about.

REFERENCES

Baron, Dennis. *The English-Only Question: An Official Language for Americans?* New Haven: Yale University Press, 1990.

Bazeley, Michael. "Bilingual Classes on the Way Back." *San Jose Mercury News.* 8 Oct. 1998: 1A.

Bradley, Barbara. Report. *Morning Edition.* National Public Radio. KUNR, Reno. 16 Oct. 1998.

California State Board of Education. *Proposition 227 Emergency Regulations.* State of California. 26 Mar. 1999 <http://www.cde.ca.gov/prop227.html>.

Citrin, J. "Language Politics and American Identity." *Public Interest* Spring, 1990: 96-109.

Colvin, Richard Lee. "Prop. 227 Delays Reading Lessons in English in L.A." *Los Angeles Times.* 9 Oct. 1998, A1+.

Connor, Kim. *Proposition 227: English Language Education for Children in Public Schools.* California Voter Pamphlet. 9 Apr. 1999 <http://www.sen.ca.gov/sor/educate/ prop227.htm>.

Crawford, James W. *Hold Your Tongue: Bilingualism and the Politics of "English Only."* Reading: Addison-Wesley, 1992.

De la Peña, Frederico. *Democracy or Babel?* Washington: U.S. ENGLISH, 1991.

Elliott, Russell R. *History of Nevada.* 2nd ed. rev. Lincoln: U. of Nebraska, 1973.

Fishman, Joshua A. *Reversing Language Shift.* Clevedon: Multilingual Matters Ltd., 1991.

Karst, Kenneth L. "Paths to Belonging: The Constitution and Cultural Identity." *North Carolina Law Review* 64 (1986): 303-77.

King, Robert D. "Should English Be The Law?" *Atlantic Monthly* April 1997: 55-64.

Krashen, Stephen D. *Under Attack: The Case Against Bilingual Education.* Culver City: Language Education Association, 1996.

Macias, R. F. "Official Languages in the United States: Policies, Polemics, and Politics." Conference paper. ERIC Number ED 316 019. 1987.

Mackey, William. F. "US Language Status Policy and the Canadian Experience." *Progress in Language Planning: International Perspectives.* Ed. J. Cobarrubias and Joshua A. Fishman. Berlin: Mouton Publishers, 1983. 173-206.

Nevada Department of Education. "Nevada Public Schools, Ethnic Reports, School Years 1982-83 through 1995-96." Fax from Robin Loder Padilla, Program Officer, to Dr. Lee Thomas, University of Nevada, Reno. 22 Oct. 1998.

News Hour with Jim Lehrer. Report. PBS. 27 Oct. 1998.

Nunberg, Geoffrey. "Linguists and the Official Language Movement." *Language* 65 (1989): 579-87.

Paul, Rodman W. *The Far West and the Great Plains in Transition 1895-1900.* New York: Harper and Row, 1988.

Perea, J. F. "Demography and Distrust: An Essay on American Languages, Cultural Pluralism, and Official English." *Minnesota Law Review* 77 (1992): 269-373.

Phinney, David. "Bilingual Ed Lacks Support." *ABC News.* 29 May 1998 <http://archive.abcnews.com/sections/us/Daily News/ bilingual980527.html> 7 Oct. 1998.

"Pope Will Be Met by Melting-pot Church in America." *Reno Gazette-Journal.* 1 Oct. 1995: 11A.

"Proposition 227: English Language Education for Children in Public Schools." California Initiative. <http://www.onenation.org./ fulltext.html> 30 Oct. 1998.

Slater, Wayne and Terrence Stutz. "Bush Wins by Landslide." *Dallas Morning News.* 4 Nov. 1998: 1A.

US Census Bureau. <http://www.census.gov/population/www/projections/ stproj.html> 1 Oct. 1998.

———. Cong. House. H.J. Re. 21. 15 Apr. 1999 15 Apr. 1999. <http:/ /thomas.loc.gov/cgi-bin/query/z?c106:H.J.RES.21:>

Wardhaugh, Ronald. *Languages in Competition: Dominance, Diversity, and Decline.* Oxford: Blackwell, 1987.

"Wave of Waivers." Editorial. *Los Angeles Times.* 23 Oct. 1998, home ed.: A16.

Zentella, A. C. "English-Only Laws Will Foster Divisiveness, Not Unity: They are Anti-Hispanic, Anti-elderly, and Anti-female." *The Chronicle of Higher Education* 23 Nov. 1988, B1+.

TRIANGULATIONS

With the crises of the millenium comes danger and opportunity, meditation and madness, and now a sense of mediated reality and virtual existence. In the years of transition we may continue to face fear and lament, longing and connection, and perhaps a growing sense of nostalgia for nostalgia. But throughout our adjustments, we open possibilities for new ways of seeing, new ways of knowing, and new ways of being in the world. The world of today, tomorrow, and yesterday is no longer one of simple coin tosses, lines in the sand, or us versus them. As we look to the future, we attempt to view our possibilities from many sides, triangulating our observations—in the hopes that we might see better and understand.

In this final section, place and perspective play a crucial role in the progression of discussions. Thomas Noerper conveys the dynamism of a Bohemian quarter in Tucson, suggesting a horizon of possibilities for similar places across the country. His vision triangulates grassroots claims to community space, promotion of intellectual and artistic expression, and resistance to institutional programming of place. Taking us from Noerper's vibrant urban locale to the stars and beyond, Jane Detweiler's "Landscaping the Final Frontier" weaves together stories of western expansion, her life experience, and narrative analyses to examine possible worlds of the expanding US space program. Through these, and other, triangulations, she suggests that the stories we tell may not just alter our perception of future landscapes, but determine what we do to them, for them, and with them.

As we look to our storied horizons, we must also consider the media for our messages and the languages we use. Beverley Curran's "Re-reading the Desert in Hypertranslation" takes us into a discussion of translation: as an act of passage and as a means to transform reality. The creation of textual spaces, and the digital media that allows us to shape such spaces, echoes Detweiler's concerns about narrative as much as it posits further connections between user and interface, text and author, storied space and the space of stories.

H. Lee Barnes concludes this volume with "Riding the Curves Into the Twenty-First Century," taking us across the American West with visions gleaned from either breakneck speed or prophetic glimpses culled from careful observation and reflection. As he explains, "The relationship of human to motorcycle, at its meridian, it atavistic. Add a desert to the equation and the relationship heads toward something spiritual." With Barnes's image of human and machine working together, we approach the curves in the road before us, unaware of the turns to come or the places that lie ahead. The familiar image of a lone person traveling on a beast of burden—human and animal in harmony—is translated, triangulated, and transposed into a different score, a variation on a theme that calls for further play and a yearning for improvisation.

Barrio Devo
Lessons in the Ethical Function
of Architecture

THOMAS E. NOERPER

On the west side of Tucson, in a downtown neighborhood and only a block from the tracks of the Southern-Pacific Railroad, there stands the ruin of an old adobe house, built in a manner typical to a Tucson *barrio*. A two-story house, it is conspicuous in towering over its low neighbors. It juts up, alone, from a too-large lot that is bare Sonora desert, a light brown, graveled roughness tinged with pink, marked by sparse, scrubby grass, a little bit of prickly pear, and a single mesquite tree that leans in affinity toward the adobe ruin. Some of the wooden shingles of the roof have given way, exposing large portions of the interior to the sun and wind and the seasonal rains of the monsoons. Without the protective covering of the roof, the tops of the walls have taken in the sky's weather, and the stucco has begun to fall away, leaving the adobe bricks, mere dampened soil of the desert, to melt back towards their source.

The ruptured surface of the house, in its failure to hold against the elements, reveals a great deal about the nature of the house, its building materials, and the kind of dwelling that occurs in such houses. The primary building material is mud, lumps of dampened desert soil baked in the desert sun. The fragile bricks are protected from rain and wind by a layer of stucco hung on chicken wire. Above is a wood frame roof shingled with corrugated iron in older houses, with wood or tar-paper shingles in those built more recently. Older houses

Tom Noerper left St. Louis, Missouri in 1987 to travel the desert southwest, eventually landing in Tucson, Arizona. There he played guitar in one of the city's loudest bands. Returning to school in his mid-twenties, he took his B.A. from Yale College; he currently studies psychology at Northwestern University.

of this style are strung with copper electrical wire wrapped in cloth insulation that hangs from porcelain insulators. Plastic-covered electrical wire appears in only a few refurbished buildings, usually remodeled as law offices. Wood, adobe, stucco, iron or tar-paper, copper wire and pipes, porcelain and window glass—each material rose out of the earth or was formed from earth, and each would almost too easily melt back into the desert.

The ruined adobe is typical of houses in the older neighborhoods of Tucson, many of which were built by the Southern-Pacific Railroad as temporary dwellings for railroad workers. Some of them are laid out shotgun fashion, with three or four rooms end to end, three or four single-story apartments to a building. Staring at the melting ruin and remembering the impermanent intentions of the company that had built much of the neighborhood, one realizes that if human beings left this place, or if everyone died, in fifty years there would be little remaining to show that people once lived here. The melting house cannot even feign permanence, but instead illustrates the ultimate vulnerability of all human building and all human works to the patient forces of nature over time. Without continued maintenance, much of Tucson would simply wash away in the heavy downpours of the summer monsoons.

Even before Spanish missions were built in the area, indigenous Americans lived within a half mile of the melting adobe site. Tucson claims to hold within its bounds the oldest continuously inhabited site in North America; however, its history is one of continual and successive displacement. Indigenous people have displaced other native people, whose culture was displaced by Spanish missionaries, until most recently Anglo-American culture has become dominant. Developers from the East brought a single rail line through the town, to be followed eventually by a single interstate route, I-10, which stretches across the lower part of the country from Jacksonville, Florida to Los Angeles. The clean desert air and year-round warmth have made it a favorite wintering spot for asthmatics, the elderly, and those transients who used to be known as "hoboes."

As in most cities, the transients and various other displaced persons tend to drift towards the downtown area, which is centered on the fork of Congress Street and Broadway. Fewer than ten blocks to the East and just north of the downtown, the University of Arizona campus sprawls out into mid-town. Between downtown and the campus lies the West University neighborhood, which together with its adjoining neighbor-hoods houses the greater part of Tucson's "neo-bohemians." Struggling artists and musicians, aging hippies, aging punk rockers, recently graduated English majors, perpetual stu-dents, radical activists, and some members of the gay and lesbian community are drawn to the area by the low rent, one another, and the proximity of the downtown area. They con-gregate in numbers great enough to make this part of Tucson the Lower East Side of the Desert Southwest. With a nod to the adjacent Barrio Anita, Barrio Viejo, and Barrio Hollywood, Tucson's roughly Bohemian quarter has been nicknamed "Barrio Devo."

Generations of renters, many in flight from their parents' suburbs, have sought a sense of authenticity in the aging temporary adobes of Barrio Devo. A strong sense of rootless-ness is suggested by the buildings being used beyond their expected length of occupancy, by their proximal relationship to the train tracks, and by the apparent imminence of their re-absorption into the desert. At the same time, the adobe houses offer also a sense of place, in the regionalism of their construction materials and design, and as an expression of the history of the growth of Tucson with the railroad. Barrio Devo exists in the tension between these two experiences: There is a sense of place, but it is someone else's place. In Barrio Devo, everyone rents, crashes with a friend for awhile, and swaps room-mates. Periodic attempts to re-locate to San Francisco or Seattle are common.

Rather than being a consequence of gentrification or rap-idly shifting demographics, displacement in Barrio Devo is more the general expression of individual neo-bohemians' re-lationship to American society. Some see themselves as hav-ing little access to, or no real place within the American middle class dream of life in the suburbs. Others have displaced them-selves by rejecting this life style. There is a consensus of dis-illusionment, a shared sense of having been born into a once-beautiful world that for them has been ruined. There is a belief in a fallen America that is centered on a childhood memory of Watergate and the assassinations of Martin Luther King, Jr., Malcolm X, and the Kennedy brothers. This disappointment is transformed by irony and cynicism into a kitschy justification of the abandonment of all heroic leaders and whatever hope they offered. Police, politicians, and judges are assumed to be the corrupt enforcers of a failed social system that benefits only its controllers. Despite the concerns of environmentalists, the degradation of the planet appears to be proceeding rapidly as ever, and the American consumer monoculture continues to assimilate all other cultures.

Barrio Devo is formed around a withdrawal from social and political institutions. Most neo-bohemians have a heightened awareness of the failure of Soviet Communism in Stalinism; of the failure of Western Europe in confronting Nazism too late; the destruction of Native American cultures; the sell-out of America's youth that was the Viet Nam War; and, the flagrant disregard for law and blatant indifference to the poor that characterized the Reagan and Bush administrations. Beyond distrust or suspicion, the neo-bohemians take it for granted that government varies from being corrupt and ineffectual to being downright malevolent. Having no investment in official institutions such as the city hall, the state and federal courts, these people withdraw as well from the public spaces set up around government buildings—Tucson's various versions of the courthouse square. To the neo-bohemians, the public architecture of these institutions symbolizes the malevolence and ineptitude of the state, the spiritual failure of the American socio-political experiment.

Similarly, the buildings on the campus of the University of Arizona could be described as the Architecture of Disappointment. In two decades the administration has continually cut funding for the once-great library system and the school's music programs, as well as other academic needs, while increasing the budget allocated for athletics and defense research such as the ethically and pragmatically questionable "Star Wars" (Strategic Defense Initiative) program. Like most large state schools, this university is always expanding, gobbling up adjacent neighborhoods and replacing them with a mixture of late-twentieth century "interesting" but uninhabitable architecture and functional monstrosities that act like billboards for the priorities of late capitalism. A number of enrolled students seek refuge in Barrio Devo from this inhuman giant of an institution.

This refusal of institutional architecture and the public space it imposes relates well to another refusal that almost defines those who are at the center of Barrio Devo's counter-culture: the refusal of café culture. Among the small group who might be seen as Tucson's neo-bohemian elite, by virtue of their commitment to unsalable art and performance, or their efforts to establish and maintain alternative social space, no one is likely to be seen hanging around in cafes and coffee houses. In Tucson, these slightly theatrical social spaces designated for the non-performance public appearance of writers, artists, actors and musicians attract those performers more committed to posing as "artiste" than they are committed to the actual activities of art production. Their theatricality is enjoyed by suburban teenagers who come downtown for an approximation of an urban experience. In contrast, the group of interest here, in the refusal of both institutional architecture and cafe culture, shows an unwillingness to participate in any social program. Barrio Devo is more than wary of leaders and of being led, avoids any participation in a community that would imply complicity in its sins. This is not to say that those who make up Barrio Devo are without the need for experiences of community: Arguably, they have provided themselves experiences of togetherness that can be considered even as edifying departures from everyday life.

* * * * *

About a block away from the duplex adobe ruin, in an identically constructed house, there lived some time ago a very old Hispanic man who would come outside every day to tend to his yard in the stiff movements of the aged. Undoubtedly, he had lived in the *barrio* since long before the most recent influx of Anglos from the mid-west, northeast, and California had made Tucson the third fastest-growing city in America. His house, like his aging body, spoke clearly of the ravages of the elements through time. The walls leaned so that the entire frame of the house was slightly twisted off of its foundation, and the single window and single door set into the wall facing the road had been pulled into trapezoids, so that there was not a single right angle to be seen in the entire building. A screen door, pulled by gravity in the direction opposite that of the doorframe, slapped in the wind against the wooden frame, leaving large gaps between the door and frame. The two shapes betrayed nothing of having once fit into each other, decades ago.

The Sonora Desert is an incorrigible, often hostile environment. The resources in time and money necessary to achieve the green-carpet lawn that says "this is an American suburb" are available to only a few people. The very region refuses homogeneity. The older residents of the city, mostly Hispanic, hold a different standard of how a yard should appear. Generally they do not grow grass, but rake the dust and gravel into small furrows reminiscent of the gravel in a Japanese rock garden. For the crooked old man in the crooked old house, the custom of raking the gravel seemed to have taken on the air of a rigid, preserving ritual of place. He raked every day, regardless of the weather, so that one day, as he raked in a blustering hot wind, the dust flew up from his rake into a cloud so large and dense that he all but disappeared within it. This scene was the promise of the little house made of dust, in which the old man lived alone, soon to return to dust himself, by himself. The constant encroachment of desert dust into the adobe houses of Barrio Devo makes the same promise; no amount of sweeping and cleaning could contain all of the dust that seeps into such an adobe. It comes through doorframes and window-frames, cracks between floorboards, sometimes through the walls. The consuming desert Earth, the startling expansiveness of the western sky and the open landscape provide constant reminders of eventual oblivion.

The open spaces of the American West, beyond suggesting the idea of finitude, are very dangerous in actuality: To be lost alone in the desert and exposed to the elements of nature can mean a quick death. Most everyone in the southwestern cities has come from somewhere else to this hostile natural environment, and the need for community becomes readily obvious, and more self-conscious. The residents of Barrio Devo, having rejected traditional community institutions and their buildings and programs, or having found no place for themselves there, have developed their own spaces and rituals. Reflecting the individual sense of "not having a place" in society, the sites for these rituals are always borrowed—someone else's place. The most important locations have been abandoned warehouses slated to be cleared for a highway expansion project, and a few night clubs and sports bars that could be appropriated for a few hours on an otherwise dead night.

The grandest of these rituals were weekend-long art and performance festivals held seasonally over a period of a few years. An art school refugee from the east coast who had been an important organizer of punk rock shows in the late 1970s and early 1980s had come to Arizona presumably to escape the crowded alienation of the East. With a group of like-minded artists and community activists, he had convinced the city government to convert an old warehouse space, waiting to be demolished for the new highway, into artists' studios and a performance space called "Dodjk."

Under themes such as "Create Yourself," the participation of over one hundred members of the community was solicited. There were punk bands and paintings, photography and sculpture, improv comedy and dance, amateur films and poets reading, performance art and installation pieces. Contributors ranged from professional makers of mainstream "Southwestern" art, university professors and students, to unschooled inspired amateurs, and children in art classes taught by the organizers. People were invited, cajoled, and otherwise pressured to work in media they had never explored. Closet artists who had never shown their work or performed were convinced to 'fess up to their art. These festivals were attended by hundreds of people over the course of each weekend, and received much positive press attention.

Roughly summarized, the ideology of the project held that the consumer culture of late capitalism demands that we sacrifice our individuality and any sense of autonomy to a life of wage slavery and leisure time programmed with the consumption of fetishized commodities and the spectacle of popular media. Time with movie, television and pop music stars becomes a commodity we purchase at someone else's rates, with wages we slave for in jobs that someone else controls. As wage slaves and consumers in a "Society of the Spectacle," (a title borrowed from Guy Debord) we find no place for autonomy, no place to create one's own life and identity. The program is set forth for us with little allowance for variation by the media and the technological infrastructure, both of which are increasingly difficult to escape while still participating in our communities. The Spectacle calls us out of our investment in the neighborhood, our own families, our own lives, and into the theater of electoral politics, the lives of soap stars and pop stars, the world of sports statistics, etc., ad nauseam.

In opposition to the Spectacle, the Dodjk festivals urged each person in the community to create: To create art, and in so doing to create a relationship with oneself; to share this expression of self with others in order to create a real sense of community—a community based on the shared value of individuals nurturing each other in striving for autonomy. Autonomy of identity facilitates autonomy in the social, political, and material areas of life, and thus we have a revolutionary vision of autonomous individuals working together in community to build a world that is an expression of that community and its values. This vision, not expressed as theory but experienced in the microcosm of the festival, was a distinct departure from the alienation of everyday life in the consumer culture. Not by identification, as in acting as a member of a theater audience, but in full participation, the members of Barrio Devo were called to interact more deeply with each other and themselves. The participants were shown that their contribution was worthwhile and empowering both to them individually and to the community.

The event gained a great deal of energy in its opposition to the values of the dominant consumer culture. The festivals were held on spring and fall equinox, and the summer and winter solstices. These pagan holidays were chosen to reconnect with the oldest cultural traditions—the ritual observation of the universal experience of the seasons—and to invite questioning of fundamental Judeo-Christian assumptions. Crossing minor legal boundaries heightened the experience of taking leave from the everyday. The fire codes did not allow for the number of occupants in the building; the event ran all night, and did not close down with bars or gallery parties; the event was held without performance permits or proper insurance. The police only just tolerated the multiple violations. Eventually, the city forbade further such events on city-owned property. The authorities could not condone illegal activities, however minor, however constructive the whole of the event might have been.

One could not return from these departures without a higher sense of self and a higher regard for the community. Each celebration served as a demonstration of the belief that even in this late period, the individual can contribute to something grand without sacrificing one's individuality. Instead, each could come away with a stronger sense of self. The Dodjk festivals were a deliberate call to the community's members to transform the everyday, to create and sustain an alternative social and even aesthetic space more humane than that of the dominant society.

It is not the theory or the idea of the "Create Yourself" fest that is so remarkable. It is the actualization of the vision that sets it apart. It is the fact that several hundreds of lives were affected in such an uplifting way, and that this was sustained over several years. It does not surprise us, but perhaps it should, that those people who experience themselves as most self-consciously disenfranchised in the status quo were so able to achieve a functioning alternative. That this neo-bohemian group, so steeped in irony and cynicism, so committed to a post-modern ethos, should so successfully bring about a festal space has some bearing on a focal question important to any discussion of architecture's role in our time.

In his book *The Ethical Function of Architecture*, and in his Philosophy of Architecture class at Yale, Karsten Harries recalls Hegel's assertion that art in the modern era no longer serves the highest needs of the spirit. Harries is unsure whether architecture in our era can function in an ethical capacity. This would be achieved by an aesthetic experience that invites us to take leave of our everyday consciousness, and to enter into the extraordinary consciousness of an aesthetic moment, only to return to the everyday with a transfigured vision of the mundane. An experience of beauty in which our culture's foremost values are idealized is to be delivered to us in the architectural aesthetic moment; this moment should return us to the ordinary world with an enhanced sense of our relationship to our time, and place, and community, and the universal experiences that bind the human community. Such architecture would deliver us to an experience of having discovered our place in our world. Further, that place would inhabit the tension between individual responsibility and participation in community. Architecture is not to be used to create the kind of collective experience that releases individuals from a sense of conscience or responsibility.

Our ability to take leave of the every-day through architecture is dependent on our ability to make such a departure at all, and so Harries asks, are we moderns able any longer to make this kind of departure in festivals? After fascism and the Holocaust, are we justifiably too wary of the group, of bad community, to allow ourselves to participate? The Dodjk festival in Barrio Devo provides a partial model for how such experiences may still be possible, and does so emphasizing an achievement of community not at the cost of individuality, but while strengthening individual autonomy. The example of Barrio Devo maintains Harries' proposed ellipse around these two poles of dwelling that may be called *private* (the adobe) and *public* (the warehouse); the appropriated warehouse and the impermanent adobe clearly correspond in function to the temple and the house, the two basic paradigms in the history of architecture. Here, Harries' two poles are occupied by the mobile renter, anxiously rootless, striving for autonomy, and an alternative community dependent on increasing individual autonomy for its project to progress. The interdependent relationship between them is the cherished, celebrated value in the Barrio Devo's festivals.

What is conspicuous about this model is that, despite the size of the community involved, *works* of architecture are nakedly absent. Certainly borrowing stages and re-appropriating warehouse space are architectural *acts*, acts that smack of a nostalgia for the functionalism of the early twentieth century. But Barrio Devo does not build. It is defined by a refusal of architecture.

So the question of whether architecture may serve an ethical function remains: Can an edifying effect be achieved in building in this time? This reflection on an actual community demonstrates the importance of a manner of dwelling that delivers us to ourselves. The essential balance between the individual and society is preserved in Barrio Devo. This balance, the prevention of the two poles of the ellipse collapsing into one, is Harries' requirement for "mythopoeic" architecture—if architecture is to be allowed to place the individual in society after the Nazi and Soviet architects demonstrated the totalitarian possibilities inherent in building.

The essential issues as set forth by Karsten Harries ring true in the ease with which this reflection on Barrio Devo falls into the scheme provided; however, there is an important discrepancy. Professor Harries' lectures are given before a group composed primarily of architecture students who come from around the world to study at Yale. The discussion is still very much one of a wealthy, educated elite building for people who are less privileged. The idea that those at the top of the hierarchy can do anything to create community from above is contrary in principle to the fundamental values that have brought about success in the Barrio Devo model.

It is useful to think of the failed housing projects that became successes only when the units were sold to their occupants. Perhaps the generation that was never very comfortable with the "Gen X" label is too strong in individuality to experience a strong sense of connection with an environment provided by someone who presumes to know better than they who must live in it. Autonomous individuals want to build their own communities, write their own stories, make their own movies, and even web sites. "Do it yourself" may be more than a slogan from the underground youth culture in which most neo-bohemians participated. It is just what is demonstrated in this reflection on Barrio Devo.

Beyond this, there are other implausibilities in the idea that a privileged elite can build well for the masses. Autonomous individuals in community with one another are bad for business: They create, rather than consume. For the markets of capitalism to remain stable, there must be multiplex movie houses, strip malls, fast-food drive throughs, and a smoothly controlled, homogeneous media simulacrum, all presenting life-style and commodity "choices" that depend on a high level of alienation and anxiety. Not because of evil intentions, but simply because of the structure of capitalism, those who control building cannot afford to build community.

This reflection has explored the experience of community within a group of people who are in part defined by an architectural act, by their refusal of institutional architecture and avoidance of programmed public spaces. If architecture is to regain some ethical function, those who design and build must understand and respond to this vision of community and what it reveals about the current situation. Beyond listening to other architects, social theorists, and philosophers of architecture, those who hope to return architecture to an edifying social function need to look to the efforts of members of their own culture who are achieving some kind of success already. The frequent use of the term "crisis" in discussions such as this suggests that architects currently are not.

WORKS CITED

Debord, Guy. *Society of the Spectacle.* Detroit: Black and Red Press, 1968.

Harries, Karsten. *The Ethical Function of Architecture.* Cambridge: MIT Press, 1996.

Landscaping the Final Frontier
Narrative Spaces
We Live and Fly By

JANE DETWEILER

*As Americans use machines to transform space
into landscape (or to reconfigure an older landscape), they also construct narratives to make
sense of this activity. (Nye 6)*

*The desert offers itself as the white sheet on
which to trace a figure. It is the tabula rasa on
which man can write, as if for the first time, the
story he wants to live. (Tompkins 74)*

*The original space travel was hitching your
wagon to a star. (folk saying)*

As the United States space program forges ahead with its
efforts to "transform [S]pace into [known and habitable] landscape" (Nye 6) in the new millennium, several western states
are among those vying to become the point of departure for
the X-33, a prototype of a next-generation spacecraft, and
the VentureStar, the type, the "Space Shuttle of the 21st Century" (Sweetman 42). Development and deployment of the latter reusable launch vehicle (RLV) sustains hopes for many of
NASA's key projects, including an international space sta-

---

*Jane Detweiler is an assistant professor in the Department of
English, University of Nevada, Reno. She conducts research
into the discipline-specific writing practices of various academic
communities, into narrative as a way of knowing, and into
rhetorical theories-as-practices. She teaches courses in rhetoric, narrative theories, creative writing, research methods, non-
fiction writing, and first-year composition.*

tion, a lunar colony, and manned Mars explorations, because it offers vast improvements on the 1970s-vintage technology of the existing, aging space shuttle fleet (Cooper 369; Becker 50; Sweetman 43. See also NASA Strategic Plan). If the old western frontier states[1]—with their large, largely empty spaces—have their way, Florida's crowded Atlantic coast will no longer serve as the primary launch pad for high-profile missions[2] into "the final frontier": dry, dusty landscape of some kind would likely replace Cape Canaveral and its usually balmy salt marsh and seascape.[3]

And, if some legislators and a development corporation in my new home state have *their* way, it will be the desert landscape of the federal test site in south-central Nevada, arid and "pockmarked by decades of nuclear detonations," in which the spaceport will be built (Shouten, "Nevada Offers"). Whether or not these advocates succeed in securing more federal dollars, two thousand new jobs, and a stronger aerospace industry for the state remains to be seen. To many observers,

Figure 1. Artist's conception of (left to right) the X-33, the VentureStar, and the Space Shuttle (NASA).

Figure 2. The VentureStar as it might appear in flight (NASA).

making the case for this siting would seem a long shot, even "shooting for the moon." With the residual risks of other R&D pushes still decaying on and under the dry soils, what would entice Lockheed-Martin, prime contractor on the VentureStar project, to set up spaceshop in this blasted area?[4] Or, for that matter, what would encourage the local populace to accept new risks posed by a spaceport, which would be located fairly near the Yucca Mountain federal test repository for nuclear waste? Despite long political odds, I suggest that the rhetorical problems of making this case for space(flight) are not as intractable as they might initially seem, given the ways that American culture "landscapes" western space with new technology, and further given narratives about the place of machines and land in human existence. Even as I write this statement, I wonder whether I want the test site to be used as a "text site," as the symbolic space where our storytelling will metaphorically hitch our wagons to the stars.

For me, Nevada's arguments in pursuit of the spaceport are both personally and professionally engaging: As the daugh-

Figure 3. The Space Shuttle in its usual landscape (NASA).

ter of an electrical engineer who has worked all his professional life in the federal aerospace effort, as a citizen who is
concerned about the politics of land use, and as a rhetorician
who inquires into how communities narrate themselves and
their shared projects into being, I watch all the new space
projects with profound, profoundly conflicted interest. In this
case, I have the strong sense that, should Nevada Test Site
Development Corporation succeed in its efforts to persuade
various parties involved in the spaceport decision, its success will have depended, at least in part, on the resonant
connection between western lands and extraterrestrial spaces
in the technological landscaping Americans have long practiced. Here I would draw attention to how the word, "landscape," functions as both noun and verb, and thus comes to
have important and multiple implications in the narrative
construction of space in the West and beyond. Not only does
this word denote physical surroundings in their natural, un-
altered state, it also points to the processes with which humans transform those physical surroundings into
"composition[s] of space" which "serve as infrastructure or
background for . . . collective existence" (Jackson 8). As historian David Nye asks us to understand, "landscape is not

merely something seen[;] rather it is part of the essential in-frastructure of existence" (6). He believes that "landscape is a shared creation and a collective responsibility," a process and a product of applying the myriad technologies that humans use to shape their world (6). As a student of serious storytelling, I am intrigued with (and, to be precise, concerned about) the ways that these technologies are both figurative[5] and literal: the *techne*, or arts, used in (re)creating spaces for human habitation include both the social habits of thinking that enable engineering and warrant specific uses of machines, as well as the more concrete construction practices with which land is "machined" into collectively conceived, devised, and used spaces. So it is that shared narrative lore makes sense of technologies, explaining the need for particular uses or shapings of space and grounding ventures out into other "possible worlds" (Bruner).

As I read the storied West, the narrative grounds for ap-plications of technology have seemed oddly "all or nothing" ventures, with the popular imagination constructing a past largely evacuated of machinery and a future utterly filled with it. That is, the wide-open basin-and-range spaces have come to be overdetermined with what would seem mutually exclu-sive "landscapings" of emptiness, stories that lead people to imagine technology in quite opposed ways, and thus to dis-place and place machineries in white American settlement activities. In the following episodes, I spin my own tale about shared conceptions of the western past, about the futures necessarily captured in that past, and about my own place as the present, tense teller of this landscape and people's figu-rative machinations.

I. (O)missions: Deserting the Past

Since it was explored by white Americans in the nineteenth century, the western desert wilderness has apparently invited narratives that ignore the presence of technology altogether, even as the extremity of this land's living conditions demands intensive use of quite sophisticated machineries to support habitation by (mostly white) non-natives.[6] What most shared popular mythologies have in common is a central plot as-sumption that emptiness requires exploration, thus the vi-sion of a desert wilderness evokes questing, a traveling to

Figure 4. Cover page of Collier's *issue in which the future of space exploration was discussed by Wernher Von Braun and other luminaries (Heppenheimer 178. See also Piszkiewicz, Sheehan for more details).*

know and thus to master the land. In the most common packaging of western spaces, the classic Western in its textual and filmic incarnations, the open range or desert, the land itself, becomes the stage for the (usually solitary) human hero who "can conquer it by traversing it, know it by standing on it. Distance, made palpable through exposure and infinitely prolonged by absence of obstacles, offers unlimited room to move . . . the possibilities are infinite" (Tompkins 75). Technological or urban features—the railroad, the six-shooter, the ore cart, the barbed-wire fence, the telegraph—these are present, perhaps, but their importance is subsumed by the sheer presence of pristine and threatening wilderness into which the few humans struggle and for which they make personal, physical sacrifices. It is as if, as the land stretches out into infinite, wild distance in shared imagination, the physicality of heroic human figures in its midst are drawn in starker relief, their resoluteness and endurance underscored "in a field where a certain kind of mastery is possible, where a person (of a certain kind) can remain alone and complete and in control of himself, while controlling the external world through physical strength and force of will" (Tompkins 75). With a sweeping rhetorical gesture, two imageries are linked to sublimate the extensive, sophisticated technologies necessarily involved in creating actual living spaces for whites in actual western landscapes: The overt trials and lurking threats of pristine wilderness, and the shaping of that land by strength of human arm and will, tend to pull narrative focus away from the machineries that enabled most white settlers to survive.

It is not just the western film that underplays the machineries of progress with which Americans manifested their destiny in the last century. Most other popular and scholarly understandings of the West have also tended to neglect the role of technology in the transformation of the land: Here, too, the narratives of emptiness and personal domination have long framed such transformation as an agrarian, highly individualized effort, one in which settlers homesteaded steadily across a largely uninhabited space, contending with the solitude and danger of the wilderness (e.g., Frederick Jackson Turner). More recently, this storyline has been adapted to account for the fact that the western spaces were, in fact, anciently inhabited by native peoples whom the settlers and

Figure 5. One conception of the space plane. Note the mountainous "western" setting (NASA).

their governments had to remove in order to empty the frontier for settlement. And the heroics of the settler-character have been refigured to account for frontier women's experience in the wilds as well.

Nye would have us consider yet another sort of landscaping tale, one less often acknowledged but perhaps all the more powerful for its relative unconsciousness: In the vast, empty frontier of the West, settlement required and received substantial application of what were for the time highly advanced technologies. Although "in the imagination the West often seems pre-technological, as if it alone among the regions remained an elemental battleground between [hu]man[s] and nature . . . the most powerful force in the settlement of the West [was] the technolog[y] that white Americans had at their command" (Nye 26). By centralizing such phenomena as the building of transcontinental railroads and telegraph communications, as well as the electrification of the western states, Nye's new narrative attempts to account for the extraordinary rapidity of migration and growth of urban areas in the West in comparison to the settlement of other American regions. Where the pattern of settlement from the Atlantic seaboard to the Mississippi readily fits into a wilderness-to-agrarian-to-urban model, western migration might best be understood in a different chronological sequence: "First came the mining west, itself a technological phenomenon dependent on railroads and other forms of advanced technology. This stimulated the urban west, particularly Denver and San Francisco. Third . . . came the agricultural west, itself split by ranching and farming interests, and, fourth, the regions that remained became significant precisely because they were undeveloped, or wilderness" (Nye 27).

In this account, the transformation of western space into human-habitable landscape has its origins underground, in the mines that opened those desert or mountain wildernesses considered impractical or impossible for farming uses. Barren vastnesses yielded valuable ores, the first white travelers found, but only with heavy investment in labor and transportation to remove these materials, then to return with all sup-

Figure 6. Another rendering of the space plane, this time with the international space station in the distance (NASA).

Figure 7. Three different designs for a reusable launch vehicle, or RLV (NASA).

plies needed to support miners and their continued excavation in deserted, wild areas: food, clothing, lumber, tools, clean water, and so on. Very quickly, mining businesses shifted their investments into labor-saving, yield-increasing technologies that sped up financial returns: Railroads replaced animal pack trains; electric lighting replaced candles and kerosene lanterns; electric or steam engines replaced human and animal lifting power (29). Here, too, prior to nearly anywhere else in America, newly designed hydroelectric dams and petroleum-powered generators were extensively employed to furnish electricity, which was then fed on grids to the remotest reaches of western interior space, miles underground—hardly to mention into the streets and homes of new municipalities that sprang up frenziedly around or above the lodes (22-43).

Such sublimation of life-sustaining, business-advancing technology still continues to mark representations of the landscape in the West. Diorama-like presentations and glass-cased collections at historical sites tend to include the merest nods to such *public*, infrastructural uses of technology as Nye describes. One enters a deserted mining town like Berlin or Bodie or Calico, and nearly all the artifacts presented are, technically, evidence of the *personal* technologies brought to bear on the problem of living as a contemporary white American in the hinterlands: the hat-stretchers, ruffle irons, concertinas, eyeglasses, pocket Bibles, compasses, buttonhooks, whetstones, sheet music, and so on that can be imagined easily into the work-hardened hands of a miner, his "girlfriend," or his wife. What might be considered public and occupational technologies are also evident, but the giant flywheels and mine elevator frames, Model Ts and railroad axles, rust motionless like strange megaliths, bespeaking none of their past uses, their contribution to what must have been substantial urban hurly-burly in the desert vastness. Wood frame houses, maintained in a conservator's semi-stasis, gradually deteriorate beneath their porcelain insulators and street side power poles. Even in similar towns where time does not wholly pretend to stand still (Virginia City, Nevada, comes to mind), the emphasis is on the romantic low-tech, as tourists are steered past glass-covered faro tables, sledge hammers, and assay paraphernalia, toward the do-it-yourself goldpanning or the authentic two-mile railroad trip. It's easy to forget, even in this land where piles of sulphur-colored mine tailings sprawl interspersed with rusting technological hulks of various kinds, that this might be considered the origin and dominant developmental site for much of human existence in the present-day desert West; the family farm or ranch, while certainly present on the scene, likely was not dominant (the tourist's "Ponderosa Ranch" and other simulations of simulations notwithstanding).

Consider, as well, how "pristine" western wildernesses have been packaged into national parks, with sophisticated transportation and reproduction technologies that make it possible first to see some remote "natural" scene, then to take representations of it home, to seem to own it, to feel as if one knows it (Nye). These primitive islands seem to remain frozen in the pastness of the past—thusly parceled out for human uses, symbolic and recreational—even as tourists drive minivans through them clad in technical or high tech clothing and shoes (See also Fenimore on this point). Most of us, I suggest, tend to omit from mental note the technologies, both symbolic and literal, involved in western adventures. The machines are hidden behind (or, perhaps, in the holster bouncing at the hip of) the large, stark figure of the emigrant who is followed, riding out toward a new, empty frontier. Somehow, technology and wilderness cannot occupy the same narrative space, though the natural threats embedded in our conceptions of desert wilderness, and with good empirical reason, have always warranted use of life-sustaining technologies. For most of the white folks migrating through and into the harsh landscape, this technology has most often been preceded by adjectives like "high," "latest," or "advanced," or, of course, these words' nineteenth-century equivalents.

II. Missions: Desert Futurisms Beyond

The physical landscape in the western frontiers lends itself to other cultural adventures into emptinesses, other efforts impelled by scarcities imagined or actual: those exploration, mapping, and settling projects launched outward into what a famous starship captain termed the "Final Frontier." To the sci-fi film as to the Western, our imagined desert lends its contours, this time for magnifying the technological features of lived existence, and upon these premises we build a place in Space. As David Fenimore notes, the extreme starkness of the western terrains has made them perfect stand-ins for filmic landscaping of space; indeed, he suggests, the actual landscape has "been so thickly overlaid with futuristic frontier narratives that many of us, gazing across the basins and ranges, cannot help but see in our mind's eye the glint of sun on curved titanium alloy, the flare of rocket exhaust, or at night the mysterious colored lights" (184). And it is, after all, usually across deserts (or their visual double, barren snowscapes) that heroes like Paul Maud'dib and Luke Skywalker carry their laser guns or light sabers, leading a ragtag group of settlers to victory in a range war, of sorts. Captain Kirk with his expendable crew member, the space marine troopers of television's "Above and Beyond," and various extraterrestrial aliens in ads have clambered on the odd, tilting shapes of Vasquez Rocks in the Mojave, or striven to cross the white flatness of the Black Rock Desert, the curved whiteness of White Sands.

In the last smidgen of this century, it was common knowledge that indeed the surfaces of various other planets do resemble the rubbled and rocky, sand-strewn and windblown topographies right here in the left half of the country—minus the plants and animals, of course. Local deserts have also been sites where new kinds of space-exploration vehicles are tested; they move from emptiness to emptiness, so to speak; and in this sense, terrestrial and extraterrestrial deserts are perhaps first landscaped to be put to use: changed, terraformed for human existence. Since robotic rovers and sojourners have crawled in actual and simulated deserts, both nearby and far away, it is not much of a leap at all to place much larger space vehicles in this patch of Earth. Our futuristic mind's eye tends to blur western landspaces and Space; in both, the tall spacecraft stands vertical, a man-made butte among the natural ones that quickly become unseen parts of the scene.[7]

Popular mythic connections between the West and Space have also been invoked for a public, political efforts at landscaping extraterrestrial spaces for human habitation. Like the emigrant advertisements of the last century, the efforts to mine public dollars for research and development have begun to use the language of conquering empty spaces, converting them for human use. The history of NASA's space programs is replete with allusions linking astronauts to cowboys, the Soviets to potential squatters on lunar lands Americans would homestead for themselves, the push to plant a flag on the Moon to staking an explorer's (or a miner's) claim. Adopting a rhetoric of sacrifice—and *competitive spirit*—that likely lent meaning to many a homesteader's struggles in the century preceding his own, John F. Kennedy exhorted the public to join him in efforts to land an American explorer on barren lunar wastes:

> The exploration of space will go ahead whether we join it or not, and it is one of the great adventures of all time, and no nation which expects to be the leader of other nations can expect to stay behind in this race for space. . . . We choose to go to the moon in this decade, and do the other things, *not* because they are easy, but because they are *hard* . . . Because that goal will serve to organize and measure the best of our abilities and skills, because that challenge is one that we are willing to accept, one we are unwilling to postpone, and one we intend to win. (Heppenheimer 185,

Chapter 7 *passim*. See also Chaikin 2, Breuer 160-
75. Emphasis in original).

In Kennedy's time and in our own, the visual rhetoric to
complement such verbal expressions has relied heavily on a
sort of natural minimalism, a deserted flatness or curvedness,
a high-country spareness that, again, foregrounds the technology involved in getting humans into such a scene, in making this landscape habitable. Here, however, the vistas of absence are sometimes truly meant to represent the complete
absence of matter[8], as in the "astronaut's eye views" captured in the famous 1952 Collier's cover (see Figure 4) or more
recent artists' mockups of the agency's anticipated space
planes and reusable launch vehicles (see Figures 5-7).
Obviously, such sceneries are crafted not just to encourage humankind to make the leap into nothingness. The language of the land rush has been yoked to the project of colo-
nizing other heavenly deserts, especially the red sands of
Mars.[9] Just as the "empty" space of the western plains and
deserts offered a blank sheet on which to write the story of
human struggle for habitation, so does the uninhabited surface of Mars provide available land—land suddenly figured as
scarce on the Earth. In a popularizer's contribution to ongoing confabulations about the need for manned missions to
explore the red planet, Robert Zubrin and Richard Wagner[10]
draw into their "Mars Direct" argument all the resonances of
futuristic western landscaping. Zubrin and Wagner's publicly
persuasive[11] "case for Mars" frames their critical response to
recent NASA project proposals, which favor investing in the
technologically complex and thus expensive intermediate steps
of a space station or lunar space colony; only when these
stages are accomplished might a similarly complex and pricey
manned Mars space vehicle be built and launched. The more
direct route would be to forego the substantial effort of providing for all human and transportation needs, roundtrip, to
Mars and back. Instead, designers would consider ways to
send unmanned machines designed to manufacture, for example, oxygen for the astronauts and fuel for their vehicle's
return trip. For humans to walk on the barren, rocky plains
of the red planet in the near term, say Zubrin and Wagner,

we simply need to use some common sense and employ the technologies we have at hand to travel light and "live off the land," just as was done by nearly every successful program of terrestrial exploration undertaken in the past. Living off the land—intelligent use of local resources—is not just the way the West was won; it's the way the Earth was won, and it's also the way that Mars can be won. (2)

Like the settlers in their Conestogas, the astronauts headed for Mars would be prepared for extended isolation in bleak, alien surroundings; also like their frontier forebears, they would have advanced technology to support their efforts.

As I consider Zubrin and Wagner's carefully articulated plans, I wonder how similar are their futurisms to those of the last century's emigrant outfitters and mining recruiters; and I wonder if I will look around many years hence and notice that the pastness of the past has yet again rendered the technology humans use familiar to the point of invisibility. Without weighing the appropriateness of transforming Martian environments in the first place, nor considering whether the money and talent expended on Mars might be used to improve conditions on the planet that would be deserted, these two modern-day emigrant recruiters spin out a homesteader's yarn, frankly elaborating on the various "terraforming" activities that must eventually be undertaken in order to establish the colony on the red planet. These writers continually downplay the sophistication of the as-yet undeveloped technologies required for human habitation beyond mere survival, such as machinery to convert the thin carbon dioxide atmosphere into breathable air, barrier materials from which to make domes, building materials that would enable underground living, ways to grow plants. Granted, articulating these designs is far beyond the scope of the persuasive task Zubrin and Wagner set themselves. Yet it seems to me that the "Mars Direct" exploration-to-pastoral narrative reiterates the time-worn plot with which the popular imagination still landscapes the West into an empty stage, within which technologies (and the sometimes environmentally unfortunate sequelae of their use) tend to, with time, vanish from public consciousness. "Mars is not just a destination for explorers or an object of scientific inquiry," Zubrin and Wagner write, "[I]t is a *world*. . . .

Figure 8. Artist's rendering of the initial Mars habitations proposed by NASA (NASA). Zubrin and Wagner criticize NASA's intermediate stages of a major space station and a lunar colony before the first trips to Mars; however, these writers agree with NASA that an early "conestoga" type craft would be similar to this one.

The resources of Mars could someday make the Red Planet a home not just for a few explorers, but for a dynamic society of millions of colonists building a new way of life in a new world. . . . a new set of utilization technologies will have to be developed and demonstrated. . . . To do this we will need a substantial base on the planet where an intense program can be carried out" (171-72). In this landscaping of newly open Space, imaginative sublimation of machineries begins even as these writers wind their argument to a close. The ending of this Martian version of the settler's epic finds the complexity of the necessary technology ultimately diminishing, as Zubrin and Wagner sketch out schemes for making bricks of Martian concrete, move swiftly into above-ground air-containing buildings, and then emphasize that mere masks will soon be all that is required for humans to breathe easily in their new, red-skyed home in rusty, rocky alien soils.

Unlikely, yes, that I will wander through historical sites on Mars, where the new century's emigrants will have put down roots. In Bradburyesque daydreams, however, I see from my imagined self's vantage the hologram-histories replaying the arrival stories, alongside collections of artifacts that evidence the personal technologies involved in bringing contemporary humans to these furthest hinterlands: stasis pods, eyeshields, gravity-increasing exercise gear, do-it-yourself emergency surgery kits, sonic cleaners, nano-ROM readers, carbon dioxide scrubber masks, hermetically-sealable oxygen-generating puptents that can be imagined easily into the work-hardened hands of a settler. The public technologies of survival infrastructure will probably be rusting away somewhere outside, strange monuments to an early high-tech urban life, vague referents to the power companies' and mining interests' pursuits, relics of the time when the red planet was not so green as it is "now." A few of the first domes, maintained in conservator's stasis, do not deteriorate (except in barely observable microcycles, to maintain the semblance of time's passage) beneath their static electricity collectors and microwave communications equipment. Et cetera.

Perhaps—I hope—the necessarily international constitution of the Martian emigrant population will texture the shared landscaping efforts with some more complicated storytelling and more reflexive technological assumptions. The narrative premises on which the popular (and in this case, aerospace professioinal) mythmaking of the Final Frontier must offer alternatives, if we are not simply to pursue what have become the customary ways of structuring natural spaces for our common existence—and to endure all the environmental problems that have attended our narrations and machinations to this point.

III. I/Entermission

As I said at the outset, I watch recent developments in the Nevada spaceport wooing with a great deal of interest, given my personal and professional histories. While as a lover of the land, I'm grumbly about the development in "my" piece of the desert, as a "hot-eyed moderate," I am usually trying to balance environmental and human concerns, and as a closet

Figure 9. Another artist's rendering of human habitations on Mars (NASA).

technophile[12] I am eagerly collecting information about the latest space exploration pursuits—technologies which could upset the balances I pursue. What I feel in reading about the Nevada Test Site as a potential spaceport is a strange mix of horror (What if the VentureStar crashes into Yucca Mountain? Or if rocket fuels get into the already potentially contaminated groundwater?), morbid amusement (variations on jokes about glow-in-the-dark astronauts run through my head), critical fascination (If the development folks make this case work, why will it have succeeded?), and excitement (I've got to get myself a seat on the bleachers to watch those spaceships blast off!). Mostly, I think about the ways that, even more than my love of science fiction and the movies, what seemed to me ordinary events of family life shaped me to be at ease with the idea of rocket ships in the desert rangelands.

My father has devoted his entire career as an electrical engineer to the national aerospace programs, working on the microwave radio transmissions that help push human inquiry outward to the stars. Before I knew all the details of what this meant, I knew that he made traveling wave tubes, tiny parts that went in radios for satellites and deep-space probes. Certificates on our family-room wall announced that he had invented several new varieties of these delicate hearing and speaking mechanisms. I connected the framed documents and his professional tinkering with the strange workscape he showed me with pride on "the Lab's" open house days. As he put it, he tested equipment in what looked to my untrained child's eye vaguely like ovens, washing machines, automated car wash arms. These unfamiliar labor saving devices were, however, draped with a scientific glamor: keyboards and switches, small glinty view ports, wires of all colors stretched here and there on plugboards, screens wrought over with phosphorescent traceries, needled gauges, and glimmery red readouts. What these machineries captured my dad often brought home to us in the form of photographs and other representations of the planets, viewed from afar and on the surface, until I had a substantial collection of Saturns and Jupiters and Mars-scapes with which to amaze my friends. Add to the mix my fascination with science fiction, and my child's world centered on a family hero who would someday

*Figure 10. Deep Space Network (DSN) 13, a 30-meter an-
tenna, at Goldstone Reservation, near Barstow (Courtesy of
JPL/Caltech/NASA.).*

make it possible for the spiderlike machines collecting rocks
on Mars to have astronaut drivers.

    Deserts have always been, for me, scenes of connection
with my father and his Space. In them, I tended to overlook
the stark oddness of human constructions that intruded. Even
though I had internalized much of the seventies' Earth First
attitude, the rocket test stands and satellite antenna networks
peeping out from behind sharp-shouldered ridges were no
more worthy of mention than our family car and the abandoned homesteaders' shacks along the interstate's sweep
through the Mojave. I would lose sight of the delicate ecosystems I had learned about in school and on TV, wanting to see
instead how wonderful Dad was (and I sometimes still do,

Figure 11. DSN14, a 70-meter antenna, at Goldstone. Note the vehicles and buildings below, which offer some visual scale (Courtesy of JPL/Caltech/NASA).

because he still is). Once we reached our destination, he could move a thirty-meter antenna—a round building, topped with a white dish as big as a house—around on its concrete pad, swirling me with him on its circular catwalk: a stately, slow, machined dance in the desert spaces where other giant satellite dishes stood picket duty, dustless in the Goldstone sun. He would lean out from the control room, grinning proudly. I would hold the railing, gleeful at the slow promenade of gleaming white bowls in their skeletal frames. Later, we stood together on the desert gravels beneath the seventy-meter antenna and watched repairmen crawl antlike more than ten stories up. There would be no dance on this giant disk: "refitting" kept it still in the blue air, rules about wearing steel toed shoes kept us have-nots on the ground. But in my mind's ear, I clung to that topmost arch over the antenna's bowl, my father beside me "adjusting the gain," both of us straining to catch the inaudible hum from the stars.

So, as teller of tales about our common spatial figures and futures, I always suspect myself; I know that for me, this landscape and these machines are troped together in familiar ways, in all the senses of this term, and hence tacitly already plotted into particular significance. At such moments of self-reflexiveness, I draw on another filial inheritance: my father's humorous, rigorous skepticism with regard to "information," its shapings and its uses. Equally impatient with the abuses of physical laws in science fiction's worlds and with the machinations of some industries in the real world, my father taught me to investigate carefully how and what we know of worlds. (Even the ones in which spacecraft on which he worked were sent to collect information about other worlds.)

It is with his relentless, caring curiosity that I suggest we take up the new terraforming of the test site and of the deserted frontiers beyond. Before the VentureStar first lifts off, we will have irretrievably linked notions about our familiar terrain to that one as yet unknown, landscaped it with dreams of machines, made its space human-habitable. Just as the "knowledge base of a tool or tool system that we call technology . . . is essentially a cognitive construct in a social setting" (Van Nostrand 32), so also is the information gathered with that technology embedded in shared notions about what is valued, accepted interpretations; it thus becomes knowledge (33-34). And it compels thoughtful people to, as Anne Berthoff puts it so gnomically, "know our knowledge," its selections and exclusions, dreams and forgetfulness.

What we do know of our potential Text Site, which might provide us symbolic and actual "essential infrastructure for existence"? Surely the technological imageries that constellated with our *other* race with the Soviets have not dimmed, though certainly it is difficult to conjure them up, out in the wilderness visible from where one is allowed to drive or stand; today, it would take an illegal flyover (or perhaps participation in a VentureStar launch) to get a sense of just what disruption past concerns over national security have entailed. Photographs and films of the mushroom clouds or of dramatic, implosive landslides tend not to remain viscerally compelling as their undeniably dangerous products decompose invisibly out there, somewhere in the scrub and sagebrush. Do we need to apply, yet again, our narrative configurations and other technologies to this thoroughly disrupted plot of ground?

What concerns me is that this time, we storytellers would not be crafting the old frontier earth itself for living space, for few would choose to live where the testing took place (nor would they, for that matter, in the landscape Earth is likely to become should humankind not devote its energies fully to careful stewardship). Instead, the Nevada Test Site Development Corporation would lead us in building a leaping-off point for the great, settle-able and sellable landscape in the sky. And we might, like Zubrin and Wagner, invoke the influential narrative "hypothesis" articulated so long ago by the historian F. J. Turner, which dictates a "no looking back" frame, again, for landscaping Space as our Final Frontier:

> To the frontier the American intellect owes its striking characteristics . . . that coarseness of strength and inquisitiveness; that practical, inventive turn of mind, quick to find expedients; that masterful grasp for

Figure 12. Artist's conception of a spaceport to occupy some flat, deserted landscape (NASA).

material things, lacking in the artistic but powerful to effect great ends; that restless, nervous energy; that dominant individualism, working to good or evil, and withal that buoyancy and exuberance that comes from freedom—these are the traits of the frontier, or traits called out elsewhere because of the existence of the frontier . . . . each frontier . . . furnish[es] a new opportunity, a gate of escape from the bondage of the past; and freshness, and confidence, and scorn of older society, impatience of its restraints and its ideas, and indifference to its lessons, have accompanied the frontier. (Turner qtd. in Zubrin and Wagner 295-96)

I have to say that I hope that it will not be such a past-evading, future-obsessed metastory into which we westerners will write ourselves along with the land we share. I am reminded of Arthur Danto's admonition that, contrary to popular belief, it is not that the future is open and the past closed; rather, people endlessly rewrite an open past to project, and thus attempt to (fore)close, the futures they would have come to pass. As teller of this tale, I offer it in trust that there must be some way to retain a "presents" of mind that neither erases technology as a central feature of the past, nor wholly populates the future with machines as demonstrations of human mastery over land. (Neither unreflexive denial nor uncritical acceptance serves us well.)

What needs considering is how, in the next century, westerners might place the outcomes of any narrative reasoning in the balance when weighing particular landswaps for anticipated technological and financial gains. Surely folks around here are cagey enough to understand the risks necessarily implied however, whenever we go about crafting Space for our spacecraft.[13]

NOTES

[1]The spaceport site list includes such western states as Texas, Utah, Washington, Oklahoma, New Mexico, Montana, Idaho, Arizona, and California; the list of non-western spaceport bidders includes South Carolina, Virginia, North Carolina, Louisiana, and Florida (Shouten, "Nevada Offers" 1).

[2]There are, of course, many lower-profile launch sites and launches: The Department of Defense and other federal agencies do

launch space vehicles from sites other than Cape Canaveral.

[3]Despite the rapid increase in population density around Cape Canaveral, this site remains a front runner for any launch effort for the same reason it was initially selected: "It . . . supplanted White Sands as the nation's principal missile center because it faced the Atlantic and had a clear range of ten thousand miles directly off the coast" (Heppenheimer 113).

[4]Shouten notes that Nevada legislators are pointing to the good weather (many flying days) and the already-secured air space over the test site as the best selling points ("Nevada Best").

[5]De Lauretis, along with Foucault, theorizes "technologies" of social construction, specifically "technologies of gender" which shape our experience of being in physically gendered bodies. In this case, I think that Nye's discussion needs a little elaboration on this point, since he tends to see technologies primarily in terms of how machines are implicated in the shaping of particular landscapes: ways of thinking about the world impel particular uses of technology. Since I find De Lauretis' arguments persuasive, I would add that the processes of social construction Nye invokes are themselves "technologies." Hence, here I mention "figurative and literal technologies."

[6]Obviously, there *are* cultural discourses that foreground for critique the presence of technology in wilderness spaces: As in other regions, in the West, environmental activists continue to point out the destructiveness of human technological intervention in desert areas. However, I argue that these critical discourses, while persuasive in local discussions centering on specific issues, have not captured the shared, national imagination in the ways that the narratives I discuss in this article apparently continue to do. In fact, the technological unconsciousness operating within the romantic visions perpetuates the problems that the environmentalists work to address. To succeed, it seems to me, activists will need to account for this in their efforts.

[7]In other representations of Space, as in the scenes Tompkins notes in western films, our eyes are also drawn to the human figure, stepped down (from the machine, in this case, rather than a horse), tramping bootprints into remote and moveless sands.

[8]I realize that cosmologists and astrophysicists would likely argue this characterization of the space between planets, noting that there might be so-called "dark matter" in what we conceive to be utter absence of matter (See Ferris 39, 121-44, 159, 327 for a good introduction to this discussion). However, until such theories find some empirical verification, this "complete absence of matter" is my story and I'm sticking to it.

[9]See also Senate/101st Congress/Document No. 101-24 for an excellent introduction, which was originally composed as a national high school debate topic resource.

[10]To be fair to their discussion, I must allow that Zubrin and Wagner actually argue for a non-RLV push to Mars: one that need not necessarily involve the preliminary steps of the international space station and/or a lunar colony that the Shuttle's successor will help to build. These writers critique the aforementioned projects for needlessly complicating the technology required, and would probably argue against putting money into the VentureStar space plane at the center of my own discussion about the siting of a spaceport in the Nevada desert. Zubrin and Wagner suggest investing the money in a non-reusable launch vehicle like the Saturn IV or V rocket. Their discussion is, however, the best current example of the kind of Mars-related narrative argumentation I am examining, which shows up elsewhere in sundry other proposals for Space program-related projects.

[11]Zubrin and Wagner's book was financially successful, a national trade bestseller for a number of weeks. It has endured mixed reactions in scientific and aerospace-technical circles.

[12]Some informants, such as my partner and my long-time friends, will offer the corrective view that I am, in their opinion, an unabashed gadget geek, and my love affair with machines tends to fixate me on earthmovers in general and those forklifts that wreak so much traffic havoc at Home Depot in particular.

[13]In case anyone reading this has the power to nominate me, I am willing to become "the first rhetorician in space."

REFERENCES

Becker, Pamela. "X-33 Program Signals New Approach for NASA." *Mechanical Engineering* Sept. 1996: 50.

Berthoff, Ann. *Reclaiming the Imagination.* Portsmouth, NH: Boynton/Cook, 1984.

Breuer, William B. *Race to the Moon: America's Duel with the Soviets.* Westport, CT: Praeger, 1993.

Bruner, Jerome. *Actual Minds, Possible Worlds.* Cambridge: Harvard UP, 1990.

Chaikin, Andrew. *A Man on the Moon.* New York: Penguin/Putnam, 1994.

Cooper, Mary H. "Space Program's Future." *CQ Researcher* 7.16 (25 Apr. 1997): 361-84.

Danto, Arthur. *Narration and Knowledge.* New York: Columbia UP, 1985.

De Lauretis, Teresa. *Technologies of Gender: Essays on Theory, Film, and Gender.* Bloomington: Indiana UP, 1987.

Fenimore, David. "Singing Cowboys on the Moon: The Exogeographic West." *Western Technological Landscapes.* Halcyon Ser. 20. Reno: Nevada Humanities Committee, 1998.

Ferris, Timothy. *The Whole Shebang: A State of the Universe(s) Re-*

port. New York: Simon and Schuster, 1997.

Heppenheimer, T. A. *Countdown: A History of Space Flight.* New York: John Wiley and Sons, 1997.

Jackson, J. B. *Discovering the Vernacular Landscape.* New Haven: Yale U P, 1984.

National Aeronautics and Space Administration. "Strategic Plan: 1997." <http://www.hq.nasa.gov/office/nsp>.

Nye, David E. *Narratives and Spaces: Technology and the Construction of American Culture.* New York: Columbia UP, 1997.

Piszkiewicz, Dennis. *The Nazi Rocketeers: Dreams of Space and Crimes of War.* Westport, CT: Praeger, 1995.

Sheehan, William. *The Planet Mars: A History of Observation and Discovery.* Tucson: U Arizona P, 1997.

Shouten, Fredreka. "Nevada Offers Desert Test Site as Home for Next Generation of U.S. Spacecraft: Project Could Create 2,000 Jobs in State." *Reno Gazette-Journal* 30 Sept. 1998, 1A.

———. "Nevada Best for Spaceport, Officials Say." *Reno Gazette-Journal* 30 Sept. 1998, 4A.

Sweetman, Bill. "VentureStar: 21st Century Space Shuttle." *Popular Science* (Oct. 1996): 42-44.

Tompkins, Jane. *West of Everything: The Inner Life of Westerns.* New York: Oxford UP, 1992.

United States Cong. Senate. *Outer Space: What Should be the United States Government Policy Toward the Region Beyond Earth's Atmosphere?* 101-24, Washington: GPO,1989.

Van Nostrand, A. D. *Fundable Knowledge: The Marketing of Defense Technology.* Mahwah, NJ: Lawrence Erlbaum, 1997.

Zubrin, Robert, and Richard Wagner. *The Case for Mars: The Plan to Settle the Red Planet and Why We Must.* New York: Touchstone, 1997.

Re-reading the Desert in Hypertranslation

BEVERLEY CURRAN

Terre, poussière, un paysage sans fenêtre, sans abri. Terre observée du silence, beauté antérieure, le désert est indescriptible. (149)/ Earth, dust, a landscape without windows, without shelter. Observed land of silence, pre-existent beauty, the desert is indescribable. (138)

—Nicole Brossard

What drove me to this obsession? The beauty of language, the character of Mélanie, the images flying about in my head as I was reading? The all-encompassing nature of Brossard's project and its confluence with my own cultural practice of revealing the process of production? My fear of the future?

—Adriene Jenik

In writing her novel, *Le désert mauve*, Nicole Brossard, one of Quebec's most important writers, and a crucial feminist writer and theorist, was interested in "translation as an act of passage . . . the transformation of a reality."[1] "My intention," she says, was "to translate myself from French to French" (1996), and in the novel, the process of translation

Beverley Curran is an associate professor at Aichi Shukutoku College in Nagoya, Japan. She is interested in the figure and process of translation in Canadian writing. A version of this paper was presented at the Joint Annual Meeting of the Western Literature Association and the Canadian Association for American Studies in Banff, Alberta, October, 1998. An abridged version appears in Style's *special issue,* Style in the Media Age, *edited by Craig Saper.*

takes place within one language, between language and body, and in the writing of a woman's tongue. Interrupting her own writing process in order to read and imagine, Brossard developed her novel as an "interactive discourse,"[2] a dialogue between two versions of a story, between two writers, one of whom is an active reader: a translator.

Brossard's provocative writing has obsessed many readers and inspired some brilliant translations. One of these is Adriene Jenik's CD-ROM translation, *Mauve Desert*. From her first reading of the English translation of Brossard's novel, Jenik realized that she had found a book that would transform her own life.[3] Much like Maude Laures, the translator within the text, the process of translation was for Jenik not entirely one of choice: "Non, je ne suis pas libre d'oublier *le Désert mauve* quand bien même il en irait de mon propre équilibre" (148)/ "No, I am not at liberty to forget *Mauve Desert* even if my equilibrium were at stake" (137). But while Maude Laures was left to imagine dialogues with the author of the novel that had seduced her, that she was driven to translate, Jenik enjoyed the luxury of knowing her author, and talking to her about translating this work into moving images.[4] As she explained in a letter to Brossard, exploring the possibility of her project at an early stage, Jenik was fascinated with, "not only the transformation from written words to image-sounds, or from French to English, but also the movement from North to South, from night to day, from your generation to mine."[5] The translation from print to electronic text recaptures that process' "root sense of movement through language . . . of language that moves" (Hayles 804).

Brossard's novel is a structural triptych, consisting of Laure Angstelle's novel, *Le désert mauve*, and a translation of Angstelle's book, *Mauve, l'horizon*, by Maude Laures. In the space between the two sites of writing, the translator imagines the possibilities of the text she has read, creating a fluid dimension of desire, a "space to swim with the words" (Brossard 1996). Alice Parker locates Brossard's prolific writing project in "the overlapping space between the epistemological crisis of modernism and the ontological crisis of postmodernism":

> Epistemology is in crisis because the production of knowledge and our access to it have undergone dras-

tic transformations in the electronic age. The emphasis for half a century has been on new modes of processing and transmitting data, while a postcolonial, global community has unsettled former power arrangements whereby information was disseminated. Ontology is in crisis because revised philosophical and scientific insights have forced us to rearticulate who/ what we are and what world(s) we inhabit. (*Liminal* 5-6)

Or as the question is posed within *Le désert mauve*, "La réalité avait un sens, mais lequel"(28)/ "Reality had a meaning, but which one?" (25).

Brossard, in a discussion with Jenik included in the CD-ROM translation, says that "before the idea of the novel had definitely shaped itself," she knew that it would be in "a hot place, where the weather, *la température*, would be almost unbearable; people would be sweating; the light would be difficult." That site became the American southwestern desert because of its beauty and danger, its timelessness and history; and because in the desert there are the "traces of the decadence of civilization" in the litter of old bottles and the abandoned, rusting cars. Brossard imagined the desert through the images and words of books about the desert, appropriating the flowers and cacti that excited her through naming, through language. Her translator, Maude Laures, too, found the desert as a dimension of her reading.

But Jenik locates the site of translation in the desert where she lives, and writes the desert from her own experience as well as from her desire:

> I live out in the desert, and essentially the desert has been seen as this kind of trashcan, a waste land for all the worst of civilization. And I feel like everything that's going on in the desert right now, and particularly Yucca Mountain, is something that people don't know about . . . and it's urgent. (Interview)[6]

In her CD-ROM translation, Jenik creates a space, "un paysage, une énigme dans laquelle je m'enfonçais à chaque lecture" (143)/ "a landscape, an enigma entered with each reading" (133). Originally conceived as a film, the interactive reading is full of movement and images, the hypertext imposed on the print surfaces of maps and the novel tattooed with the inked notes of Jenik, the active reader. The process of production is consciously on display, as Jenik "shows the seams" of her work by including scenes of the video shoot and her correspondence with Brossard about the project within her translation. "I was a layer in that progression that needed to exist in order for the person that was watching the CD to feel that they were the next level," says Jenik (Interview). And indeed, as Sue Ellen Case points out, "The pleasures of the text are located neither in plot nor in character, but in an obsession with a prior print text that performs its own obsession with a depiction of a particular terrain and images of people and things within it" (648).

That obsession, though, does not prevent Jenik from translating the desert closer to her own desires as a reader. The trajectories within the novel and the CD-translation still link the desert with Montreal, but Jenik links Maude Laures with Brossard by using Brossard's voice as the voice of the translator on her CD-ROM, and adds another dimension to her translation: her own hypertext-making. In Mélanie's car, the user finds three maps in the glove compartment: Mélanie's Map, a road map of the desert site of Mélanie's story; a walking map of Montreal, where Brossard and Maude Laures, the translator, live; and the location of a library of texts which juxtapose the desert, nuclear waste disposal, intelligent machines, and lesbian desire. The Maker Map is inscribed on a close-up of Jenik's face, locating Jenik in the text through her reading, and the text located within her through the making of her translation[7]:

> I felt it was important for me not to hide my subjectivity behind the work. It was important to me to implicate myself, as an English speaker, mainly; and important that I position myself geographically, in order to continue that cycle so that the person watching the CD would include themself in it, too. (Jenik Interview)

Brossard's print triptych is "a pretext and a post-text, with a long analysis of translation as a third term that mediates between them" (Parker, *Liminal* 130); hypertranslation extends the novel's investigation of "narrativity as interactive discourse" (130) by translating the translator, situated simultaneously inside/outside the story, present "in the medium of their dissolution" (Joyce 237).

In the first screen, filled with the sound of insects and then cars, and the blinking neon of a motel sign, a woman's voice (Jenik's) gently cautions the reader to drive carefully: "As you drive *Mauve Desert*, I hope you keep in mind where you sit and what drives you to understand."

> The introductory screens are placed in such a way that all background material about the book, the characters, and how to drive the CD-ROM can be impetuously passed in one's rush to drive *Mauve Desert*. If this happens you are driving at your own peril, since you may not be able to piece together what is happening. My hope is not to produce confusion or obfuscation, but rather to set up a situation in which, like Mélanie, you learn that even in interactive media there are consequences for your actions. (AJ)

The CD drives the story off the page, off the main road, and into the desert (*désir*), the dimension of desire. The reader, drives with Mélanie, Angstelle's 15-year-old narrator whom Jenik describes as "Brossard's picture of a desiring force" (AJ), tuning in the radio for French, English, or Spanish versions of the story, or reaching into the glove compartment to select a map, Mélanie's notebook, or a revolver. As Jenik intended, the reader is always conscious of her own activity, her own presence within the site of the story as Mélanie's eyes seek hers in the rear view mirror.

Jenik conflates the landscapes of reading and reality in hypertranslation to offer another version of the desert/*désir*, and another form of translation which, as Carolyn Guertin describes it in "Hovering Between: Canadian Hypertextual Discourse," is "not simply a different language, but a different way of seeing. . . . The creation of a new interactive intertext involves the visualization of a different potential reality that is inherently collaborative." As Michael Joyce further specifies,

> Multiple [electronic] fictions quite literally require collaboration by the reader of the hypertext to give

meaning to the texts through her constant textual intervention and shaping, her construction of successive interpretive frameworks, and her responses as a reader. This is to say that with electronic texts slippery notions, which have become hallmarks of postmodern criticism—like the notions of interpretive community or intertextuality—no longer enjoy the luxury and repose of theory. . . . Rendered in the pure light of ground zero, the intertextual polylogue . . . is perceived as the sometimes tiresome process our desire claimed it to be. (234-36)

In the car with Mélanie, the reader must relinquish control, unable to leave until the driving sequence is finished (a little more than a minute). This can be unsettling for hypertext users who enjoy the choice offered by the medium as one of its most liberating features. Jenik intends to slow the reader down, so that she might think about the process she is engaged in, and find time to linger with the language. She describes her own experience with hypertexts as comparable to her relationship with an Advent calendar: "I would quickly open all the doors to see what was behind them and, after a brief moment of glee, close them all back up. Since I had 'seen' inside all the windows already, the power of the delightful daily ritual was diffused" (AJ). User control was an issue that Jenik struggled with from the very beginning of her translation:

People that I was conferring with . . . said that what makes media "interactive" is you can bail out at any time; you can click away wherever you want; you always have the option to go wherever you want; that's what makes it different from a linear medium: the control is with the viewer.

But I also took a lot of time to notice how I interacted when I was using CDs, and there's this sense that you have to look at everything, so I think you're almost burdened by the possibilities. . . . So I felt I needed to carve some kind of space however small or short—I mean, you're in the car for a minute and a half—in which people weren't concerned about where else they could go, or what else they could do, so that they actually had the chance to be really there, and have the language flow over them and through them. (Interview)

The speed, the tendency towards excess, marked in the 15-year-old Mélanie and in Angela Parkins, the woman who fascinates her, is a feature of reading hypertext, where the pace of information far exceeds that of writing which "takes time, takes a perspective, includes memory." Jenik slows time down, as Maude Laures did within her own translation, to let the reader realize the difference between sensation and emotion: "you need time to build the emotion and to live with it" (Brossard 1998).

The viewer also has no control over longman (*l'homme long*), the scientist linked to the nuclear tests and the death of Angela Parkins. In Brossard's novel, longman is segregated in numbered chapters, and in the translator's series of files on characters, places, and dimensions of the novel, there are no words for him, just blurred images. Maude Laures' translation made longman a more substantial threat by rendering him as "o'blongman." Jenik's CD-ROM shifts the desert from Arizona to Nevada to foreground the nuclear tests, and she connects both longman and Angela Parkins to the Yucca Mountain nuclear waste disposal site project. Jenik explains that in the course of trying to understand longman's "narrative purpose,"

I stumbled upon news articles about the US Government's desire to bury 80,000 metric tons of high-level radioactive waste in the desert. My "update" of Longman focuses a lens on this decades-in-progress history of hosting nuclear experiments in the desert: from the 1940's and 50's test bombings conducted by Los Alamos Laboratories in New Mexico (referred to by Brossard in *Mauve Desert*) to the plans to geologically isolate high-level radioactive waste in Yucca Mountain in Nevada . . . . In this "fact is stranger than fiction" script adaptation, I position Longman as chief mathematician at the DOE-sponsored Yucca Mountain Site Characterization Project. In my narrative . . . is Longman's certainty (read: ego) that the go-ahead

is given to bury . . . hazardous material in the side of
Yucca Mountain. Currently (in non-fictive space) the
site is being studied by the DOE in order to prove its
suitability and safety for long term storage. (AJ)

As Jenik explains, "I read longman as an historical figure,[8]
but also in terms of scientific ethics; and what kind of pressures go on in scientific communities" (Interview).

Jenik links longman with the Yucca Mountain Nuclear
Disposal site in Nevada, but he is not just a threat to ecological equilibrium; longman threatens the reader, undermining
her sense of freedom and choice. Skimming Mélanie's map,
the cursor will suddenly change shape, and become an icon
of radioactivity. Without warning, longman interrupts the
reading process with a rapid sequence of black and white
photographs and distorted sound. His interruptions cannot
be controlled and after the ninth one, longman shuts down
the computer and the reading process: the reader cannot forget about reality.

"Le désert est indescriptible," begins Brossard's novel, as
she imagines the desert, as that "grand nu à l'horizon qui
tente"(87)/"that great nude on the horizon enticing" (81),
translating the Nevada/Arizona desert of cacti and and nuclear
test sites into a landscape of woman's desire. But how does
lesbian love and the sensual environment of body and nature
make sense of nuclear weaponry and ecological destruction?
In the intimate connection between the woman reading and
writing, between their tongues and their bodies, is found an
ecological consciousness, for if "dreams are narratives made
of those words which arise from the flaming of things within
us, their opposite is the poisoned world of the 'exploited earth'"
(Weir 61). Does the hypertext make us more aware of our
belonging to a network of being beyond the human, or make
us more aware of our body and what technology can do to it?

In Jenik's CD-ROM translation, the uncomfortable light
of the desert is modulated into the desire of a woman writer
and her reader to *tutoyer* in the flickering light of the computer screen. Maude Laures' worktable was covered with print
texts and coloured pens, but among the dictionaries, under-
lined pages, newspaper clippings and file folders there was
no computer. Her eyes may have squinted into the "harsh
light of March" or closed against the blinding reflection of

snow, or light ricocheting off a car bumper, but she would
have to imagine "light as a wave encouraged by the heat on
the skin":

> Comment pourrais-je déserter Mélanie? Comment
> entrer dans l'angle de son regard et m'éviter la lumière?
> Comment oublier l'instant? Car c'est bien là l'histoire
> de ce livre. L'instant porté par un seul symbole: la
> lumière. (100)/ How could I desert Mélanie? How to
> enter the angle of her gaze and spare myself the light?
> How to forget the instant? For therein lies the story of
> this book. The instant formed by a single symbol: light.
> (141-2)

Jenik writes by the same light her reader reads by: "Electronic texts are read where they are written; they are written
as they are read" (Joyce 235). Jenik's reader is urged to think
about her desire as they drive through the landscape of their
desire:

> From the very beginning in my voiceover, I talk about
> where you're sitting. I was trying to figure out ways to
> keep pointing out to a person about their own body
> and where they are sitting and what they are doing.
> When I show Maude Laures' lips, I want people to think
> about their own lips as they read . . . There's a part on
> my [Maker] map where it says if you squint your eyes
> you can see me in 3-D. Whether or not you can, I like
> thinking about people squinting their eyes. (Jenik In-
> terview)

If the process of translation is a somatic one, to be taken on
"body to body," it is also a landscape seldom foregrounded,
hidden under the "unforgivingly previous" so-called "original."
Like the desert it is "sises à l'arrière-plan de nos pensées (177)/
sited in the background of our thoughts" (161).

The link between war weaponry and computer play may
be implicit in Jenik's re-reading of the desert, but she is fully
conscious that the majority of gaming software uses the computer interface as a gun or weapon of destruction, and that
"it is not a coincidence that all these war games go on in a
country which has not had a war fought on its soil in over

seven generations. Anonymous destruction with no apparent consequences has demonstrated appeal" (AJ). Nuclear tests and hazardous waste disposal take place in spaces like the desert, "sited in the background," spaces that can be imagined empty, so remote and detached they are from us. Lorna Myher, Mélanie's mother's lover, who grew up in Ajo, where "[t]ous les jours, un grand nuage de fumée toxique arrêtait le temps au-dessus" (91)/ [e]very day a great plume of poisonous smoke stopped time" (85). In Jenik's translation, Lorna is black, making race visible in her image of the lesbian, and in desert life. Her choice is significant, according to a 1987 study which

> concluded that race is a major factor in the location of hazardous waste in the United States: three out of every five African and Hispanic Americans . . . and over half of all Asian Pacific Islanders and American Indians live in communities with one or more toxic wastes sites. Seventy-five percent of residents in the rural Southwest, mostly Hispanic, drink pesticide-contaminated water. (Warren 11)

The Spanish that names so much of the southwestern desert landscape—the *saguaro, senita, ocotillos,* and *arroyo*—appears within Brossard's text, one of three languages (along with French and some English) which make up Angstelle's text. Her translator, Maude Laures, increases the code-switching in her version of the story, adding more Spanish phrases to her text, and Japanese, too, perhaps to magnify the echo of nuclear destruction in longman's beautiful equations written in the language of mathematics, in his recitation of poetry in the "dead" language of Sanskrit. Jenik considers Spanish "the language of the desert," but also feels its effect in her translation coming from her perspective as

> an Angeleno urbanite, someone living in polylingual space . . . . Another language was spoken in Los Angeles before English. Issues of sovereignty, language repression (as evidenced by the English Only movement), bilingual education, and cultural appropriation are battlegrounds in both Québec and California. (AJ)

In the first driving scene (and the last), Jenik overlays Spanish, English, and French, the voices of women speaking the same words at the same time in their different linguistic postures. In other scenes, the reader can choose the language of the text by using the car radio to select Spanish, French, or English.[9] Jencik hopes that if

> the driver is curious about the different soundtracks, they will venture on the same road again, and experience that road differently, even though visually it remains the same. This would bring the driver full-circle back to the original metaphor of driving on the road, an essentially repetitive experience that is influenced by how we feel, [and] what we are thinking. . . . (AJ)

The radio retells the story in different languages and voices; when choosing a language, the driver is also choosing another relationship to language.

The driving metaphor of the interface is pervasive in Brossard's novel and the media invocation of the electronic network, the "information highway." Although feminist hypertext critic Carolyn Guertin resists that metaphor as an example of the linear, territorial thinking that undermines the roots of hypertext as response rather than authority (Interview), Jenik appropriates the metaphor and extends it into her desert landscape, choosing some of the names for the 16 roads located on the maps from books and "desert road names gathered during [her] desert wanderings" (AJ). Others, such as Yucca Mountain, have political as well as metaphorical significance. Still others, like Hum Hollow, refer to the computer, and conflate landscapes. "The hum of the computer, the idle of a car engine, and the ambient sound of insects (computer/bugs?) bec[o]me strangely the same in this virtual desert travel/*travail(le)*" (AJ).

Roads cross the desert, and motels offer temporary shelter from the heat and glare to visitors with business to conduct before they leave. In Brossard's novel, Maude Laures imagines Angela telling Mélanie the story of man's conquest of the desert:

> —Le désert est un espace. Un jour des hommes y venus et ils ont affirmé que cet espace était enfin conquis.

Ils ont dit souffrir de leur conquête, Ils ont souffert
car le désert ne permet aucune erreur. Mais les
hommes ont confondu l'erreur et la souffrance. Ils ont
conclu que leur souffrance pouvait corriger l'erreur
de la nature, la nature même de l'erreur. (136-7)/ —
The desert is a space. Man came there one day and
claimed that this space was now conquered at last.
They claimed they suffered over their conquest. They
suffered because the desert suffers no error. But men
confused error with suffering. They concluded that
their suffering could correct the error of nature, the
very nature of error. This is how they hooked into
death. (127)

To some, the desert has become almost synonymous with
death—the end of the road—when it is really a place great
with life. Mélanie wanted to slant her desert story towards
the light; in her turn, Maude Laures bent the lines of her
borrowed text into her own life, diving into the story and sur-
facing with her own version: "j'appuyais sur le pan fragile de
mes pensées pour qu'elles soient penchant de l'instant, pour
que ça compte vraiment la réalité" (184)/ "I was leaning on
the fragile side of my thoughts to make them penchant of the
moment, to make reality count for real" (169). Jenik, too, joins
in "the struggle against perfect communication, against the
one code that translates all meaning perfectly, the central
dogma of phallogocentrism" (Haraway 176) and creates her
version of the mauve desert which we read where she writes,
amid the hum.

NOTES

[1]From an interview with Nicole Brossard, which took place in
Montreal on April 23, 1996.

[2]Alice Parker uses this term in her article, "The Mauve Horizon
of Nicole Brossard" (109).

[3]Jenik says that she knew "from the first paragraph" that
Brossard's novel would transform her: "I was in a bookstore getting a
bunch of books for my vacation, and I was getting another book out
and *Mauve Desert* fell down on the floor. I went to pick it up to put it
back and looked at the cover, and read the back, and threw it on my
pile of books. It ended up being the only book I read on my vacation
and I knew from the first page, from the first paragraph, that . . . I

was going to spend a lot of time with this book" (Interview). In the novel, the translator, Maude Laures, discovers Angstelle's novel in a used book shop in Montreal: "Dis, que peut-il se tramer dans ton regard que tu n'as pas su comprendre quand le temps était aux premières lectures et que tu annotais ce livre insolite trouvé dans une librairie de livres usagés?" (121)/ "Say, what can be plotted in your gaze that you were unable to understand during the initial readings when you annotated this unusual book found in a second-hand bookstore?" (114).

[4]Brossard, who willingly gives her translators space to "swim with the words," was very open to the project at the onset, saying, "I just want to fall in love with all the female characters" (Jenik 1998).

[5]From Adriene Jenik's unpublished thesis concerning the making of her CD-ROM translation of *Mauve Desert*. Hereafter referred to as AJ.

[6]From an interview with Adriene Jenik which took place on February 24, 1998, at the University of California, San Diego. An abridged and annotated version of this interview, "Obsessed By Her Reading: An Interview with Adriene Jenik" is forthcoming in Issue 6 of *Links & Letters: Word and Screen*.

[7]Jenik describes her Maker Map as a way to extend "the frame of vision of the project to include my own progress/process. These process elements also needed to be considered when thinking of the possibilities of an "interactive" piece. In my process section, MakerMap, which seeks to uncover the generational, cultural and shifting-horizon erspective of my translation, I would be revealing my own position as a woman maker." As Brossard has written, "To write *I am a woman* is full of consequences." I began to feel that my relationship with Brossard, my dreams and questions, the off-shoots of narrative contained within the actor's stories were all better suited to more quiet, individual and personal contemplation" (AJ).

[8]In Brossard's novel, longman (*l'homme long*) is certainly linked to J. Robert Oppenheimer, the director of the original atomic bomb project at Los Alamos, New Mexico (1942-45) and his "amoral formulas" (Parker, *Liminal* 131). As Karen Gould points out in her discussion of *Le désert mauve*, Brossard's "evocation of the first atomic explosion ("Now we are all sons of bitches") and . . . [historical] reference to Oppenheimer's apocalyptic vision borrowed from the Bhagavad-Gita ("Now I am become Death, the destroyer of worlds") . . . expose the sterility and deadly sense of fraternity that characterize man-as-symbol in her text" (99).

[9]The user (who is momentarily conflated with Mélanie) can choose among five different radio channels, each channel opening a different sound file which corresponds to that particular road. When the

driver chooses English they hear an English voiceover by Lora Moran, who plays the physical Mélanie throughout the piece. The French selection is voiced by Québécoise actor, Nathalie Derome. The performance artist, Elia Arce, provides the voice for the Spanish channel. There is also an AM channel, which provides "a paranoid soundscape filled with huckster preachers, letters to G. Gordon Liddy, and southern California accident reports" (AJ), and an FM channel plays "meditative and genre-crossing" compositions by Mary Feaster.

REFERENCES

Brossard, Nicole. Personal Interview. Feb. 1998.

———. Personal Interview. Apr. 1996.

———. *Le désert mauve*. Montréal: l'Hexagone, 1987. Trans. by . Susanne de Lotbinière-Harwood as *Mauve Desert*. Toronto: Coach House Press, 1990.

Case, Sue Ellen. "Eve's Apple, or Women's Narrative Bytes." *Modern Fiction Studies* 43.3 (1997): 631-50.

Gould, Karen. *Writing in the Feminine: Feminism and Experimental Writing in Quebec*. Carbondale: Southern Illinois University Press, 1990.

Guertin, Carolyn. E-mail interview. June, 1998.

———. "Hovering Between: Canadian Hypertextual Discourse." <http://www.ualberta.ca/~cguertin/Guertin.htm>.

Haraway, Donna. *Simians, Cyborgs, and Women: The Reinvention of Nature*. New York: Routledge, 1989.

Hayles, N. Katherine. "Corporal Anxiety in Dictionary of the Khazars: What Books Talk about in the Late Age of Print When They Talk about Losing Their Bodies." *Modern Fiction Studies* 43.3 (1997): 800-20.

Jenik., Adriene. Personal Interview. February, 1998.

———. *Mauve Desert A CD-ROM translation*. Los Angeles: Shifting Horizon Productions, 1997.

———. Unpublished thesis.

Joyce, Michael. *Of Two Minds: Hypertext Pedagogy and Poetics*. Ann Arbor: The University of Michigan Press, 1995.

Parker, Alice A. *Liminal Visions of Nicole Brossard*. New York: Peter Lang, 1998.

———. "The Mauve Horizon of Nicole Brossard." *Quebec Studies* 10 (1990): 107-19.

Warren, Karen J. "Taking Empirical Data Seriously: An Ecofeminist

Philosophical Perspective." *Ecofeminism: Women Culture Nature.* Ed. Karen J. Warren. Bloomington: Indiana UP, 1997. 3-20.

Weir, Lorraine. "Daphne Marlatt's 'Ecology of Language.'" *Line* 13 (1989): 58-63.

Riding the Curves
Into the Twenty-First Century

H. LEE BARNES

It's chilly and damp. The season hangs on, an unusual winter, the wettest perhaps since the Great Basin was the Sea of
Lahontan. The southern sun casts intense shadows on the
cliffs. The view is dramatic, especially the snow-capped peaks
of the Spring Mountains. Although it is winter, snow is unusual, for seasons here are usually defined not by such obvious manifestations but by shadow and temperature, by fleet-
ing subtleties, by the direction of the wind or undulating spires
of heat shimmering in the distance.

Come spring the foothills will color up, not verdant, not
that, nor green exactly, but an olive tone dotted with orange
and white and yellow, some red—no clichéd painter's pallette,
but more the delicate effect of spotting caused by flicking a
bristled brush over a canvas. You must look closely to see it,
as much of the living desert is implied, like ellipses in the
middle of a sentence, within the bare spaces. The bruised-
red, muted-ochre bluffs warm like hot pads. Climbers burn
palms on the rock. Sage and rabbitbrush fatten. At dusk
streaking birds and flitting bats feed. The cliffs turn cheese-
pale in moonlight. Coyote, red fox, and Mojave rattlers haunt
the arroyos to prey on rabbit and field mice. Shadows seem
less poignant during the hot arid season, and shade of any

*H. Lee Barnes teaches English and creative writing at the
Community College of Southern Nevada where he serves as
fiction editor for* Red Rock Review. *His short fiction has appeared in numerous literary journals, most recently in the*
Clackamas Literary Review. *He received the 1991 Arizona
Authors Association award in fiction and the 1997* Clackamas
Literary Review *fiction award.* Gunning for Ho, *his collection
of short stories about Vietnam is expected from the University
of Nevada Press in early 2000.*

kind is a benison. The desert becomes (there is no other word for it) the "mythic" test of endurance. The Mojave in August could humble Hercules and Atlas.

Year round, Red Rock is, by degrees, damper than the valley to the east and measurably cooler. A westerly flows down from the peaks. I set my kickstand and sit atop the fence at Red Rock Overlook. Here, August 14, 1997, in a hundred degree-plus, a student artist, an Oregon emigre, an ex-convict for rape, drove a ten-year-old girl to the overlook. The law defines his act as sexual assault, which seems an insipid tag. Language, meant to be malleable, has become a sort of filter to soften the harshness of truth, a verbal rubber room in which predators bounce off the walls a couple of times and transform themselves into victims. Nature would never tolerate such distortions. The deer would never confuse the lion with the rabbit. I cannot pass this spot now without imagining the entreaties of a young girl. Red Rock has survived wagon wheels, cliff climbers, clamoring tourists, brush fires, and buried bodies. Now this. There is something—a blemish, an energy. A stain, perhaps.

* * *

I'm a sucker for places with colorful names. Pahrump, Amargosa, and *Death Valley*. (Top that one.) The place is magical, spiritual to some. Physicists suggest a peculiar ionization of the air creates the spiritual phenomenon, which seems a pretty provincial explanation coming from erudite scientists who probe the mysteries of an expanding universe, of subatomic space, of creation itself. What essence fills the dotted lines science can't scratch names on? Rumble down a desert road on your way to Death Valley, and you'll know ions have nothing to do with what you feel. Movement and air merge into a stream that washes time away. Gravity holds you to *terra firma*, but this travel is more akin to flight. Ironically, at eighty miles an hour everything slows.

You see distant mountains as a raptor must, with a clarity that is at once shocking and faithful. You note complexity, character, the play of light and shadow on rocky shelves where the crooked arroyos retain enough moisture to sustain a few cactuses, a bush or two. On one of these peaks a Paiute hunting party once paused to watch ox-drawn wagons with white

Red Rock

bonnets crawl across the desert floor. The braves slumped forward on their unshod mustangs. One said, "Well, there goes the neighborhood." "Must be the ions," another said. The others nodded, which is universal. We all nod at bad news.

* * *

Motorcycles are basic, a primitive piece of technology that survives, though some people, for no good reason, would regulate them as if they were handguns. (After all, both kill, don't they?) But bikes defy legislation, just as they defy common sense. They serve as symbols that say good common sense is not really so great. Motorcyclists don't ride about with cellular phones welded to their ears or bran muffins stuffed in their mouths. They ride. Like their machines, they are throwbacks.

The relationship of human to motorcycle, at its meridian, is atavistic. Add a desert to the equation and the relationship heads toward something spiritual. What terrain could be more hostile to an asphalt surface or an open motor-driven machine than the high desert? Harsh winters, sweltering summers, windstorms, flash floods. Hostile. Though highways evolved to accommodate cars and trucks, motorcycling redefines the experience of travel. An age-old urge is reborn, a desire to traverse the land for no greater reason than to flow into the horizon. It is about going there, not getting there.

For eighty years highways were little more than bituminous streams, a way to the coast, to Tinsel Town where gods and goddesses lived a fabled American dream, the great theme dream. The Great Basin remained a hole in Manifest Destiny, land traversed merely to reach paradise, a gap between the hyper-bustle east coast and laid-back, golden California. Except for mining, we were safe for a while, and while we did damage, as we sapped resources and marred the land, we learned to appreciate it and to love it, came to feel guilt for the damage we'd done.

Distance became a part of our character, just as it is characteristic of the land. We became a land of individuals, friendly but slightly aloof. While Californians adhered to "lifestyles" and Easterners bathed in cultural elitism, Westerners lived a kind of cloaked existence. Now, heading toward the twenty-first century, we are experiencing an invasion. The covered wagons aren't passing through, and they come from all directions—Winnebagos and U-Hauls. We are the hunting party on the mountain top nodding our heads.

* * *

Once a brown-gray blanket of smog layered San Bernardino and Riverside and pressed like a giant fist against the steep wall of Cajon Pass. It was Los Angeles air pushed inland. The west rim of the High Desert pushed it back. You could feel air tickle the throat as you descended. It tasted of freeways and traffic jams, smelled of rush-hour commuters and fifty-cent-a-gallon gasoline pumps. That was twenty-five years ago. Now the fist has uncoiled; its fingers grope farther east. The fine Joshua trees that line the highway near Victorville are choking, smogged out, their trunks darkened with soot as if burned.

It's hard not to like Joshua trees. They fit the cliche "so ugly they're cute." They're kind of like the sea otter of the desert. It's not a point to be argued, just an observation. The

Joshua Tree with Red Rock in the background.

plant is one of the taller native to the Mojave and is perhaps the symbol of the High Desert as the saguaro is the symbol of the Sonora. Of course they're not limited to the Mojave, but you won't find them in Vermont. They're not really trees, but one would be a good test for a tree hugger. Hell, they stand in their space with open arms waiting to be hugged. Go ahead. Try one.

Joshua trees talk to one another. About what? Tourists. As in, "What's that stupid tourist looking at?" People look at them, they look back. They share a lot of laughs. You can see one smiling at an approaching tree hugger.

Their job is to entertain tourists, and they work at it. At night, of course, they sit down and gossip about litterbugs and other miscreants. This is when they share a laugh or two, especially over tourists who actually think of them as trees. Even Joshua trees know they are yuccas. How do they know this? They do yucca things—grow shallow roots, shed spines, store water—those sorts of things. Oh, and they don't smoke. They're definitely against cigarettes.

Once a month Joshua trees hold square dances.

* * *

One of my favorite stretches of highway is between Las Vegas and Cedar City, Utah. For a sheer thrill, going at eighty-five miles an hour on two wheels at dawn through the Virgin River Gorge is akin to skipping rope inside the jaws of a saltwater crocodile. The surface of the road disappears in the shadows of sheer wall and suddenly reappears as a curve illuminated in the blinding horizontal sun. Below, a hundred feet down a steep bank, the Virgin River gurgles. The gorge challenges you, says, I'm here—the test, of course, is not one of good common sense. This passage was not meant for anything as mundane as common sense. This is why people want to legislate against motorcycles. People such as these want to legislate out everything that's pleasurable. People like these should be made to hug Joshua trees.

* * *

I'd like to print up some cards that read, "You're right. This isn't New York." One of the things we in the Southwest know about New Yorkers is that their ancestors didn't come here on horseback, on foot, or in covered wagons. Theirs were generally the ones who preferred the confines of the known and noisy to the unknown and sedate. This principle applies to Bostonians as well, and Philadelphians. Perhaps it applies to the whole eastern seaboard population and every human living between there and the Great Divide.

I would also place alongside the highway signs for tourists that warned, "Beware of Joshua trees. Approach with caution. They have been known to kill." These would be small signs, and the print would be small print, and I would hope the tourists had poor eyesight and that the Joshua trees were feeling frisky and bit mean. Bet the Joshua trees would get a yuk out of a sign like that.

It's not that I don't like tourists. We need them. But every year the desert suffers more and more sullying. People shoot saguaro and yucca, ride four-wheelers over virgin sand, set brush fires, kill coyotes and rattlesnakes. This is a secret paradise, and as The Eagles proclaimed in their *Hotel California* album, "You call some place Paradise, kiss it goodbye."

We, the most prolific of nature's predators, don't understand the nature of predators or appreciate their ability to survive in this delicate environment. Do we need a mass migration of Easterners who want to pillage paradise, to trample the predators? It's bad enough that Californians cloned from cellular phones and Toyota 4-Runners arrive in record numbers to "share" the Las Vegas experience. Well, there's only so much to share. Ask the desert tortoise. It's enough to make you want to raise an army of Joshua trees and declare war.

* * *

The first time Larry and I rode together was through the loop at Red Rock on a glossy winter morning, a Sunday. Sunlight edified the mountains like stage lights illuminating a set, and a soft dew clung to the sage and covered the shaded side of rocks and boulders. Other than one jogger, we were the only ones there. We stopped just to look at the shadows on the mountains, stood silent for several minutes. There was no need for talk. I can close my eyes and see it, not in detail, but in impressions. The land impresses itself upon you.

You take the loop slowly, especially in the late spring and early summer, for the thrill is in seeing—the quick appearance of a stone face seemingly aflame, the rabbitbrush in yellow bloom, the pale, bell-shaped yucca flower. In the desert even a bee seems special. How long one must fly and how hard one must work to bring pollen to the hive! So few flowers. In a normal spring, the sight of one bee warms you, but in spring following a wet winter with wildflowers profuse as pancake batter, the sight of so many bees electrifies you, and green-winged hummingbirds with brilliant red throats, and geckos doing pushups on rocks.

Tourists and cliff climbers come out. Shutterbugs stand over the moat-like arroyo that divides the desert floor from the stone mounds where wind-etched striations create a dizzying optical illusion. If you stand and stare long enough, you'll swear either you or the rocks are moving. Seeing simply isn't enough. You spread your feet apart for balance and descend the steep path. Along the route you pass a dead rodent, its carcass covered by bluebottle flies. Rock climbing is a little like motorcycling without the speed. Handholds and footholds must be gauged with caution. The ascent is rough on the hands, but the porous rock feels good. The sensation isn't one that can be explained; it must be experienced. Suspend doubt. Try it. Get to the top, look in four directions, and take in the air.

* * *

I look at Larry, twenty-five years my best friend, and he smiles back. We're on motorcycles heading north. His smile says that he understands. He sometimes articulates it obliquely, talks about the calming effect, existing within the experience, or sometimes concretely when he sees the shimmering dance of sunlight on salt flats. I'm more direct. I say that if God were human, He/She would mount a strong motorcycle, find a desert highway, and twist the throttle. We don't mention that this may be changing, that the encroachment is a noose.

If we could organize a force of a few hundred thousand yuccas and cactuses, have them form a ring at our borders, stand ready, perhaps we could stave off the onslaught. The flaw in such an idea is that cactuses and yuccas do not form armies. Though they do battle with the elements, fight harsh

Sourthern Charleston Range from Red Rock.

winds and endure terrible droughts, they are not aggressive. Nor are they mobile. They merely are. They stand and wait to become victims. We cut down acres and acres of them and call it development. We put golf courses near retirement communities and executive homes. We seed for grass, dig holes for swimming pools, and plant trees so people from California will have something to hug, so those from New York can migrate to a land that will never be home, will never be *like* New York.

Coming from Lee Canyon, Larry and I hit the straightaway. We could throttle out and slash through air, but instead we slow down. Up here scrub juniper grow beside the Joshua trees. It's warming and the desert is two or three weeks from blooming. Evidence of a colorful spring to come is everywhere. Quills on Joshua trees are thick and long, a rich green. Taking it all in, we crawl along hugging the shoulder at about fifty miles an hour. Below in the distance on the east side of the interstate is a depression of alkaline flats and sagebrush land cut by arroyos.

At the interstate we stop and drop the kickstands. Scattered about the ditch beside the road are glass bottles and plastic bags, paper napkins and aluminum cans. Litter. The white man has littered this land since he first crossed in covered wagons. Congress wants to bury nuclear waste in Nevada. Why? Because it's desert. More litter, deadly litter. Trucks rumble past, shaking the earth. Cars whoosh by. In between intrusions we are swallowed by the silence and the expanse of the land.

We ride south. Somewhere between the Paiute reservation and the Mt. Charleston turnoff Las Vegas comes into view. A haze similar to that which once was blockaded by the west shelf of the High Desert rests like gossamer silt over the valley. In midst of all this haze are the theme hotels, the next generation of entertainment for Americans, sinking pirate ships that rise again, kings and knights who dual at dinner, plastic Pharaohs and plastic treasure—virtual unreality. This is the city of the twenty-first century, Hollywood's replacement. Will Americans see the desert as a theme park? Will we have cartoon characters on TV modeled after Joshua trees and saguaro?

Larry doesn't say so, but he's feeling the noose. He shakes his head. I nod. The universal response to bad news. Later I mention riding the same route in two weeks to catch the desert in early bloom. And so we will.

* * *

As a twelve-year old in Tularosa, New Mexico, I had an English teacher who insisted we spend hour upon hour each week diagramming sentences. Her mind had simply frozen on images of branches that grew prepositions and indirect objects, dependent clauses and participial phrases. That which we read, we diagramed. She never explained stories or asked us to explain any. One day she wore to class a silver necklace that bore an amber-colored crystalline stone. She removed it from her neck and held the chain between forefinger and thumb. The stone oscillated before her.

She asked if we knew what it was. "Tourmaline," I said. "Topaz," guessed another. She shook off our answers. This, she explained, holding it so close to her eyes she went cross-eyed, was nothing we'd ever see again.

"It comes," she clarified, "from silicate heated instantly to temperatures in excess of ten thousand degrees Fahrenheit."

She said the stone came from near ground zero at Alamo, New Mexico, where a bomb called Trinity was exploded. July 16, 1944, she'd been awakened before dawn by a thunderous explosion. In a straight line, Tularosa was less than thirty miles from ground zero. She spread the chain and slipped it over her neck. It was her only story.

East of Tularosa lie stretches of ground where the white silicate encroaches on the sage lands, dry grassland where ranchers graze cattle. From there I was able to see into the flats. Dozens of times I looked out into the white dunes hoping for a glance of Alamo. I never caught sight of it, but it became the germ of a story. The pristine desert, the war, the bomb, the lives affected, raw stuff turned into a novella *The Mind Is its Own Place,* a simple story about a tangled issue.

The government tested "the bomb," every kind, in the desert—above ground, below ground. The same government sees the desert as a storage bin for atomic waste, an atomic dump site—something for the twenty-first century and beyond. A few years back, when I was in Vermont for some post-graduate studies, I was participating in a group discussion about social problems, in particular homelessness. I told my "peers" they had little concept of the true extent of homelessness, that to them it was so much social theory, because Vermont and New Hampshire and Maine truly had no homeless problem, that the cities of the Southwest did have real problems, that, indeed, in Las Vegas homeless franchises were being packaged and sold. My peers felt my attitude was callous. I said my immediate concern was a nuclear dump site in my backyard. They asked where I'd dig one if not in the Nevada desert. "In Vermont," I said. They were appalled.

No wonder Joshua trees don't grow in Vermont.

* * *

South of Kingman, Arizona, clump grass covers the hard desert floor. By the 1920s, much of what was once savannah had been over-grazed, but this year, prompted by an unusually mild but wet winter, the grass is making a comeback. I leave the interstate and circle a hundred and thirty degrees south onto the Widow Maker, which will take me through Wikiup and Wickenberg and into Phoenix. This is the most treacherous and loveliest of highways.

The sun is out, however the air is cold, not burning cold, but damp and inclement. Is it *El Niño*? or are the weather patterns shifting as we head toward the millennium? Have we created a gas screen, a greenhouse that's warming the atmosphere and oceans? The upper Sonora seems peculiarly affected by cool temperatures. Pistils sprout from the tentacles of octillo, but have not yet bloomed, and except for wild flowers, mostly bluebells, budding beside the highway, the desert seems dormant. The normally thick palette of orange and yellow, the striking reds, the subtle white remain in hibernation, awaiting a spring warmth that's already two weeks late.

Winnebagos, like grunting overfed boars, crawl along the route. The French have saying about someone taking up too much air, a reference to an individual's sense of self-importance. Winnebagos take up too much air. Their drivers have every right to use the road, but are not content with doing just that. They take possession of the highway, dictate the pace of traffic and are protected by every conceivable amendment to the Constitution and all the bylaws of the AARP. At the millennium's end, their machines are technology's version of the covered wagon. "Circle up, boys, and man your rifles. The enemy is here."

The one in front of me sputters and spurts noxious fumes, its bumper a mass of stickers—"Impeach Clinton," "If Guns Are Outlawed, Only Outlaws Will Have Guns." "Every Day's a Holiday. I'm Retired." The license plate is from Ontario, Canada. I wonder how quickly the driver would invite an American to keep his nose out of Canadian politics.

After ten minutes of taillight tag, I see a short straightaway. I downgear and swing into the oncoming lane. The snowbird buries his accelerator to prevent me from passing. My bike at near full throttle, I'm eyeball to eyeball with him. He glares out his side window and mouths the word "Sonovabitch." On his tongue it is one word. Where are the Apaches when you need them? How they must now lament allowing passage to the first of those Conestogas! I wish I had a bumper sticker that read "Impeach Pucks."

I'm reminded that a few years back Canadian environmental writer Farley Mowat was detained and returned to Canada from a United States port of entry, Detroit. He was on a list of "excluded persons"; his offense, as near as anyone can tell, was writing books championing endangered species—*Never Cry Wolf, A Whale for the Killing*—or was it his antiwar sentiments—*And the Birds Sang No More*? Had his baggage been labeled with "NRA" and "Impeach Carter" stickers, he might not have been sent back. But he had no such stickers. Mowat was turned away. Here more than a decade later in the state where Edward Abbey wrote in support of eco-terrorism and Frank Waters penned Hopi philosophy into a counterculture *Testament*, an invasion of Canadian retirees may, in part, dictate politics in the Borderlands.

The foreign dollar means that much. Is this the irony of the twenty-first century—a fascist from Canada snowbirding in Arizona to enjoy mild winters and the privilege of packing an assault rifle? Should we move a division of Joshua trees to the north to guard our borders from boors? The snowbirds may be too well armed for that, and it may be too late.

A few vagrant clouds float east. I can enjoy the horizon. It's mine and not mine. It strikes me as contradictory that this nation would rally so quickly when Pearl Harbor was invaded and now gripe about Mexican aliens who work me-

nial jobs none of us want, yet keep open the border to vener-
able gray-haired invaders with platinum credit cards and
unyielding notions of who deserves what. The Eagles wrote
that lovely song about naming Paradise and kissing it goodbye.
The traveler in my rearview mirrors is unaware it's Paradise
he's passing through. He's just looking for a good $5.95 buf-
fet and a place to plug in his Winnebago for the night so he
can watch *Married with Children*. He's found his theme park.

The desert smells of mold. Clouds mingle on the horizon.
The temperature drops. I stop at the Cowboy Cafe in
Wickenberg. Here is the best apple pie in the Borderlands. I
grab a seat by the window to eat pie and drink coffee while
watching the Winnebagos drift by at twenty-five miles per hour.
The occupants don't stop for the best apple pie on the road.
They don't stop to look at saguaro or cholla. They head for
Phoenix or Tucson, for cities. It's comfort they want. Here in
Arizona the Joshua trees don't entertain travelers. Why
bother? I hope travelers never discover the apple pie at the
Cowboy Cafe. Still, I can't help but hope one tries to hug a
saguaro. In fact it should be required of them. Call it sensitiv-
ity training.

The Carefree Highway is just that—no snowbirds or
Winnebagos. Ignoring the double-five speed limit, I hold the
throttle steady at seventy. Paloverde are leafing. The low sun
highlights the west side of the saguaros that spread over miles
of rocky hills. Joshuas are the comedians of the desert, but
saguaros are strictly high drama, opera singers belting out
the final note on the closing aria of the best silent opera you've
ever heard. Divas, prima donnas.

At Lake Pleasant turnoff I stop to take in the view where
water flows down concrete viaducts to canals in Phoenix. Here
clump grass has grown thick and dark green. In the summer
all of this will dry, thickets of tinder waiting for a lightning
storm or carelessly discarded cigarette. I remember one year
during graduate school seeing the aftermath of an Arizona
brush fire—ancient saguaros charred and dying, blackened
skeletons of paloverde. It had been dry, and there were no
storms, no lightning, just one lone driver who flicked a cigarette out of a window.

* * *

In the afternoon I ride to Estrella Mountain College fifteen miles southwest of Phoenix to give a reading. As I near the college, a coyote trots across the roadway in my path. I slow, and he slows. I slow some more. He stops. He's in charge of the moment and knows it. The thick fur of his tail flutters in the wind as he lifts his head, sniffs the air and moves on.

Later I can't resist riding by back road to the flats. Communities surrounding Estrella Mountain are an amalgam of farmland, pastures, ranches, raw protected desert and planned communities. Here people don't want growth. Yavapai and vaqueros and farmers, Latinos and suburban commuters live in a pristine setting far away from McDonald's and Robinson's May. The mountains are lush with yucca and cactus and sage, the foothills on fire with wildflowers. The air smells of sage, a scent that clears my nose as if I haven't been breathing until now. Atop an incline I slow the motorcycle and look over my shoulder. I see the twentieth century city bleed into the twenty-first and wonder what happened to the nineteenth. I shake my head and twist the throttle. The road is straight through the pass. I am the sole person navigating it, and I think, this is rare, so very rare.

* * *

It's late April and the temperature no more than sixty degrees. The wind blows. My friends and I sit in the park at Summerlin, "a master-planned community," and listen to jazz, mostly fusion, at the City of Lights Jazz Concert. People mingle—black-skinned, brown-skinned, white-skinned. The audience has set aside normal tensions and biases to exist, at least for the moment, harmoniously. Music and art can affect us that way.

Beyond the crowd, beyond the blaring loudspeakers, I see ochre mountains still tipped with snow and white clouds sailing east and alkaline flats. An ethereal horizon bleeds into a pale blue sky. Closer I notice the red-tiled roofs and white plaster houses meant to be harmonious with the landscape. I'm looking at another theme park, looking at the twenty-first century. It has come. I lie back, close my eyes, and try not to think as I listen.